ONE HUNDRED YEARS

New York Yankees™

THE OFFICIAL RETROSPECTIVE

Edited by Mark Vancil and Mark Mandrake

RARE AIR BOOKS

A Division of Rare Air Media

NEW YORK YANKEES
ONE HUNDRED YEARS | OFFICIAL RETROSPECTIVE

Created and Produced by Rare Air Books

Copyright © 2002 by Major League Baseball Properties, Inc. All rights reserved. Compilation © 2002 by Rare Air Media. Edited by Mark Vancil and Mark Mandrake. Produced in partnership with and licensed by Major League Baseball Properties, Inc. and the New York Yankees. No part of this book may be used or reproduced in any manner whatsoever without written permission except in the case of brief quotations embodied in critical articles and reviews. For information contact Rare Air Media, PO Box 167393, Chicago, Illinois, 60616-7393.

A Ballantine Book
Published by The Ballantine Publishing Group

All rights reserved under International and Pan-American Copyright Conventions. Published in the United States by The Ballantine Publishing Group, a division of Random House, Inc., New York, and simultaneously in Canada by Random House of Canada Limited, Toronto.

Ballantine and colophon are registered trademarks of Random House, Inc.

www.ballantinebooks.com

Library of Congress Cataloging-in-Publication Data can be obtained from the publisher upon request.

ISBN 0-345-46090-1

Manufactured in Italy

First Edition: May 2003

2 4 6 8 10 9 7 5 3 1

ACKNOWLEDGMENTS

In times of stress what emerges from any organization is the substance of its individuals. In the world of sports that substance is often called "heart." It defines the winners as well as the losers, and though it often is hard to describe, it also is self-evident. Throughout the making of this book that unmistakable something flowed from everyone who became a part of the process. At Rare Air Media, Nick DeCarlo showed himself to be more than a creative talent. As the late nights blended into the early mornings, Nick never backed away from demands that were often at the far end of reasonable. His efforts can be found on every one of these pages. Ken Leiker proved to be more than a man of immense talent. His passion helped drive the entire project, and his gentle grace is apparent to all of us fortunate enough to be around him. John Vieceli once more showed himself to be a friend and one of the best designers in the country. Paul Sheridan stood by us throughout; Frank Fochetta's will forever be a part of our collective experience; and Andy Pipitone weathered more than a few late nights. At Major League Baseball, Don Hintze again showed why he is the absolute best in professional sports at what he does. Don balances leadership and compassion with a fundamental desire for excellence. This project would not have happened without him. We asked some remarkably talented writers to produce essays and analysis within a very narrow window, and none of them disappointed: Bill James is one of baseball's most-respected statisticians, historians, and authors, but it is his integrity that defines him; Robert W. Creamer wrote the definitive book on Babe Ruth, *Babe, The Legend Comes to Life*, and ranks among the finest sports writers of his generation; lifelong Yankees fan Peter Golenbock has written five bestselling books; Donald Honig has written more than 30 books about baseball and is widely recog-

nized as one of the game's preeminent historians; Leonard Koppett was inducted into the writers' wing of the Baseball Hall of Fame in 1992; Ray Robinson is the author of numerous books, including *Iron Horse: Lou Gehrig in His Time*; Keith Olbermann is the host of two daily sports shows on the ABC Radio Network and contributes to CNN; Pat Jordan wrote the highly acclaimed *A False Spring*, an account of his experience in the minor leagues; Ken Shouler's baseball knowldege and passion once more showed through; and Roger Kahn, author of *The Boys of Summer*, who was described by professor Stephen Jay Gould as "the best baseball writer in the business." Accompanying their words are more than 200 photographs from an array of talented artists. They include Walter Iooss Jr., a friend and an immense talent. At *Sports Illustrated*, Prem Kaliat walked us through the greatest sports photography collection in the world. At Corbis-Bettman, Michael Bacino helped us navigate thousands of shots, and at TimePix, Hilary Johnston showed us where to find more than a dozen crucial images. Getty Images, the New York Yankees, the Baseball Hall of Fame, and Major League Baseball also helped locate critical shots, often at a moment's notice. All this work came together thanks to the commitment and support of everyone at Ballantine Books, specifically Gina Centrello, Anthony Ziccardi, Bill Takes, Zach Schisgal, Patricia Nicolescu, and Barbara Greenberg. Lastly, the love, tenderness, and presence of my girls — Laura, Alexandra, Samantha, and Isabella — remain gifts beyond my imagination. As always, the best of me comes from them.

— Mark Vancil

To George M. Steinbrenner III, without whom a book on Yankees greatness would be much less great. The Boss ostensibly will have his modesty offended by this tribute. But for the winning tradition he helped restore to sports' most successful team, as well as for the support he has shown me personally and professionally — sincere thanks.

Of the Yankee Stadium front office, Glenn Slavin was indispensable on this project, as an editor, as photography coordinator, and as a friend. The paragon of professionalism, Glenn subjugated his own interests time after time to accommodate us. Lonn Trost, with his legal acumen and profound advice, always found a way to squeeze publishing dilemmas into an impossible calendar. Lou Rocco never let the photography awards go to his head and has continued to get the best shots in the face of much adversity, as have Eileen Barroso and Bernie Nuñez.

To the ballplayers, managers, and coaches — most particularly Joe Torre, Reggie Jackson, Whitey Ford, Derek Jeter, David Wells, and Don Zimmer — whose insights and narrative skills helped shape many of these pages. Yogi Berra and Phil Rizzuto lent us not only their cooperation, but that of their grandchildren: Gretchen Berra and Jennifer Rizzuto Congregane served as Yankees photo assistants, helping shoot, organize, and deliver some of the content that follows.

It's tough to summarize in a few sentences the continued patience and understanding shown by my family through myriad crises (real or imagined) in recent months. Most heartfelt appreciation to Hanley, Melissa, Janet, and particularly to Jackie — my wife and my life.

— Mark Mandrake

SPECIAL THANKS

Scott Mondore, Jeff Idelson, and W.C. Burdick at the National Baseball Hall of Fame; Don Hintze, Rich Pilling, and Paul Cunningham at Major League Baseball; former and current Yankees staff Brian Cashman, Anthony Incampo, Deborah Tymon, Michael Tusiani, Arthur Richman, Jeff Jackson, Jayna Rust, Kristen Aiken, and Neil Schwartz; other ballclub executives Dick Bresciani, Larry Cancro, Debbie Matson, and Bernadette Repko; Dave Kaplan of the Yogi Berra Museum; Larry Burke and Mark Mravic of *Sports Illustrated*; David Durochik; Pat, Dave, and Steve Goley at Professional Graphics, Inc.; Tom Keegan, Bob Nightengale, and Pete Palmer for their help and friendship.

PHOTOGRAPHY
Photography except as noted below ◦ Corbis Bettman Archives

Eileen Barroso/New York Yankees	13	Peter Read Miller/*Sports Illustrated*	92–93
Tomasso DeRosa	91, 246	Ralph Morse/TimePix	46, 58, 169, 176
John Dominis/TimePix	168, 172–173	Carl Mydans/TimePix	121
David Durochik	4–5	National Baseball Hall of Fame Library, Cooperstown, NY	30
Bob Gomel/TimePix	48		
Hulton Archive/TimePix	128	New York Yankees	1, 14, 17, 25, 31, 50–51, 61, 76–78, 108
Walter Iooss Jr.	2–3, 15, 20–21, 64–65, 67, 85, 87, 96–98, 103, 142–144, 149, 218		113, 131, 146, 149, 156, 206, 209, 234
		Hy Peskin/TimePix	80, 116–119, 215
Walter Iooss Jr./*Sports Illustrated*	69, 148	Eric Schweikardt/*Sports Illustrated*	112
Mark Kauffman/TimePix	78	Ezra Shaw/Getty Images	18, 111
Mark Kauffman/*Sports Illustrated*	70	Eugene W. Smith/TimePix	127
Heinz Kluetmeier/*Sports Illustrated*	110, 145	Shannon Stapleton/Reuters/TimePix	31
David Leeds/Getty Images	157	Ray Stubblebine	28–29
Neil Leifer/*Sports Illustrated*	239	Time, Inc.	237
Richard Meek/TimePix	18	Ron Vesely	90
Ronald C. Modra/*Sports Illustrated*	68	John Z. Zimmerman	49, 51

TABLE *of* CONTENTS

FOREWORD

The bad part about working for George Steinbrenner has been well-documented. He settles for absolutely nothing less than being the best and always winning. Now I don't care how good you are, you can't win every single day. But still, that is a philosophy I respect, and not only because George is my boss. Find me another owner who cares as much about being the best as he does.

I feel privileged not only to have been on George's list of potential managers after the 1995 season, but also to have been the one he eventually chose. That three guys ahead of me had to say no first doesn't hurt my feelings. When you're talking about Sparky Anderson, Tony La Russa, and Davey Johnson — those people had won World Series. To even be included on that list, I was fortunate. Our Yankees media advisor, Arthur Richman, whispered into George's ear that I should be among those names, and for that I'll be forever grateful.

In my years in this sport, I've been a member of four organizations. There always will be a special place in my heart for each of them. The Braves, because they were the first club I signed with, and because I got to play alongside Hall of Famers like Warren Spahn, Hank Aaron, and Eddie Mathews. I had my best playing years with the Cardinals, and I guess you could say that I matured in St. Louis. I won the MVP in 1971 with the Cards, but personal success didn't

diminish my desire to play in a World Series. I had joined a team in Milwaukee that had been to two Series, in 1957 and 1958, but didn't go back again in my six years there. Then I went to St. Louis, where the Cardinals had been to the Series in 1967 and 1968. I arrived in 1969, and the team didn't go to the World Series in my six years there. Those Braves and Cardinals teams had awesome talent, and I left each one feeling empty for not having a chance to play in the Fall Classic.

I went to the Mets in 1975 as a player, which was a bittersweet situation. We didn't have the personnel to compete, really. But I do owe them for giving me my first chance to be a manager. That opportunity came in 1977, a year after the Mets' general manager Joe McDonald asked me if I'd be interested in playing for the Yankees. I told him no, not if it would keep me from getting a chance to manage. Getting my foot in the door as a manager with the Mets, of course, opened up everything that happened for me later.

I remember going back to St. Louis to manage in 1991, and the first speech I gave to the players. I was looking up at their nine World Championship banners and made reference to the fact that only one team had more championships than the Cardinals: the New York Yankees. Never did I dream that the Yankees would be in my future. But the next ballclub that hired me to manage was the Yankees. I know now that I came to the Bronx under a lot of pressure. But I never felt the demands or criticism that went with this job. I guess it's a good thing that I was so focused. This was not a job you could do if you were worried about the fallout of failure.

This has been an opportunity that has worked out well for all involved — George Steinbrenner, me, the players, and the fans. I never anticipated being here seven years. It's absolutely insane when I think about it. With all the player movement in the modern era, to achieve what we have done is simply amazing.

My years with the Yankees have been the best time I have had in baseball, and that's from a guy who played the game pretty efficiently for 16 years. Nothing has come close to the thrills I've had in this uniform, in this ballpark. To see Yogi Berra just happen by your office once or twice a homestand, dropping by to chat with you, calling you "Kid" — it's sometimes hard to keep in perspective the greatness that goes with this ballclub.

George should take much pride in his legacy with the Yankees, and I believe he does. Many teams have proved that throwing money at players doesn't make a winning team. George has dedicated himself, all his energies, to keeping a winner on the field. In this era, when players change teams on such a regular basis, it's extremely difficult to stay ahead of the pack. Keeping the core of a team together is important, and George has enabled us to do that, to have the tools to be in the hunt every year.

I'm pleased that during my watch, the Yankees have made the city and our ownership proud. And not just that the team has won, but how we have carried ourselves. That's something that transcends whoever is custodian of the team. To me, that's the most important factor in remaining competitive and winning: How you carry yourself.

I'm as fulfilled as anyone by what's happened with the Yankees these past seven years, and I will always be appreciative to have been a part of it.

— *Joe Torre*

George Steinbrenner, Rudolph Giuliani, and Joe Torre (left to right).

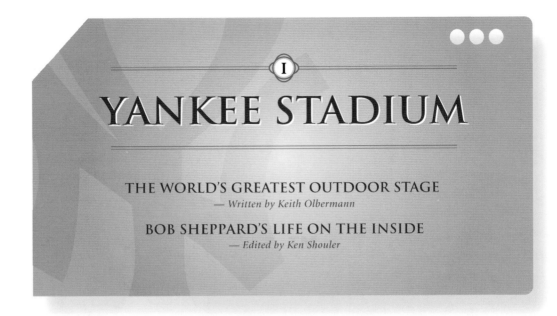

YANKEE STADIUM

THE WORLD'S GREATEST OUTDOOR STAGE
— *Written by Keith Olbermann*

BOB SHEPPARD'S LIFE ON THE INSIDE
— *Edited by Ken Shouler*

In the 20th century no outdoor entertainment venue in the world showcased a more

diverse cross section of the cultural experience than Yankee Stadium.

From Popes and evangelists to rockers and pugilists, the Stadium became the ultimate outdoor stage.

And no one worked it better than the Yankees, winning 26 World Championships and dominating

to a degree unmatched by any team in any sport anywhere on earth.

Written by Keith Olbermann

The original blueprints for Yankee Stadium were found in the archives of the Osborn Engineering Company of Cleveland some 30 years ago. The images on the crackly sheets were Yankee Stadium all right, down to the unique facade and the flagpoles on the roof. But the roof on the blueprints was one continuous oval. Yankee Stadium, as originally designed, was to be an enclosed, triple-deck arena. Imagine where the upper deck ends in left field and clone it around the perimeter of the outfield to where the upper deck ends in right field — that's what the Stadium was supposed to be. The place might have seated 100,000 for a baseball game.

Between the time Osborn Engineering designed the Stadium and the building contract was awarded to White Construction on May 5, 1922, the plans were scaled back. In the less ambitious project, the upper deck didn't even extend to the foul poles, much less ring the stadium.

The Stadium officially opened on April 18, 1923, just 284 working days after construction began. A crowd of 74,217 was admitted inside, and newspapers reported that another 15,000 were turned away. On that day and on many to come, Yankees owners Jacob Ruppert and Cap Huston no doubt regretted their decision to scale back the project.

YANKEE STADIUM FACTS

- The Stadium, designed by the Osborn Engineering Company of Cleveland, Ohio, and constructed by New York's White Construction Co., was built in only 284 days.

- On opening day, official attendance was marked at 74,217.

- In 1959, the Yankees unveiled the first electronic message board.

- After the renovation of the Stadium in 1976, a new 560-foot-long scoreboard would boast baseball's first "telescreen" used to provide instant replays of the action by employing a then-remarkable nine shades of gray.

- The largest single home game crowd took place on May 16, 1947, a night game against Boston that drew 74,747 fans.

- A ball hitting the foul pole in the 1930s was in play, not a homer.

- The New York Giants football team called Yankee Stadium home from 1956 to 1973.

- The "Bloody Angle" between the bleachers and the right-field foul line during the 1923 season, was very asymmetrical and caused crazy bounces. Eliminating this in 1924 caused the plate to be moved 13 feet and the

deepest left-center corner to change from 500 to 490 feet.

- In memoriam of the tragic death of Thurman Munson, his locker remains empty to this day, with the number 15 still posted on top.

- From the years 1923 to 1946 the Yankees dugout was located on the third-base side of the Stadium.

- The signature of the Stadium, the facade, which ran along the roof of the old Stadium, was replaced by an exact replica that runs

atop the scoreboard above the bleachers.

- The first night game was played at Yankee Stadium in May 1946.

- The original Yankee Stadium dimensions included an amazing distance of 490 feet from home plate to center field (1923–1936).

- The original placement of Monument Park was in the outfield as part of the playing field.

- After the remodeling, the Stadium hosted three consecutive World Series.

- During the 1936 season and continuing through the 1937 season, the wooden bleachers were replaced with concrete ones.

For foes their stadium was Dracula's castle. No team came in without a clutch in the throat, a sweating in the palms, a fear in the eyes."

For foes their stadium was Dracula's castle. No team came in without a clutch in the throat, a sweating in the palms, a fear in the eyes."

— JIM MURRAY. *Los Angeles Times* sports columnist on Yankee Stadium

Before we proceed much further, let us take a minute to discuss the word *stadium*. In its original form, it did not connote what it does today. *Stadium* is one of the oldest words in the English language. The British borrowed it from the Romans, who had adopted it from the Greeks. It is found in British texts dating to the 12th century — but not as a synonym for *arena*. *Stadium* was, in fact, a precise measurement. The running track at the first Olympics nearly 2,900 years ago was exactly one stadium long. Scholars of ancient

should be without being ridiculously oversized. Think of the 1959 World Series games at the Los Angeles Coliseum, where some fans were so far from home plate that they could see the ball hit before they heard the crack of the bat. Think of the circular ashtray stadiums built in the 1960s and 1970s; only the absence of piles of rocks kept the spectator from thinking he was at the bottom of a quarry. Think of Cleveland Municipal Stadium, which had room for more than 84,500 for a baseball game. The 7,290 that watched Len Barker's

Greece believe the word has an even unlikelier origin: It was a compound of the word *stadios*, which meant "fixed," and *span*, which meant "the limit of physical activity before one's muscles would spasm." Thus, a Greek stadium wasn't just a given distance, such as a yard or a mile. It also was the longest, the largest, the farthest, the most an athlete could achieve — the exact moment one had reached his physical limit.

Given that definition, maybe everyone can understand the meaning of Yankee Stadium. It was not only bigger than any other baseball facility that had been built, but time has proved that it was about as big as such a place

perfect game there in 1981 looked like raisins in a bowl of rice pudding.

Yankee Stadium, after the upper deck was extended in 1937, and certainly after the place was remodeled in the mid-1970s, was just the right size. It was the envy of every other franchise in the major leagues, and a model for every park built over the next 40 years. It even changed the terminology of a baseball arena. The nine homes built for major league teams prior to Yankee Stadium consisted of four "Parks" and five "Fields." Sixteen of the 20 built after Yankee Stadium and both of those remodeled were called "Stadiums."

Across the Harlem River from where Yankee Stadium would be built stood the Polo Grounds, home of the storied New York Giants of the National League. The original Polo Grounds, a 20-year-old, two-tiered, wooden structure, burned down on the night of April 14, 1911, and Giants owner John T. Brush quickly commissioned a new park. He ordered a baseball park to be built unlike any other in the industry — a gigantic bowl that would seat 54,000.

The project was finished in 10 weeks. The Giants celebrated with a National League championship in 1912, and the cover of that year's World Series program shows a center field view of a magnificent new arena, replete with 132 friezes along the roof and 44 heraldic banners fluttering atop it. However, the place had flaws. In hurriedly shaping his team's new home, Brush had become the first owner to separate fans from the game. There was enough room in foul territory to dig a moat. The place seemed unwieldy and lumpy. The friezes, depicting classically sculpted ballplayers holding logos of the National League teams, were a little overdone but provided some character to the park.

John J. McGraw,
manager of the New York Giants.

After the friezes were ripped out in the 1920s, the Polo Grounds took on the appearance of a faded horserace track.

The Polo Grounds and the men who controlled the Giants had much to do with why Yankee Stadium was built. Yankee Stadium in baseball lore is "The House That Ruth Built," but the truth of the matter is, Babe Ruth had less to do with it than John McGraw.

McGraw was the player-manager of the Baltimore Orioles in 1902 — that was the American League's second season — and he owned a piece of the team. The volatile McGraw clashed frequently with league founder and president Ban Johnson, not to mention with umpires. After Johnson suspended McGraw in midseason for knocking down an umpire, McGraw pulled off one of the greatest stunts in business history. Wary of the Orioles' chances of survival and fed up with Johnson, McGraw contacted the New York Giants' ownership and sold them on a proposition almost too good to be true. McGraw released the Orioles' top players, including stars Roger Bresnahan and Joe McGinnity, and the Giants quickly signed them up. McGraw, the executive, then fired McGraw, the manager, and released McGraw, the player. As the heart of the Baltimore team bolted for New York, with McGraw locked in as the Giants' new manager, McGraw sold his share of Orioles stock to a Giants employee, which forced the Orioles into receivership.

The Baltimore team survived the 1902 season, then was sold for $18,000 to New York politicos Big Bill Devery and Frank Farrell, who moved the franchise to Manhattan. The mess McGraw made in Baltimore had been dumped on his own doorstep.

McGraw and Brush constantly worked behind the scenes to sabotage the relocated American League club. Every time the new team found a lot suitable for construction of a permanent home field, political cronies of Brush and McGraw managed to have New York City cut new streets through the site.

Devery and Farrell had no choice but to build a temporary field in Washington Heights, where Broadway meets 168th Street — wilderness territory in the early 1900s. The park, catty-corner to The Deaf and Dumb Asylum, had a rickety grandstand that sat only 16,000 and, some claimed, swayed when the wind blew. The outfield grass was so sparse and the terrain so rugged that the field became known as "The Rockpile."

Despite their substandard environs, the Highlanders, as they were called at the time, contended for the American League pennant in 1904. (They fin-

HOME RUNS

No player has ever hit a fair ball out of Yankee Stadium. Four have hit balls more than 500 feet, every one before the Stadium was remodeled in 1976. There are kings of distance for each of the five sectors of the Stadium —left field, left center, center field, right center, and right field. Mickey Mantle, Jimmie Foxx, Frank Howard, Babe Ruth, Jay Buhner, and Barry Bonds have hit the longest balls ever in Yankee Stadium.

Foxx and Howard hit the longest homers to left field. On June 25, 1932, Foxx, playing for the Philadelphia Athletics, belted a Lefty Gomez pitch into the upper grandstand, 525 feet from home plate. Howard, playing for the Washington Senators, hit a pitch from Pete Mikkelsen on July 18, 1965, that traveled 440 feet and was 70 feet high when its flight was impeded by a general admission seat in row five of section 34, near where Foxx's ball landed, about 520 feet from home. Bill Jenkinson, who has been estimating the distance of home runs for more than 20 years and is writing a book on Ruth's homers, credits Foxx with the greater distance. Unlike Howard's towering fly, Foxx's ball was a line drive, which if unimpeded would have traveled farther.

Joe DiMaggio hit three balls into the distant left-center field bleachers, one each in 1939, 1941, and 1950. Each touched down 460 to 470 feet from home plate. DiMaggio likely was robbed of more home runs because of the dimensions of his home park than any other player in

baseball history. DiMaggio hit 148 homers at Yankee Stadium —the distances at the time in left center were marked by 415- and 457-foot signs — and 213 on the road. The longest homer to left center remains a 492-foot shot by Buhner that soared over the left field bullpen on July 25, 1991. Buhner played for Seattle at the time.

Mantle hit two balls into the center field bleachers. On June 21, 1955, he hit the first ball that cleared the 20-foot hitter's background screen at the 461-foot marker. Landing eight rows behind the screen, the distance was measured at 486 feet. On August 12, 1964, Mantle's towering drive off Chicago's Ray Herbert crashed into the empty bleachers 15 rows behind the screen. Measured at 502 feet, it was the longest home run to center field at the Stadium.

From 1923 through 1937, the center field fence was 487 feet from home plate. On May 31, 1924, Ruth hit a ball just to the right of dead center, 12 rows into the stands. Ruth's favorite target was right center field, where the distance to the fence ran from 350 feet to 429 feet. The

bleachers beyond extended 80 rows high. According to Jenkinson, who gathered information from several of New York's 14 newspapers of that era, Ruth reached the 74th and 75th rows of the bleachers six times, distances of 500 to 505 feet.

In right field, Mantle hit two balls off the upper deck facade. The first, off Washington's Pedro Ramos on May 30, 1956, hit the facade on its downward flight, coming within 18 inches of clearing the roof. Mantle at the time called it "the best ball I ever hit left-handed." On May 22, 1963, Mantle hit an 11th inning, game-winning homer off Kansas City's Bill Fischer that struck the facade. "It was the hardest ball I ever hit," Mantle said. Taking into account the ball's vertical distance, 108 feet, and linear distance, 387 feet, it was estimated that Mantle's drive traveled 535 feet. That remained the longest ball ever hit at the Stadium through the 2002 season despite a similar shot by Barry Bonds that landed deep in the right field upper deck.

ished 1¹/₂ games behind Boston.) The Giants, meanwhile, ran away with the National League pennant. When it became apparent that New York's American League upstarts could be in the World Series, which had been born a year earlier, Brush and McGraw announced that the Giants would not participate. Their explanation: The Highlanders played in a "minor" league. In truth, the Giants had nothing to gain and everything to lose by playing the Highlanders in the World Series. Had the Giants not kept interfering, the Yankees, as the Highlanders came to be called, might have been able to build a suitable park before 1910. They could have gotten an arena splendid for the time, something like Crosley Field in Cincinnati, League Park in Cleveland, maybe even an Ebbets Field or a Fenway Park. They might have gotten their own version of Wrigley Field: heavy on the quaint, light on the magnificence. But the constraints of architecture would have made building a place like Yankee Stadium impossible in 1907, or even in 1917.

BUHNER   DIMAGGIO   FOXX   BONDS   HOWARD   MANTLE   RUTH

BOB SHEPPARD

has been the public address announcer at Yankee Stadium since 1951. His deep, distinguished voice is as famous as the great ballplayers he has introduced. Sheppard announces a player coming to bat in such a dignified, almost reverent cadence that one might think he was introducing Moses coming off the mountain with the Ten Commandments. Reggie Jackson, echoing Billy Crystal's description, said Sheppard's words sound like

"THE VOICE OF GOD"

as they reverberate through the Stadium.

Sheppard has many warm memories of Yankee Stadium:

"One of my favorite times was Roger Maris hitting his 61st home run up there into the right field seats off Tracy Stallard on October 1, 1961. It impressed me so much that within 15 minutes I wrote a short poem about the event. The poem was called 'Roger Maris Says His Prayers.' Here it is:

> *They've been pitching me low,*
> *They've been pitching me tight.*
> *I've grown so nervous, tense, and pallid*
> *But my prayers are full of joy tonight,*
> *Thank you Lord*
> *For Tracy Stallard*

"I handed it over to Mel Allen, who was in the next booth to me. He read it over the radio before the game ended and he said, 'If you want copies of Bob's poem, write to Yankee Stadium.' I was deluged with mail in the coming days."

❀ ❀ ❀ ❀

"Of all the names I have announced, my favorite is Mickey Mantle. My other favorite names are Alvaro Espinoza, Jose Valdivielso, Salome Barojas, and Shigetoshi Hasegawa. "Mickey Mantle has a nice ring to it because the two 'Ms' make it alliterative and the 'I' sounds very good. Mickey Mantle is the perfect name. I just loved announcing his name. "Shortly before he died, we were both being interviewed on a television program. All of a sudden, he turned to me and said — on the air — that every time he heard me announce his name, he got goose bumps. And I felt the same way about announcing him."

❀ ❀ ❀ ❀

"I don't get to know the players well; I rarely go into the locker room. But Reggie Jackson and I have had a fairly warm relationship. "One day I received a phone call from a Catholic nun who had recently been stricken with a heart attack, and she had been watching the Yankees a lot on TV during her recovery. She asked if I could get her an autographed baseball. And I knew her well and told her I would try. "I asked the clubhouse man, Pete Sheehy, and he said they had run out of autographed balls. I started to walk out of the room. Reggie was in a corner locker and he said, 'Bob, what's wrong? You look sad.' I said, 'No problem.' And he said 'Tell me.' I told him I needed an autographed ball for this nun who was stricken. He reached back into a duffel bag and pulled out a ball from an All-Star Game he had been in, signed by every player on the team. He said, 'Here, give this to the lady.' "When Reggie was elected to the Hall of Fame, he wanted to write an acceptance speech. He knew I was a speech professor (at St. John's University) and he said, 'I need some help.' So I helped him write it."

❀ ❀ ❀ ❀

"When Johnny Unitas passed away, I gave a eulogy about him. The great Giants-Colts overtime championship game of December 28, 1958, came back to me. I can remember thinking late in the game, *The Giants have won it*, and they punted down toward the home plate area of the field, to the 20-yard line. "Unitas had to go 80 yards and the Giants were a good defensive team. But he started a great drive and I kept announcing, 'Unitas to Berry,' 'Unitas to Berry,' 'Unitas to Berry.' I wanted to scream into my microphone, 'Would somebody cover Berry.' I felt I was stuttering, 'Unitas to Berry.'"

❀ ❀ ❀ ❀

"For the appearance of two Popes, in 1965 and 1979, I volunteered my services not only as a public address announcer but as a professor of speech and a Catholic lector. I was a lector in my parish and a trainer of lectors in the diocese of Brooklyn. "I submitted my request to the archdiocese, and the monsignor wrote to me and said, 'We'd love to have you, but we've already hired and invited the lectors for the Pope.' One of them was Helen Hayes, the great actress, and the other was a well-known performer. They were looking for big names. So the Popes missed me, and I missed the Popes."

When the Polo Grounds burned in 1911, the Yankees graciously put aside their differences with McGraw and Brush and allowed the Giants to use their little Hilltop Park while the Giants' new park was being built. Two years later, as McGraw steered his old buddy Tillinghast L'Hommedieu "Cap" Huston into a partnership with the brewer Jacob Ruppert to buy the Yankees, the Giants returned the favor. The Yankees were invited into the Polo Grounds as tenants, an arrangement that lasted from 1913 until 1920. By that time Ruppert and Huston had made enough money to buy Babe Ruth from the Red Sox, and in 1920 the Yankees outdrew the Giants in their own park by 100,000 fans. McGraw, by now in virtual sole control of the Giants, ordered the Yankees out of the Polo Grounds.

About this time, multimillionaire William Waldorf Astor died suddenly and left to his heirs a 10-acre plot on the Bronx bank of the Harlem River, across from the Polo Grounds in Manhattan. The river often flooded the tract, which discouraged development. Ruppert, though, saw the land's potential and offered $600,000 for it. The Astor heirs, facing a huge inheritance tax, were ecstatic to sell.

Suddenly, the Yankees were building a stadium virtually next door to the Giants, and the New York City fat cats that long had been in cahoots with McGraw switched their allegiance. The Yankees convinced the city to extend public transportation to their Bronx locale. While the elevated train line in Manhattan that had made the Polo Grounds accessible would be dismantled, the new city-owned subway system would run directly under Babe Ruth's new home.

Of course, without Ruth, Yankee Stadium might have become a canyon of empty seats, as was the case with the stadium that opened in Cleveland a decade later. That one, built on the hope that Cleveland would be awarded the 1932 Olympics, was so ponderously large that the hapless Indians moved in at the end of July 1932 and moved out at the end of the 1933 season. Until 1947, they could afford to open the gates and turn on the hot dog grills at Municipal Stadium only on Sundays and holidays, and later for night games.

But the Yankee Stadium turnstiles have never ceased to click regularly. Fans initially drawn by the exploits of Ruth also found a hometown hero in Lou Gehrig. Then came Joe DiMaggio; followed by Mickey Mantle and a grand cast that included Yogi Berra, Whitey Ford, and Roger Maris; followed by the likes of Thurman Munson, Reggie Jackson, Don Mattingly, Derek Jeter, Bernie Williams, and Jason Giambi. As often as not, the team in pinstripes was magnificent. The original Stadium played host to 73 World Series games in 42 seasons, including 11 Series-deciding games. From 1976, when the remodeled Stadium opened, through 2002, the Yankees played host to 23 Series games, including five that decided a champion.

YANKEE STADIUM FIRSTS

- **GAME:** April 18, 1923 (4-1 win over Boston)
- **CEREMONIAL FIRST PITCH:** New York Governor Al Smith
- **PITCH:** Bob Shawkey (ball)
- **VICTORY:** April 18, 1923 (4-1 over Boston)
- **LOSS:** April 22, 1923 (4-3 to Washington)
- **BATTER:** Boston's Chick Fewster (grounded to short)
- **YANKEE BATTER:** Whitey Witt
- **HIT:** Boston's George Burns (April 18, 2nd-inning single)
- **YANKEE HIT:** Aaron Ward (April 18, 3rd-inning single)
- **RUN:** Bob Shawkey (April 18, on Joe Dugan's single in 3rd)
- **HOME RUN:** Babe Ruth (April 18, three-run homer in 3rd)
- **ERROR:** Babe Ruth (April 18, dropped fly ball in 5th)

From Ruth's Stadium-christening home run in 1923, to Don Larsen's perfect game in the 1956 World Series, to Roger Maris' 61st home run of the 1961 season, to the Yankees' implausible comebacks against Arizona in the fourth and fifth games of the 2001 Series, Yankee Stadium has been a worthy stage for some of baseball's most remarkable events. Men that come together and wage competition for a common good forge a brotherhood, and the Yankees celebrate such kinship on a grander scale than any other team in sports. They call it Old-Timers' Day in baseball, a celebration that first became an annual ritual at Yankee Stadium. And only at Yankee Stadium has Old-Timers' Day remained a highlight of the summer, an unbreakable legacy.

Magnificent as the Yankees' achievement has been over the years, the Stadium has shown a capacity for more, playing host to many memorable events that did not involve baseball, or sports of any kind. The paint was still wet in some places when the first championship boxing match was held in a jerry-rigged ring atop the infield on July 24, 1923. In 1938, the immortal heavyweight Joe Louis avenged the only loss among the first 69 bouts of his career, beating Max Schmeling ("In one round!" to quote the immortal radio call of the raspy Clem McCarthy) beneath the glare of temporary lights. It was one of seven bouts that Louis won at Yankee Stadium. Rocky Marciano won three bouts there. The Stadium played host to 30 championship bouts, the last in 1976 when Muhammad Ali knocked out Ken Norton in roughly the same location where Willie Randolph fielded ground balls.

NO-HITTERS
❧ BY ❧
YANKEES PITCHERS AT YANKEE STADIUM

Monte Pearson	Cleveland	August 27, 1938	13-0
Allie Reynolds	Boston	September 28, 1951	8-0
* Don Larsen	Brooklyn	October 8, 1956	2-0
Dave Righetti	Boston	July 4, 1983	4-0
Jim Abbott	Cleveland	September 4, 1993	4-0
Dwight Gooden	Seattle	May 14, 1996	2-0
** David Wells	Minnesota	May 17, 1998	4-0
** David Cone	Montreal	July 18, 1999	6-0

* Perfect game, Game 5 of World Series
** Perfect game

NO-HITTERS
❧ AGAINST ❧
THE YANKEES AT YANKEE STADIUM

Cy Young	Boston	June 30, 1908	8-0
Ray Caldwell	Cleveland	September 10, 1919	3-0
Bob Feller	Cleveland	April 30, 1946	1-0
Virgil Trucks	Detroit	August 25, 1952	1-0

Yankee Stadium has been home to two football franchises called the Yankees. It housed the Giants of the National Football League from 1956 to 1973, and was the venue for what many contend is both the greatest and most significant game in professional football history. When the Giants and Baltimore Colts played the first overtime game in NFL history, under the lights of primetime tel-

evision, for the 1958 championship, they were in Yankee Stadium.

College football came to the Stadium six months after it opened and returned every year through 1951. The Army-Navy game was played there in 1930 and 1931. Notre Dame and Army met at the Stadium in 1928, and in the bowels of the ballpark that day the great Fighting Irish coach Knute Rockne

NEW YORK FOO

Memorable non-baseball events at Yankee Stadium

- **November 12, 1928:** Notre Dame football coach Knute Rockne at halftime of game with Army made famous "Win One for the Gipper" speech.

- **June 22, 1938:** World heavyweight boxing champion Joe Louis knocked out Max Schmeling in first round, avenging only previous loss.

- **June 17, 1954:** Rocky Marciano defended world heavyweight boxing title with 15-round decision over Ezzard Charles. Marciano would defend title twice more at Yankee Stadium.

- **July 20, 1957:** Rev. Billy Graham held revival meeting attended by 92,000.

- **December 7, 1957:** Cardinal Spellman of New York celebrated Mass.

- **December 28, 1958:** Baltimore Colts defeated New York Giants in overtime 23-17 for NFL championship. Some regard the game as greatest in NFL history.

- **October 4, 1965:** Pope Paul VI celebrated Mass on first-ever papal trip to North America.

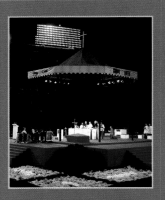

stirred the team with his "Win One for the Gipper" speech, later immortalized on the big screen by Ronald Reagan, the actor who became President of the United States. The short-lived Gotham Bowl pitted Baylor versus Utah in 1961, and Nebraska versus Miami in 1962. In the 169th and final college football game played at the Stadium, Eddie Robinson's Grambling Tigers pounded Morgan State 33-0 in front of 34,000 in 1983.

The Stadium has served as a soccer pitch for the great Pele, who first played there in an exhibition game and later as a member of the New York Cosmos. What we know as the warning track that circles the perimeter of the field originally was part of a 400-yard running track sanctioned by the Amateur Athletics Union.

TBALL GIANTS

- **September 28, 1976:** Muhammad Ali defended his world heavyweight boxing title with controversial 15-round decision over Ken Norton — final bout held at Yankee Stadium.

- **October 2, 1979:** Pope John Paul II celebrated Mass in second papal visit to North America.

- **June 21, 1990:** South African civil rights leader Nelson Mandela welcomed with huge celebration.

- **June 22, 1990:** Billy Joel performed first of two concerts on successive days.

- **August 29, 1992:** Irish rock band U2 performed first of two concerts on successive days.

- **June 10, 1994:** Pink Floyd performed first of two concerts on successive days.

- **September 23, 2001:** "A Prayer for America" service held in wake of September 11 terrorist attacks on United States.

Yankee Stadium's vastness has long been appreciated by the world outside of sports. The Jehovah's Witnesses staged their annual conventions at the Stadium from 1950 through 1965, and again in the 1990s putting 123,707 souls into the place on one particular day. Two Popes held Mass there, Paul VI in 1965 and John Paul II in 1979. On Sunday, September 23, 2001, with the pyre of the World Trade Center still smoking, a non-denominational prayer service at the Stadium impacted a community struggling to get back onto its feet. Billy Graham crusaded on the infield as early as 1957, and in the kind of variety that only Yankee Stadium could have handled, Nelson Mandela and Billy Joel appeared there on consecutive days in 1990.

28

As much and as many as it has accommodated, Yankee Stadium was meant for baseball games. Such isn't the case with the other four stadiums built before 1966 that remain in use in the major leagues. Though built for the Red Sox, Fenway Park was shared in 1914 and 1915 by the Sox and the Boston Braves; in fact, the Braves won the World Series in Fenway in 1914. Dodger Stadium was shared by the Dodgers and Angels from its opening in 1962 through 1965. Shea Stadium, which opened in 1964 and is the fifth-oldest park in the major leagues, was occupied by both the Mets and Yankees in 1974 and 1975. Venerable and beloved Wrigley Field, seemingly forever linked to the Cubs, actually was built as Weeghman Park in 1914 for the Chicago Whales of the Federal League.

MONUMENT PARK

○ ○ ○ ○ ○ ○ ○

In the outfield at Yankee Stadium, and as a tradition that has continued since 1932, the team's all-time greatest are honored with plaques and monuments. On May 30 of that year, the first monument was dedicated to the memory of manager Miller Huggins, who had died suddenly three years prior.

The first plaque was placed on the center-field wall in April 1940 as a tribute to Jacob Ruppert, the former owner who built Yankee Stadium and who guided the team to their first pennant and world championship.

In 1941, a monument was erected to honor the untimely passing of Lou Gehrig, and eight years later, in 1949, to honor the late Babe Ruth. In the 1990s, two more monuments would be placed: one for Mickey Mantle erected in August 1996 and one for Joe DiMaggio in April 1999. Both centerfielders had plaques hanging that were taken down in favor of the monuments after their passing.

In the 1940s, a plaque was added for general manager Edward Barrow. In 1976, two more plaques were added to memorialize managers Joe McCarthy and Casey Stengel. In the 1980s, plaques were dedicated to Yankees greats Thurman Munson (1980), Roger Maris and Elston Howard (1984), Phil Rizzuto (1985), Billy Martin (1986), Lefty Gomez and Whitey Ford (1987), Yogi Berra and Bill Dickey (1988), and Allie Reynolds (1989). Two non-uniformed Yankees legends had their plaques put up recently: the "Voice of the Yankees" radio announcer Mel Allen in 1998 and the "Voice of Yankee Stadium" Bob Sheppard in 2000.

Plaques commemorating the visits of Pope Paul VI in 1965 and Pope John Paul in 1979 were dedicated in Monument Park by the Knights of Columbus.

Most recently, the sixth monument was added on September 11, 2002, to pay tribute to those who were affected by the events of September 11, 2001.

Monument Park was once part of the playing field, located in straight-away center on the warning track about 10 feet in front of the wall. In 1985, after the left-center field fence was moved in, the Park became an area for up-close fan viewing. The popular Stadium feature was expanded in 1988 and a special walk honoring the Yankees players and managers whose numbers have been retired was added.

Beginning in 1932, plaques and monuments have been dedicated to the following:

PLAYERS: Yogi Berra, Bill Dickey, Joe DiMaggio, Whitey Ford, Lou Gehrig, Lefty Gomez, Elston Howard, Reggie Jackson, Mickey Mantle, Don Mattingly, Roger Maris, Thurman Munson, Allie Reynolds, Phil Rizzuto, and Babe Ruth

MANAGERS: Miller Huggins, Billy Martin, Joe McCarthy, and Casey Stengel

OTHERS: Jacob Ruppert, team owner, 1915–1939; Ed Barrow, front office executive, 1921–1945; Mel Allen, "Voice of the Yankees," 1939–1964; Bob Sheppard, Yankee Stadium public address announcer, 1951–present, September 11th Commemorative

Thus Yankee Stadium is unique among ballparks of any significant age in this one area: No major league baseball team except the Yankees has ever called it home. Lost in the simplicity of this fact is its profound meaning for the feel of the place, the continuity of its image, and the resilience of its popularity. From Notre Dame's Four Horsemen to two Popes to the rock band U2, everyone has been welcomed and afforded a key to the place. But only the Yankees reside at Yankee Stadium, sometimes in pin-striped person, always in spirit.

For New Yorkers, taking an out-of-town fan to the Stadium for the first time is almost as enjoyable as being able to go back and experience anew one's own first visit. Films have been made and many words written that attempt to capture the essence of the place's imposing beauty. Each seems merely to echo the observations of William O. McGeehan, the correspondent who covered the Stadium opening in 1923 for the *New York Times* and wrote, as both reporter and goggle-eyed fan, the following:

"Once inside the grounds, the sweep of the big stand strikes the eye most forcibly. It throws its arms far out to each side, the grandstand ending a way over where the bleachers begin. In the center of the vast pile of steel and concrete was the green spread of the diamond, and fewer ball fields are greener than that on which the teams played yesterday."

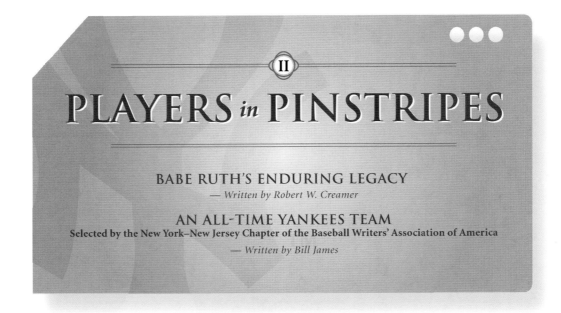

II

PLAYERS *in* PINSTRIPES

BABE RUTH'S ENDURING LEGACY
— *Written by Robert W. Creamer*

AN ALL-TIME YANKEES TEAM
Selected by the New York–New Jersey Chapter of the Baseball Writers' Association of America
— *Written by Bill James*

Babe Ruth was the first New York Yankee player to go from baseball fame to American legend, but he wasn't the last. From Ruth, Gehrig, DiMaggio, and Mantle to Reggie Jackson and Derek Jeter, there has always been something unique about those wearing Yankee pinstripes. It is within this context that award-winning author Robert W. Creamer examines in the following essay the enduring relevance of Ruth. Baseball historian and legendary analyst Bill James dissects the 25-man all-time Yankees team as it was voted by the New York–New Jersey Chapter of the Baseball Writers' Association of America. James also lends his unique skills to analyze other great players, some of whom were lost in the shadows of their more-famous teammates.

AL **LEADER** IN

RUNS **8** TIMES

ON BASE % **10** TIMES

RBI **6** TIMES

HR **12** TIMES

SLUGGING % **13** TIMES

WALKS **11** TIMES

Sultan of Swat

BABE RUTH

Written by Robert W. Creamer

Babe Ruth has been dead for more than 50 years, and he has not swung a bat at a pitch in a major league game since 1935. And still we talk about him. How come?
His storied record of 60 home runs in a season was broken more than 40 years ago. The lingering glamour of the "Babe's 60" has been trampled and all but obliterated by sluggers racing toward and beyond that once magical mark.

Ruth's career record of 714 homers was surpassed a generation ago. His incredible slugging average for one season, a record that lasted 80 years, is gone. His near-legendary number of walks in one season, most of them intentional or nearly so, has been topped. When the Babe retired he held 56 major league records, but that majestic castle of achievement is crumbling.

And still we talk about him. In 1973, 25 years after Ruth's death, the columnist Red Smith wrote that the Babe seemed "insistently alive," and after 30 more years it continues to be that way. "Babe Ruth" seems to jump into print and discussions almost every day. Why is he recalled so vividly? What was it about Ruth — what *is* it about him — that keeps him so alive?

The answer is *impact*. Ruth made an impact on everyone who saw him, from his schoolboy days at St. Mary's Industrial School for Boys in Baltimore to his final burst of three home runs in one game in Pittsburgh, a few days before his playing career ended. He simply dominated the scene wherever he was, on and off the field, with his size (at 6-feet-2-inches and 235 pounds he was a very large person for his day), his big round face, his booming voice, his infectious, outgoing personality, his extravagant behavior, the dramatic scope of his accomplishments on the ballfield, the way he changed baseball, and perhaps, beyond everything else, the way he created the image of the New York Yankees that continues to this day.

Ruth made the Yankees. Before he went from Boston to New York, in January 1920, the Yankees were nothing. The now glamorous team name was only seven years old when the Babe arrived — New York's American League club had been called the "Highlanders" for 10 seasons before that. From the club's inception in 1903 through 1919, it had never won a pennant, had finished second only twice, and in most seasons was a drab, mediocre team. Some years it was worse than mediocre. The encyclopedic *Total Baseball* claims that in

1913 the new manager, Frank Chance, inherited "the weakest lineup the New York Yankees will ever have." The Yankees had been last in 1912. Under Chance they edged up to seventh in 1913, one game above last place, and in 1914 they climbed into a tie for sixth place.

Jacob Ruppert and Cap Huston bought the club after the 1914 season, and things began to improve, if slowly. Ruppert and Huston, men about town in Manhattan, had looked into buying John McGraw's New York Giants, at the time baseball's most famous team. McGraw turned them away, so they bought the Yankees, who in 1913 had abandoned their old hilltop stadium to play in the big, modern Polo Grounds as the Giants' tenants. The Yanks finished fourth in 1918 and third in 1919, but they were still considered a second-rate team.

Then Ruth arrived, and the baseball world changed. One must appreciate the situation. Ruth had come into the big leagues as a left-handed pitcher and he proved to be a great one. In his first full season, in 1915, he won 18 games. He followed that with 23 victories in 1916 and 24 in 1917. He had 13 wins in 1918 in a war-shortened season during which he also played the outfield much of the time. As a pitcher, he won three games without a loss in World Series competition, including a 14-inning, 2-1 masterpiece in 1916 that was the longest World Series game played in the 20th century. He pitched 29 consecutive scoreless innings in Series play, breaking the great Christy Mathewson's record set 13 years earlier. Ruth's record lasted for 43 years.

Ruth was one hell of a pitcher, but that wasn't all he was in those days. During his first three seasons as a pitcher, Ruth hit nine home runs — four in 1915, three in 1916, and two in 1917. Even today that many homers by a pitcher might attract attention. Back then, in the dead-ball era, it was sensational. The American League home run leader in 1915 was an outfielder named Braggo Roth, who played for Chicago and Cleveland and hit seven home runs; three more than Ruth, four more than Ty Cobb, and two more than Shoeless Joe

Jackson. The National League leader was Gavvy Cravath, who hit 24.

And here was a 20-year-old rookie, a pitcher, with four home runs in 1915. Beyond that astonishing development was the way Ruth hit them, the power he displayed. Ruth's first major league homer, hit in May 1915 in the Polo Grounds where his Red Sox were playing the Yankees, landed in the upper right field stands; a gargantuan poke in that era and particularly impressive because, as an awed sportswriter pointed out, the young pitcher hit it "with no apparent effort."

Ruth hit another home run in the Polo Grounds a month later, prompting another journalist to intone: "His name is Babe Ruth. He is built like a bale of cotton and pitches left-handed for the Boston Red Sox. All left-handers are peculiar and Babe is no exception, because he can also bat."

He hit his third homer that season into the distant right field bleachers in Boston's Fenway Park, where only one ball had ever been hit previously, and his fourth sailed completely out of Sportsman's Park in St. Louis, breaking a plateglass window on the far side of the street. In that game in St. Louis, Ruth also had two doubles and a single, drove in three runs, and pitched a complete game in a 4-3 victory.

Ruth hit only three homers in 1916. They came in successive games, noteworthy any time but amazing in 1916, particularly because one of them was a pinch-hit, three-run, game-tying blast. Of his two home runs in 1917, one was the first ever hit into the center field seats at Fenway Park. The other was something of a command performance: He was pitching in New York, in front of a crowd largely made up of newly inducted soldiers (this was during World War I) who had been brought to the ballpark as a farewell treat before shipping out. The soldiers wanted to see Ruth hit one. The Babe, who loved interacting with the crowd, tried to accommodate them. He brought them to their feet with a roar in the sixth inning when he drove a long "foul home run" over the right field roof before settling for a single. When he came to bat in the ninth inning, the soldiers beseeching him

"As soon as I got out there I felt a strange relationship with the pitcher's mound. It just felt like the most natural thing in the world. Striking out batters was easy."

— BABE RUTH

to belt one, he came through, hitting his second and last homer of the year.

By that time, even though Ruth had hit only nine home runs in his career, he was being called "The Home Run King." In spring training of 1918, the Red Sox stopped at an Army camp to play an exhibition game, and Ruth put on a show in batting practice, knocking five balls over the right field fence. People just didn't hit a ball that far that frequently in those days, and for the assembled soldiers it was like watching a sudden explosion of skyrockets. Cheers of delight erupted every time a ball sailed beyond the distant fence.

That was the season Ruth began playing the outfield when he wasn't pitching, and he tied for the American League home run title with 11. In 1919, as Ruth completed the transition from full-time pitcher to full-time hitter — he started 15 games on the mound and won nine — he hit 29 homers, two more than the previous major league record. He was just 24, yet he had become the most compelling figure in the game. "The more I see of Babe," said the respected Boston sportswriter Burt Whitman, "the more he seems a figure out of mythology."

And at that point Ruth was sold to the Yankees.

Think of the impact. The Yankees were improving, but in a city dominated by McGraw and the Giants, who had finished first or second 13 times in 17 years, the Yankees still were nothing. Far more people went to the Polo Grounds to see the Giants play than to see the Yankees. Now, suddenly, stunningly, the lowly Yankees had Babe Ruth, the game's best and most popular player — and Ruth came through for them far beyond their wildest dreams.

He started slowly in the 1920 season, as though for dramatic effect. Opening Day was in Philadelphia. The Yankees' regular center fielder had been injured, and Ruth persuaded manager Miller Huggins to let him play that position. He hit two singles, but also dropped a fly ball in the eighth inning with two outs and two on. The homer-less spell persisted in

"When you figure the things he did, and the way he lived and the way
he played, you've got to figure he was more than an animal even.
There was never anyone like him. He was a god."

— JOE DUGAN, Ruth's teammate, 1922–1928

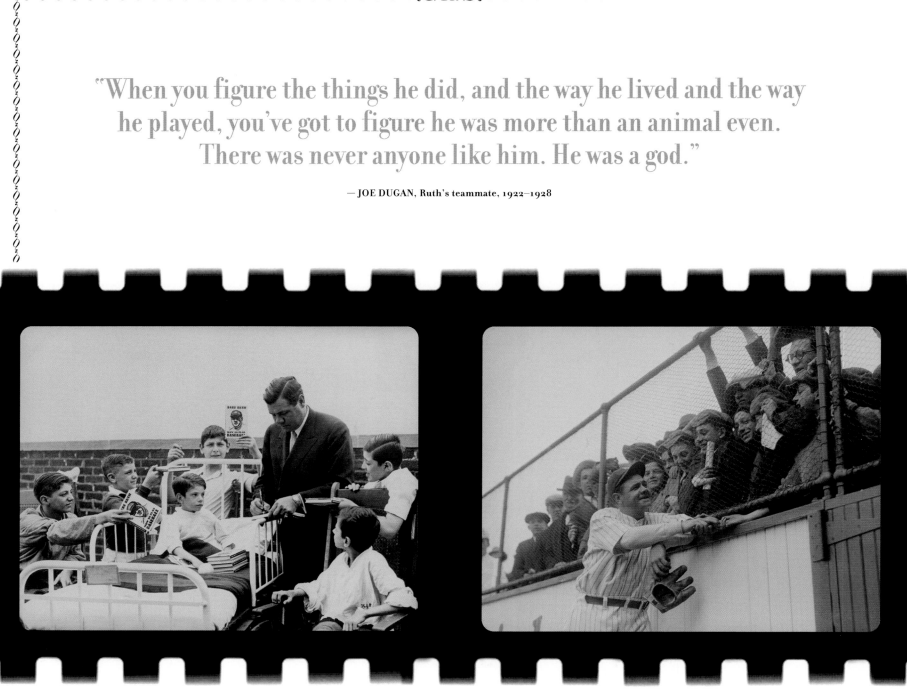

Philadelphia and then in Boston, where the Yankees lost three games to the Red Sox before returning to New York for the home opener. A big crowd turned out that afternoon, but Ruth's New York debut was a fizzle. He suffered a pulled rib cage muscle during batting practice, struck out in the first inning, and was taken out of the game, a great disappointment for the fans. Ruth didn't play again in that greatly anticipated weekend series, and in the first game upon his return he struck out twice and made an error.

Some were murmuring: "How good is this Babe Ruth?" The "Ruthless Red Sox," as sportswriters had begun to call the Boston team, were leading the league, and the Yankees, with Ruth, were in the second division. Boston came

to New York for a five-game series and won the first game, the fourth straight time the Red Sox had beaten the Yankees in the young season.

As the calendar turned to May, Ruth began to deliver. On the first day of the month, he hit his first home run of the season, and the Yankees beat the Sox. By the end of May, he had struck 12 home runs; far more than any other major leaguer had ever hit in one month, and as many as any other American League player, other than the Babe, had hit in a full season since 1903.

He hit a dozen in June. He mounted a 26-game hitting streak, even though he was walked intentionally game after game. His batting average climbed into the .390s before settling at .376 by the end of the season. Ruth

> "I saw him transformed into the idol of American youth and the symbol of baseball the world over, a man loved by more people and with an intensity of feeling that perhaps has never been equaled before or since. I saw a man transformed into something pretty close to a god."
>
> — HARRY HOOPER, Ruth's teammate, 1914–1919

passed his 1919 home run record in the middle of July and finished the season with an utterly astonishing 54 homers, 35 ahead of the second man, George Sisler, who himself hit a remarkable 19. The Yankees were in the middle of the pennant race for a change, and in the end they finished third — a game short of second and three games behind the first-place Cleveland Indians.

Spectators poured into the Polo Grounds to see Ruth, many of them fans new to the game, drawn by the siren call of the Babe's explosive hitting. Season attendance at major league ballparks in the early decades of the 20th century was much less than it is now. In the post–World War I glow of 1919, the year before Ruth joined the team, the Yankees had set a club record by drawing 619,000 spectators to the Polo Grounds, 24 percent above their previous high. In 1920, with Ruth, they drew 1,289,000. Not only was it the first time a major league team had drawn a million in a season, but it was also 42 percent better than the previous record, set a dozen years earlier by McGraw's Giants.

Ruth's impact on baseball in 1920 was far greater than any player's previously or since. Beyond the record number of home runs and the record attendance for which he was largely responsible, he changed the way major league baseball was played. Whether the owners had altered the baseball from "dead" to "lively" is still debated, but there is no doubt they made changes with the intent of benefiting the hitters. They banned trick pitches such as the spitball

"I swing as hard as I can and I try to swing right through the ball. The harder you grip the bat, the more you can swing through the ball and the farther the ball will go. I swing big, with everything I've got. I hit big or miss big. I like to live as big as I can."

— BABE RUTH

and the emeryball, and they ended the long-standing practice of letting scuffed, dirty balls remain in play. Other players rushed to copy Ruth's swing-for-the-seats style. As home run totals began to soar, managers shifted their strategic approach from the traditional bunt-steal-sacrifice mode of creating runs to the long ball. Even McGraw, high priest of "old-school" baseball, followed along, despite the disparaging comments he made about Ruth and his style of hitting. Casey Stengel, who played three seasons for the Giants, said, "McGraw was the best manager I ever saw at adapting from the dead ball to the lively ball."

Ruth's performance in 1920 shook baseball at its moorings, and nothing was ever quite the same again. Even the Chicago Black Sox scandal, the shocking revelation late in the 1920 season that eight players on the 1919 White Sox had been paid to intentionally lose the World Series, was little more than a blip

on the baseball screen. Attendance dipped briefly, then soared in the Roaring '20s, Ruth's big decade. Fans jammed into ballparks, enticed in good part by the home run efflorescence.

Ruth's popularity was enormous. Hank Greenberg, who a decade and a half later became a renowned home run hitter, said that when he was growing up in the Bronx, Ruth was the hero of every boy in the neighborhood. Harry Hooper, who had been a teammate of Ruth's in Boston, said, "I saw him transformed into the idol of American youth and the symbol of baseball the world over, a man loved by more people and with an intensity of feeling that perhaps has never been equaled before or since. I saw a man transformed into something pretty close to a god."

Throughout the 1920s Ruth remained center stage, usually heroically but sometimes as the bad boy. He had an even better season in 1921 than he did

Babe Ruth, Miller Huggins, and Lou Gehrig during spring training in 1929.

"I have only one superstition:
Touch all the bases when I hit a home run."

— BABE RUTH

in 1920, hitting 59 homers to break the home run record for the third year in a row and leading the Yankees to their first pennant. As the author Robert Lipsyte noted, "It is often overlooked that the home run king was probably the most complete player of his time — not only was he a superb major league pitcher, but his fielding and base-running were far above average too." Players who watched the left-handed Ruth fool around at third base during spring training in the 1920s marveled at his agility. The legendary New York sportswriter Red Smith said, "A person familiar with Ruth only through photographs and records could hardly be blamed for assuming that he was a blubbery freak whose ability to hit balls across county lines was all that kept

him in the big leagues. The truth is that he was the complete ballplayer, certainly one of the greatest and maybe the best one of all time." The Yanks finished first again in 1922 and 1923, won the first of their many World Series championships in 1923, won three pennants in a row from 1926 through 1928 — six pennants in eight years was unprecedented success — and won World Series titles in 1927 and 1928.

Ruth was on a rollercoaster ride of both popularity and disapproval throughout those years. He was suspended by the baseball commissioner for the first six weeks of the 1922 season for his flagrant disregard of a rule that prohibited offseason barnstorming tours, and four more times that season, for

1920

BABE RUTH'S FIRST SEASON WITH THE YANKEES

GAMES	142
AB	458
RUNS	158
HITS	172
DOUBLES	36
TRIPLES	9
HOME RUNS	54
RBIs	137
WALKS	150
STRIKEOUTS	80
BATTING AVERAGE	.376
ON BASE PCT.	.532
SLUGGING PCT.	.847

YANKEES HOME ATTENDANCE 1919	YANKEES HOME ATTENDANCE 1920
619,000	**1,289,000**

shorter periods, as a result of his hot-tempered misbehavior. After he was ejected from a game for throwing dirt on an umpire, Ruth climbed over the dugout roof and charged into the stands after a heckler. In another game he ran in from the outfield to curse an umpire who had called a play against the Yankees. He fought with a teammate in the dugout. People were both repelled and entranced. A contemporary observer, Paul Gallico, wrote, "There has always been a magic about that gross, ugly, coarse, gargantuan figure of a man and everything he did."

Ruth reformed and had great seasons in 1923 and 1924, but he got in serious trouble again in 1925. In spring training he was so involved with "booze and broads," as his friend and teammate Joe Dugan told me, that he developed an ulcer, collapsed, was hospitalized, underwent surgery on his abdomen, and missed the first two months of the season. Upon his return, with his first marriage breaking up in a glare of publicity, Ruth played poorly, defied his manager, Miller Huggins, was suspended from the team, and fined the then-enormous sum of $5,000, an amount about equal to the yearly salary of most players at the time.

As a player Ruth reformed for good after that, but his eminently public private life — his extravagant appetite, his uninhibited manner of living, his separation from his wife, her death, his marriage to his second wife — fasci-

"I never saw the Babe make a mistake in a ballgame. Ruth always knew, instinctively, what to do on a ballfield."

— ED BARROW, Yankees general manager, 1921–1945

nated people. Ruth's play on the field and his essentially good nature kept his popularity high despite the trouble he often found himself in. "There wasn't a mean bone in his body," said a teammate. Another added, "He was the kind of bad boy it's easy to forgive." Red Smith observed, "His natural liking for people communicated itself to the public."

Through it all, Ruth kept hitting home runs. Except for his two troubled seasons — 1922 and 1925 — he led the league in homers every year from 1918 through 1931, and he continued to hit them with a splendor and sense of dramatic timing that made them unforgettable. "There are a hundred stories illustrating his sense of theater," Smith said. Ruth hit the first home run in Yankee Stadium, on Opening Day in 1923, when that still-splendid ballpark was first opened to the public. He hit the first home run in the first All-Star Game. He set a home run record for the fourth time in 1927, outdueling teammate Lou Gehrig and hitting 60. He hit three home runs in a World Series game in 1926 and again in 1928. Reggie Jackson is the only other

player in the 20th century that hit three homers in a Series game.

In the 1928 Series, St. Louis Cardinals fans hooted at Ruth as he stood in right field, and in turn he cheerfully pantomimed that he was going to hit a homer his next time at bat — and he did. Ruth enjoyed doing extravagant things like that. In the late 1920s in Boston, he reacted to a box-seat fan loudly taunting him during a game in nearly empty Fenway Park by looking at the fan, pointing toward the right field seats, and hitting a ball there.

Ruth's most famous "called shot" came in Chicago in 1932 during a turbulent World Series between the Yankees and the Cubs. In the third game, with the score tied and the Cubs players and fans riding him unmercifully for a misplay he had made in the outfield, Ruth grinned, indicated he was going to hit a home run, and sent a tremendous shot to dead center field — at that time the longest home run ever hit in Wrigley Field. Ruth's performance that day has been exaggerated, misinterpreted, and distorted by Hollywood movies, television re-creations,

714
CAREER HOME RUNS

"He was one of a kind. If he had never played ball, if you had never heard of him and passed him on Broadway, you'd turn around and look back."

— WAITE HOYT, Ruth's teammate, 1921–1930

1330
CAREER STRIKEOUTS

and misinformed commentary, all keyed to the question of whether he pointed to the exact spot where he intended to hit the ball and then hit it there. Almost certainly, Ruth didn't point to the exact spot in distant center field. What is significant is that in a World Series game in front of a huge, jeering crowd, he challenged Chicago and the Cubs, clearly implied he was going to smack one, and did smack one; not a cheap shot but a titanic homer that proved to be the game-winning run and the turning point of the Series. It was epic. Ruth, who relished such moments, loved it. He said later, "I never had so much fun in my life. That's the first time I ever got the players and the fans going at the same time."

Even as his career neared its end, Ruth created an unforgettable memory. In 1935, his last season, playing out the string with the Boston Braves, out of shape, aching, and making one last road trip before retiring, he somehow roused a final flash of his remarkable ability and hit three home runs in a game against the Pirates in Pittsburgh. The final homer, his 714th, the last hit of his career,

was a colossal poke over the right field roof of towering Forbes Field, the first ball hit that far in Pittsburgh. Guy Bush, who was pitching for the Pirates, said later, "I never saw a ball hit so hard before or since. It's probably still going."

At that point no one except Ruth had hit 700 home runs, no one else had hit 600, no one had hit 500, no one had hit 400. Ruth had 350 more home runs than the man with the next biggest number, and 400 more than the man in third place. He was indeed the king of the home run.

Ruth's hold on the public hardly diminished after he left the stage in 1935. In the ensuing 13 years before his death from cancer at age 53, he continued to pop into the spotlight. When he went to Ebbets Field with his wife in 1938, to see the first night game played in Brooklyn, his presence created such a tremendous stir in the crowd that it was reported in New York newspapers the next day, along with what happened on the field that night: Johnny Vander Meer's second successive no-hitter. The publicity-conscious Dodgers

"All players should quit when it starts to feel as if all the bases run uphill."

— BABE RUTH

soon convinced Ruth to be their first base coach for the rest of the season. Even then, potbellied and in his 40s, he put on a daily show for the fans, taking batting practice with the team and usually putting a ball or two over the fence. He would take infield practice too, at first base, where he displayed surprising grace for a man of his age and portly appearance, deftly scooping low throws out of the dirt.

He remained a public figure, a notable, a celebrity. He was Babe Ruth. He was news during World War II when he batted against Walter Johnson or played golf with Ty Cobb in fund-raising events. He was in the public eye when he made an impressive motion picture appearance playing himself in the 1942 movie *Pride of the Yankees*, about his dead teammate Gehrig. Ruth's own death in 1948, after a long and painful illness, was very much a public event. There are elderly people today who remember where they were when they heard that Ruth had died, the way they remember where they were when they heard of Pearl Harbor or John F. Kennedy's assassination or September 11. Ruth's casket lay in state in the cavernous area under the stands in Yankee Stadium before his funeral Mass at St. Patrick's Cathedral in New York, and an estimated 75,000 people passed it to pay their final respects. In pre-television America, when most major league ballplayers, most professional athletes, were seldom recognized in public, everyone knew Babe Ruth.

"He was one of a kind," said his teammate Waite Hoyt. "If he had never played ball, if you had never heard of him and passed him on Broadway, you'd turn around and look back." Ruth handled it all very well. He was naturally at ease in crowds, relished the acclaim and affection, and reacted cheerfully. Simply put, he liked people and they loved him.

Ruth's towering presence didn't disappear with his death. Whenever a slugger began to hit homers at a rapid pace, a comparison inevitably was made

Crowds of mourners jammed the sidewalks on August 19, 1948, to watch the funeral procession for Babe Ruth as it moved toward St. Patrick's Cathedral in New York. Ruth's widow requested that the funeral procession and service be open to anyone who wished to attend.

between his growing total and the number Ruth had on the same date in 1927, his record home run season. In 1961, when Roger Maris and Mickey Mantle made their determined and successful (for Maris) assault on Ruth's 60 homers, Ruth was mentioned in print and on the air almost as often as Mantle and Maris were. A dozen years later, when Hank Aaron steadily approached and eventually surpassed Ruth's career home run total, the same thing happened. Aaron said in 1974, "I can't recall a day this year or last that I did not hear the name of Babe Ruth." Years after his death, the Babe was as alive in people's minds as Roger and Mickey and Hank were.

Ruth remained in mind for the rest of the 20th century. When Ken Burns made his nine-part television documentary *Baseball* in 1994, one of the segments was devoted to Ruth. In 1995, on the 100th anniversary of the Babe's birth, Hofstra University on Long Island held a three-day seminar on the subject of Ruth. In 1998 the long-gone Babe was in the news again when Mark McGwire and Sammy Sosa engaged in their spirited home run duel in which both surpassed the records set by Ruth and Maris, and which ended with McGwire hitting 70 homers, a figure that seemed as magical as Ruth's 60 — except that it was to be surpassed three years later by Barry Bonds' 73.

In 1999, ESPN had a yearlong countdown on television of the 20th century's "100 Greatest American Athletes," culminating in, so to speak, a competition between Ruth and Michael Jordan for the No. 1 spot. Jordan was the choice, although Ruth's adherents argued that the time bias was vastly in Michael's favor. Never mind. The old century ended and the new one began, and Ruth was still on people's minds. As Red Smith said, "There won't ever be a second Babe Ruth. Never another like him."

MICKEY MANTLE

Among the four great superstars of Yankees history, Mickey Mantle is the eternal adolescent. He came to the major leagues as a 19-year-old of seemingly limitless ability — and no matter what he accomplished, he would always be regarded by many as the player who was supposed to be better.

Mantle was almost 6 feet tall, blond, strikingly handsome, broad-shouldered, immensely powerful, and able to accelerate instantly and run like the wind for a short distance. He was a likeable man with a ready wit and an easygoing manner. We also can say he was a "natural hitter," a result of countless hours of batting practice he took in his youth from either side of the plate, depending on whether his father or his uncle was pitching. Mantle could read a curveball when he was 19.

When Joe DiMaggio retired, Mantle stepped in as the Yankees center fielder, a mantle — pun intended — which should not be wished even upon one's enemies. Mantle became a greater player than DiMaggio. The differences between the two are fairly subtle. Mantle's .298 batting average is about as impressive, in the context of his time, as DiMaggio's .325, or, for that matter, as Babe Ruth's .342 and Lou Gehrig's .340. Mantle batted .298 in a time when the American League batting average was .256; DiMaggio hit .325 in

"Son, nobody is half as good as MICKEY MANTLE."

— **AL KALINE**, responding to a taunting fan who said Kaline was not half as good as Mantle

Mickey Mantle		Joe DiMaggio
536	HOME RUNS	361
.298	BATTING AVERAGE	.325
2,415	HITS	2,214
153	STOLEN BASES	30

an era when the league average was .276. Adjusting both to a league average of .270, Mantle's average would be about .314, DiMaggio's about .318, Ruth's .324, and Gehrig's .322 — not really much difference.

Nor is there much to separate Mantle and DiMaggio in terms of power. Considering that DiMaggio played only 13 years and lost three prime seasons because of World War II, his 361 home runs are almost as impressive as Mantle's 536. DiMaggio was a better defensive center fielder than Mantle, which is not a put-down. DiMaggio was a better center fielder than almost anyone else. DiMaggio struck out less than Mantle — and almost everyone else — and as a result, he hit huge numbers of doubles and triples. He put a lot more balls in play than Mantle did.

The number of runs a team scores is essentially determined by how many runners it puts on base. Because he walked so often, Mantle was on base more than DiMaggio was — a lot more. DiMaggio's on-base percentage was 44 points better than the league norm; Mantle's was 92 points better. Mantle's walks won more games for the Yankees than DiMaggio's defense — or at least than DiMaggio's defensive advantage.

Mantle had many other virtues as a player. His .801 career stolen-base percentage is 15th best all time. Mantle stole five times as many bases as DiMaggio did, and he grounded into considerably fewer double plays. Mantle could not sustain his speed like DiMaggio did, but he could run faster in a short burst than almost anyone.

Mantle was adored by millions of fans, but he never reached the acceptance that DiMaggio did with the cognoscenti — if it's not too absurd to refer to old sportswriters as cognoscenti. DiMaggio demanded, deserved, and received respect. Mantle adopted an "Aw Shucks" personality, never demanded respect in the same way, and never received it. But he deserved it. He frequently played in pain, and he played magnificently.

> "I didn't think a guy could be that good. Every time I looked up,
> that big guy was on base or flying by me on a homer."
>
> — CHARLIE GRIMM, Cubs first baseman, after Gehrig hit .529 in the 1932 World Series

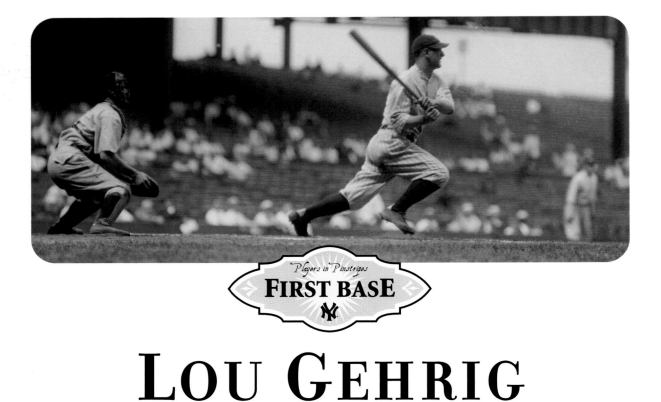

Players in Pinstripes
FIRST BASE

LOU GEHRIG

Let us suppose that the final, sad chapter of Lou Gehrig's career had not come about as it did, that his time in baseball had ended in a normal fashion. What would the final years of his career have been like? What would have been his final totals?

There are no definitive answers to these questions. But one thing is quite apparent: Had he not been stopped by illness, Gehrig would have set major league career records for runs scored and RBIs, and he would hold those records today by large margins. Babe Ruth held the career RBI record (2,213) and was passed only by Hank Aaron. Gehrig, despite losing out on possibly five years of his career, is fourth on the all-time list.

Comparing where they stood in RBIs at age 35, Gehrig was 270 ahead of Aaron, and 280 ahead of Ruth. Gehrig turned 35 in 1938, and he began to fade in the second half of that season. His career ended in the first month of the 1939 season.

Until developing the disease that would later kill him, Gehrig raced ahead of Aaron and Ruth in RBIs at a stunning pace. Aaron became a regular at age 20 and Gehrig at age 22, which afforded Aaron about a 200-RBI head start as they settled into their careers. At 28, Gehrig had 995, Aaron 991. At 30, Gehrig had 69 more than Aaron. At 32, Gehrig led by 137, and at 34 by 253. Gehrig pushed his advantage to 270 in 1938, even though, by his standards, it was a so-so season.

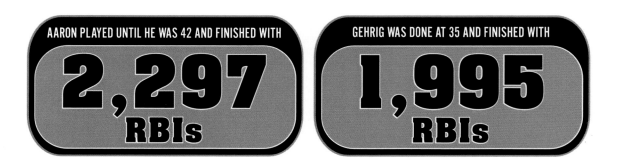

AARON PLAYED UNTIL HE WAS 42 AND FINISHED WITH	GEHRIG WAS DONE AT 35 AND FINISHED WITH
2,297 RBIs	**1,995** RBIs

Aaron played until he was 42 and finished with 2,297 RBIs. Gehrig was done at 35 and finished with 1,995. How high might Gehrig have taken that total?

The toughest part of answering that question is figuring out how long Gehrig would have played. If you would know that, you could pencil in the other numbers based on his career path and be satisfied with your projection. But you could miss by years guessing when Gehrig might have retired.

In good health, Gehrig certainly would have played every game in 1939, 1940, and 1941, at which time he would have been 38. Aside from poor health, it is difficult to fathom any reason why he would have left the lineup before 1942. By the end of the 1943 season, Gehrig might not have been playing every game, but almost certainly he would have still been playing. He would have been 40, and few stars of his magnitude retire before that age. Ruth, Aaron, Ty Cobb, Willie Mays, Honus Wagner, Stan Musial, Ted Williams, Tris Speaker — they all played at least until 40. Only a half-dozen true superstars in history retired before the age of 40, three of them Yankees (Gehrig, DiMaggio, and Mantle).

Now you come to a question that is impossible to answer: Would Gehrig have played through World War II? By 1943 the United States was in the thick of war, and great stars such as DiMaggio, Williams, and Bob Feller were in military service. Gehrig probably was too old to be drafted into service. He could have volunteered, but few men of his age did. It is reasonable to assume that a healthy Gehrig would have been one of the best players in the American League in 1943 and would have continued playing through the war years, through 1945, when he would have been 42. Gehrig probably would not have been driving in 150 runs a season during the war years, for two reasons: He was getting older, and offensive statistics were dropping sharply before the war and diving during the war.

Gehrig's career batting average, frozen at .340, probably would have dropped to about .328. His home run total, based on conservative assumptions, would have approached 700 (it is 493). His RBI total would have been about 2,850 — approximately 550 more than the all-time record. That is a phenomenal total, but certainly within the realm of possibility, based on Gehrig's rate of achievement.

Gehrig would have set numerous other records that would remain today. He would have scored more than 2,700 runs — hundreds more than the existing record; he would have been just short of 4,000 hits; and he would have had about 7,150 total bases — 300 more than Aaron's all-time record. And Gehrig would have drawn almost 2,500 walks, again, hundreds more than the existing record.

As it is, Gehrig had 13 100-RBI seasons, a record he shares with Ruth and Jimmie Foxx, and 13 consecutive 100-RBI seasons, a record he shares with Foxx. It is safe to assume that Gehrig, in continued good health, would have had 17 or 18 100-RBI seasons.

What about his record for consecutive games played? He certainly could have extended it to 2,700 or 2,800. It likely would have reached 3,000. If that had been the case, Cal Ripken Jr. would not have broken Gehrig's record in 1995. Ripken would have had to play every day until early in the 2001 season to have passed Gehrig.

The fact is that Gehrig's name almost certainly would be throughout the major league record book for batting feats — and perhaps it would be the most prominent name in the book — had he not been struck down in his prime by the disease that now carries his name.

7 — 150 RBI SEASONS

8 — 200 HIT SEASONS

3 — .700+ SLUGGING PCT. SEASONS

JOE DiMAGGIO

"You have to grow up with baseball to play it well" — Babe Ruth said it and Joe DiMaggio illustrated the point. DiMaggio grew up in a time and place when serious baseball was being played. His older brothers were ballplayers, and at the age of 18 DiMaggio played 187 games in the Pacific Coast League, just one notch below the major leagues.

Unlike Mickey Mantle, who arrived in the majors as a raw package of formidable ability, DiMaggio knew how to play the game long before he first caught sight of the New York City skyline. Just weeks after his first game, DiMaggio had jaws agape all over the American League. The moment they saw him, everyone in the baseball world realized that DiMaggio was very special.

DiMaggio was among a handful of players in baseball history who did everything well. Swinging a heavy bat, he drove long, arching line drives, and hardly ever struck out. He ran not only fast but with unparalleled grace, his strides melting one into another as he dashed over the vast, empty acres of center field at Yankee Stadium. He threw exceptionally well, and he played hard all the time.

A right-handed hitter in a park where the left field fence arched out to 400 feet before it reached center field, DiMaggio probably lost more home runs than any other player in history. He hit only 148 home runs in Yankee Stadium, and 213 on the road. He hit more road home runs than Mel Ott did, and in a much shorter career. Had he played half the time in just about any park except Yankee Stadium, DiMaggio likely would have hit 50 home runs in a good season.

For another player, Yankee Stadium's dimensions might have been a major detriment to his value. For DiMaggio, it simply emphasized other features of his game. If his long drives did not become home runs, they often became doubles or triples — and a showcase for his legendary grace. The huge left-center field area in Yankee Stadium was the perfect place for DiMaggio to display his fielding range.

After he retired, a myth grew that DiMaggio never made a baserunning error. This, of course, is silly; DiMaggio made many baserunning errors. The only people who never make mistakes are the people who never do anything. That myth started in the 1950s, when Willie Mays came along — arguably the only other "perfect" player in major league history. Mays stole bases, which DiMaggio did not, so some sportswriters of the day started the story that DiMaggio "never" made a mistake on the basepaths, trying to put him back on equal footing with Mays.

This assertion, while palpably false, is indicative of the effect DiMaggio had on those who saw him play. He came from hard times. He grew up poor, and he wasn't handsome or glib or witty. Baseball was what he had, a life raft. He learned to demand respect, and he learned dignity. He embodied dignity; he was dignity. It was one of DiMaggio's weapons — and he brought along every weapon he owned every time he went to the ballpark. The man did not like to lose.

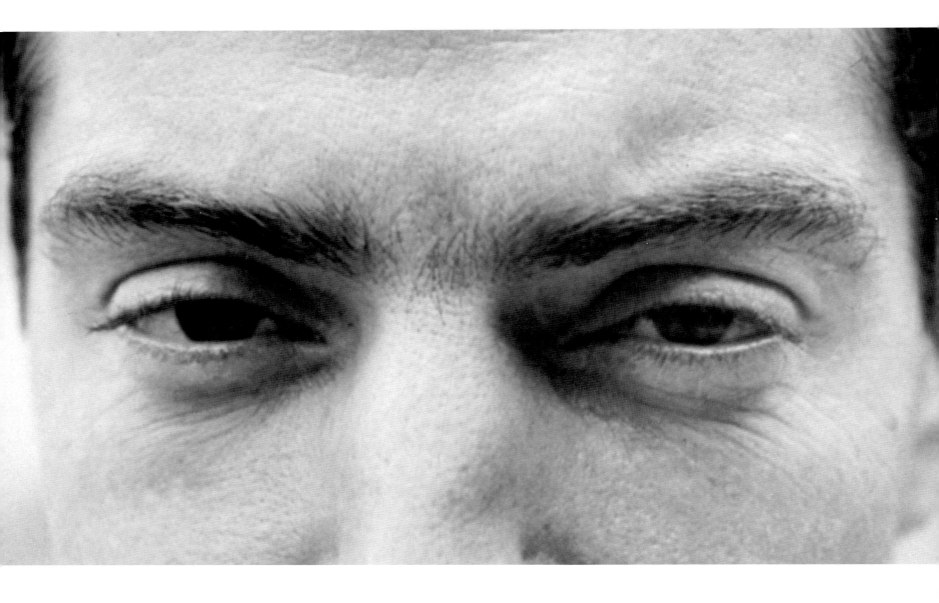

"There was nothing they could teach Joe D. When he came to the big leagues, IT WAS ALL THERE."

— JIMMY CANNON, New York sportswriter

In a cold, logical analysis unpolluted by emotion, Babe Ruth remains the greatest baseball player the world has ever seen.

Players in Pinstripes
RIGHT FIELD
NY

BABE RUTH

Funny thing about Babe Ruth: He's been dead and buried for more than half a century, yet he keeps having bad years. Roger Maris hit 61 home runs in 1961, breaking Ruth's season record of 60. The same year, pitcher Whitey Ford stretched his streak of scoreless innings in the World Series to 32, breaking a record Ruth had held since 1918.

In 1974, Henry Aaron broke one of Ruth's big records, number of home runs in a career, and others have picked off a few of Ruth's lesser records. In 2001, Rickey Henderson broke Ruth's record for career walks, and Barry Bonds broke Ruth's records for walks, slugging percentage, and road home runs in a season.

Ruth is like a giant block of marble. Chip away and chip away, and what is left is a giant statue. Ruth lives on not only in the records he still holds, but in myth, in legend, and in the minds of the millions who grew up in the shadow of his memory.

In a cold, logical analysis unpolluted by emotion, Ruth remains the greatest baseball player the world has ever seen. Why? Because Ruth won more games for his team than anyone else has. Ruth hit .342 in his career, a tremendously impressive average — but Ty Cobb hit .367 and Rogers Hornsby .358; even Riggs Stephenson hit .336. Hitters do a lot of things other than hit singles. Cobb's batting average represents 60 percent of his value as a hitter, Hornsby's represents 55 percent of his batting value, and Stephenson's 59 percent. In Ruth's case, so many of his hits were home runs and he walked so often that his batting average represents only 38 percent of his offensive value. When you add to that Ruth's achievement as a pitcher, he remains clearly the greatest player the game has ever had.

Why Ruth was the greatest player ever can be discussed on a different level. What made the man so special? The answer can be summed up succinctly: He had an enduring disrespect for rules. Ruth didn't acknowledge rules until he found from experience that they applied to him. It is a thread that ran throughout his life, and it goes a long way to explain why he was always ahead of the crowd.

A few years ago, a traveling baseball exhibit showcased one of Ruth's bats. Dave Henderson, a 1980s-era major league outfielder, studied the bat and discovered what everyone had missed for 60 years: The bat was corked. The end had been sawed off and glued back on. Any number of sportswriters assured us that Ruth never would have used a corked bat. Of course Ruth would have used a corked bat — unless someone stopped him. Indeed, the Babe was caught using an illegal bat in August 1922.

Ruth pushed and tested every rule and convention ever presented to him. Remember the story of when the President of the United States came onto the field to be introduced to the Yankees? They all held their caps in their hands and spoke respectfully to the President.

"How are you, Mr. President."

"Nice to meet you, sir."

"I'm honored to meet you, sir."

Then the President came to the Babe, who mopped his brow and remarked casually, "Hot as hell, ain't it, Prez?"

Remember the story about Ruth at a dinner party being offered asparagus? "No thanks, ma'am," he said politely. "It makes my urine stink."

Ruth knew the rules — he just tried to ignore the ones that cramped his style. Flouting the rules tied Ruth's life together, the major events as well as the minor anecdotes. As a child, he was sent to live in a supervised residence — St. Mary's Industrial School for Boys — because he refused to go to school.

Major League Baseball instituted a rule in 1911 prohibiting players on the World Series teams from touring on All-Star teams during the offseason. Commissioner Kenesaw Mountain Landis was adamant that the rule would be enforced, yet Ruth nonetheless organized an All-Star team after the 1921 Series — and was suspended for the first six weeks of the 1922 season as punishment.

Have you heard of the "Bellyache Heard Round the World"? Ruth missed a third of the 1925 season allegedly because of abdominal distress caused by poor eating habits. The Babe long had laughed off warnings that his unhealthy diet was going to harm him.

Remember the story about Ruth dangling Miller Huggins, the diminutive Yankees manager, off the caboose of a moving train? Of course it was unacceptable behavior — but Ruth had a deep-seated dislike for authority figures.

Ruth's reluctance to accept rules without at least making an attempt to bend them is precisely what made him the hitter he was. When Ruth was in his teens, the men who taught baseball to youths virtually prohibited an uppercut swing. The old-school coaches taught that uppercutting, while it might afford a batter more distance when he connected and produce some home runs,

was allowed to swing with an uppercut because he was a pitcher, and no one took his hitting style seriously. They are dead wrong. Ruth swung contrary to the norm because it was not in his nature to do what he was told. In that way, Ruth was about as American as you can get. This is not a nation of obedient people who blindly respect leaders and convention. Americans like to push the

Ruth did this better than most. Some of his challenges are to be admired; some are to be deplored. But there is no mistake that his refusal to swing a bat in the conventional manner of the times altered the course of baseball. He took the home run from a rarity to an omnipresent threat, and as a result the game's popularity soared.

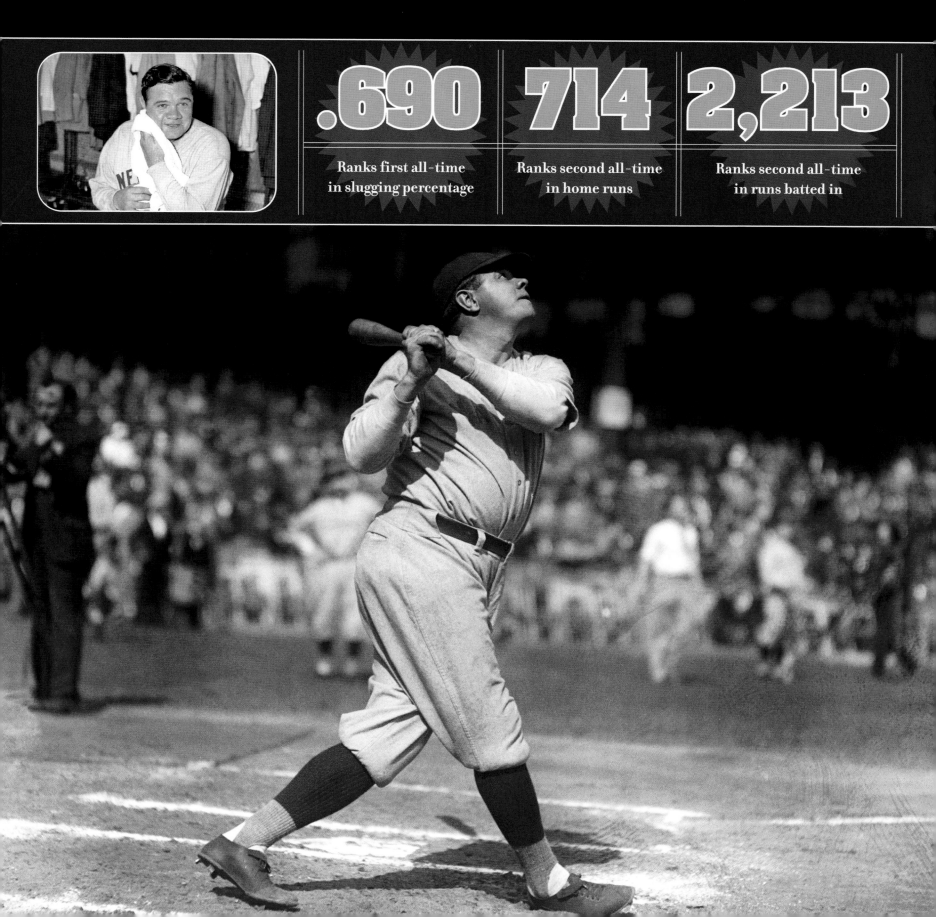

.690	714	2,213
Ranks first all-time in slugging percentage	Ranks second all-time in home runs	Ranks second all-time in runs batted in

REGGIE JACKSON

If you could go back and see the young Reggie Jackson the way a scout would see him, the first thing you'd notice would be Jackson's throwing arm. As a young man, Jackson could fire bullets from the warning track to third base. Of course he couldn't hit the broad side of a barn. But that was Reggie — he would get your attention.

Few players have ever had such an interesting combination of strengths and weaknesses as Jackson had. By the time he was 30, he had lost his powerful arm, but his skills remained a jumble of the spectacular. He could hit a baseball 500 feet, but he also led the league in strikeouts in each of his first four seasons, and over his career struck out 650 times more than any other player in major league history. He was fast as a young player and sometimes did clever things on the bases, but he wasn't a base-stealer or a consistently good baserunner. He never was close to leading the league in stolen bases, but he did lead once in times caught stealing.

Jackson led American League outfielders in errors as often as he did in strikeouts. His career fielding percentage compared to the league norm for outfielders (.967 versus .980) is among the worst in history. Many of his errors resulted from the same cause as the strikeouts: Reggie would try the impossible. He didn't mind failing when striving for the spectacular, a trait that all great performers share.

Because Jackson did some things stunningly well, many regarded him as a superstar. Because he struck out a lot, committed fielding errors, and made mistakes on the bases, some did not regard him as a very good player. On October 18, 1977, Reggie won over a lot of his critics. That's the night he hit three home runs on three pitches in the sixth game of the World Series — after batting .353 with two home runs in the first five games. Jackson lived for the big stage and the chance to do some-

thing special, and he often did. In addition to his 1977 achievements, he also was the MVP of the 1973 Series.

As a player, Jackson was a lot like Sammy Sosa is. But Jackson didn't hit 60 homers a year, because, unlike Sosa, he didn't play in the funny-number era that began in the 1990s, and he didn't play half his games in Wrigley Field. The difference between Jackson and an average outfielder over the course of his career was 55 errors. What's 55 errors against 1,700 RBIs? Same with Jackson's strikeouts. If a player has 2,597 strikeouts and 563 home runs, is he outstanding? Of course he is. If you take away the home runs and the strikeouts from Jackson, his career batting average is .301 and his on-base percentage is .424.

Statistical analysts do not warm to the idea of clutch hitters because they can't predict who will come through in a clutch situation. The guy who hits .450 in the clutch one year can just as well hit .150 the next. If it's not predictable, is it really a skill? It is one thing to say that it isn't a skill, but that's very different than denying that Jackson had many more than his share of dramatic, high-impact home runs, doubles, and baserunning credits.

Jackson doesn't need extra credit to prop him up as a star. He created runs; that's the bottom line for a hitter. Five hundred sixty-three home runs, 18 more homers in postseason play, five World Championship rings — the man came up big an awful lot. As for the rest of the Reggie package, any real baseball aficionado can live with it.

Jackson doesn't need extra credit to prop him up as a star.

HE CREATED RUNS; THAT'S THE BOTTOM LINE FOR A HITTER.

Players in Pinstripes
CENTER FIELD

BERNIE WILLIAMS

During the 2002 American League Division Series, the television network broadcasting the games offered fans an opportunity to telephone in and cast their ballot for the Yankees' most valuable player. There were three choices, and Bernie Williams wasn't one of them. He did get 204 hits, score 102 runs, and drive in 102 runs. He was third in the league in hitting with a .333 average, and he did draw 83 walks, hit 37 doubles, and play center field in his usual stellar manner. But ...Williams didn't do anything out of the ordinary for him, just what he does every year.

Here is a trivia question: When was the last time that Ken Griffey Jr. out-hit Williams? Answer: 1994, when Griffey hit .323 and Williams .289.

The best way to understand why Williams is taken for granted is to remember what they taught you in the Army about camouflage. (If you were not in the Army, just follow along.) Anything that breaks up the silhouette of a person, they teach you in basic training, makes the person more difficult to see. The same concept applies to a ballplayer. If a player is accomplished in three, four, five areas, it is harder to recognize the breadth of his total accomplishment. Williams spreads his accomplishment all over the statistical map. He hits doubles and home runs, he draws walks, he hits for a high average, he runs well, he plays a key defensive position, and he bats from both sides of the plate. If you really think about it, the following is not an outrageous statement: Williams does more things well than anyone else playing Major League Baseball today. He tends to be overlooked in discussions of the best players because his talent isn't isolated in one area — it's everywhere.

The other thing you learn in the military about camouflage is that some-thing that moves attracts the eye. Let's apply that to baseball. If a player is good one year, great the next, fair the year after, great again two years later, that play-er tends to draw rave reviews because the media is taken by how well he plays when he plays well. Yet a player who is consistently good year after year tends to fade into the scenery, just like the stationary object in our camouflage les-son. That is Bernie Williams — so steady and unwavering he goes unnoticed.

In Yankees history through the 2002 season, Williams ranked ninth in hits, seventh in home runs, fifth in doubles, seventh in runs scored, 10th in RBIs, seventh in batting average (in 1,000 or more games), seventh in on-base percentage, and seventh in slugging percentage. Yet few ever think to list him as one of the greatest Yankees. He plays the position that DiMaggio and Mantle played. Yes, DiMaggio and Mantle were better players than Williams is, although Williams probably will finish with more hits than either of them. Here is another perspective: Earle Combs, a fine Yankees outfielder in the 1920s and 1930s, clearly was not as good a player as Williams is, yet Combs is in the Hall of Fame. Perhaps Williams will get there, too.

RANK IN YANKEES HISTORY THROUGH 2002 SEASON

9

HITS

RANK IN YANKEES HISTORY THROUGH 2002 SEASON

7

HOME RUNS

RANK IN YANKEES HISTORY THROUGH 2002 SEASON

10

RBIs

RANK IN YANKEES HISTORY THROUGH 2002 SEASON

7

BATTING AVERAGE

DAVE WINFIELD

Throughout the 1970s, the American League fought the perception that the National League had more talent. There wasn't a good reason behind this misconception. The American League won the World Series in 1970, 1972, 1973, 1974, 1977, and 1978, but the National League won most of the All-Star games and seemed to have more stars. As Billy Martin said after the Yankees traded Bobby Murcer to San Francisco for Bobby Bonds: "The National League does a better job of promoting its stars than we do. When Bobby Bonds was in the National League, I thought he could walk on water. You know what? Bobby Murcer is a better player than Bobby Bonds."

In his eight full seasons with the Yankees, Winfield had 812 RBIs. That's more than Eddie Murray, Mike Schmidt, or anyone else in the major leagues for that span.

Dave Winfield, after eight years with the San Diego Padres, joined the Yankees in 1981 with the reputation for being able to walk on water. Winfield almost certainly was the best player in the National League in 1979. He led the league in both total bases and RBIs, despite playing for a terrible team in a pitcher's park. The Yankees in those days faced more left-handed pitchers than any other team, and the right-handed hitting Winfield was an ideal fit in the middle of their lineup, surrounded by left-handed power hitters.

Winfield led the Yankees in RBIs in his first season, but he did not fare well in postseason play, going 10 for 55, including 1 for 22 in the World Series that the Yankees lost to the Dodgers in six games. Reggie Jackson left the Yankees after that season, and Winfield was expected to replace Jackson's performance and presence. However, the Yankees never again got to the World Series with Winfield in their uniform, which he wore until early in the 1990 season.

The Yankees played a lot of good ball with Winfield in their lineup. They won 91 games in 1983, 97 in 1985, and 90 in 1986. During the 1980s, the Yankees had the best record in the major leagues. Yet the measure of success in the Bronx is the World Series, and the Yankees kept falling short. For that, Winfield received much of the blame. The man was a consistent run-producer, accounting for 116 RBIs in 1983, 114 in 1985, and 107 in 1988, yet it never was

quite enough to satisfy his critics. Winfield was judg the standards of Jackson, Ruth, Mantle, DiMaggio — he was expected to meet those standards with F Wynegar catching and Bobby Meacham playing short The challenge for Winfield was daunting, and it's a c to him that he continued to excel.

In his eight full seasons with the Yankees, Wir had 812 RBIs. That's more than Eddie Murray, Schmidt, or anyone else in the major leagues for span. Winfield also was among the top 10 in the n leagues for those years in home runs, runs scored, and doubles. He won Gold Gloves because he wa and had a powerful throwing arm, although those watched him play every day saw a lot of balls drop ly in front of him.

Winfield was a tall, graceful, and powerful athlet ran like the wind once he got his long legs in motio was the best athlete in baseball, in the sense that i wanted a player who also could play basketball, foo and track, he would have been the first man to choos was an athlete's athlete who had his choice of profess sports, and he selected baseball. Like the greatest Ya who preceded him, Winfield is in the Hall of F although he never is afforded as much acclaim as the ers are, largely because the Yankees' World Champio ledger shows a gap for the 1980s.

Players in Pinstripes
CATCHER
NY

YOGI BERRA

Everyone knows Yogi. How many athletes are famous enough to be featured in TV ad campaigns 40 years after they have retired? How many athletes are quoted regularly by the president of the United States?

Yogi was a short, funny-looking guy with knobby features who had a way of bollixing up the English language that would occasionally render the obvious profound. Come to think of it, that's still a description of Yogi.

He grew up in St. Louis at a time when the Cardinals signed all the good athletes in the area. They signed Yogi's boyhood pal, Joe Garagiola, to a bonus contract, but would not pay the same amount for Yogi because, well . . . *Does that man look like an athlete?* Garagiola, Yogi, and their pals knew that Yogi was the best athlete in the group, but he just didn't look the part. Yogi wouldn't sign with the Cardinals for less than what Garagiola got, so instead, he signed with the Yankees.

Bill Dickey "learned" Yogi all of his experience, as Yogi would say in one of his earliest Yogi-isms — and Yogi surpassed Dickey as the greatest catcher in Yankees history, perhaps even in baseball history. Whether Yogi was greater

than Johnny Bench is a tough call. And whether Yogi was greater than Josh Gibson is impossible to know. But to claim that Dickey was better than Berra, frankly, is preposterous.

Dickey's career batting average was .313; Yogi's .285. Batting average is a useful and important statistic, but generations of fans have been inclined to draw too close a connection between a high batting average and a good player. If a high batting average always meant a good player, then a team with a high batting average would always win, and a team with a low batting average would always lose. A cursory look at the team batting average lists will show you that's not the way it is. A hitter's job isn't to compile a high batting average, but rather to create runs. If you focus on the "runs" categories rather than the batting average, Berra's advantages are apparent. He scored far more runs than Dickey (1,175 to 930) and drove in far more runs (1,430 to 1,209).

For every 162 games played, Dickey scored 84 runs and drove in 109; Berra scored 90 and drove in 109. The numbers are almost identical, but not the value. First, Dickey played in about 130 games a year; Berra in about 145. Second, the value of a run depends on how many runs it takes to win a game. Dickey played in an era when runs were plentiful and it took a lot of runs to win; Berra in an era when runs were not as plentiful and each one had more of an impact on a game.

Berra's Yankees never scored more than 914 runs in a season; Dickey's Yankees in various seasons scored 1,067, 1,065, 1,062, 1,002, 979, 967, 966, and 927. Dickey had one season, in 1939, in which he scored 10 percent of the Yankees' runs. Berra had seven seasons in which he scored 10 percent of the Yankees' runs, and two seasons, in 1950 and 1952, when he scored 13 percent of the runs.

Dickey had four seasons in which he drove in 10 percent of the Yankees' runs, and one season, in 1937, when he drove in more than one-eighth of the total. Berra had 12 consecutive seasons, from 1948 to 1959, in which he drove in at least 10 percent of the Yankees' runs, and five seasons in which he drove in one-eighth of the total.

The test of greatness isn't just scoring a lot of runs. It's scoring a lot of runs and winning a lot of games and championships. Dickey played for teams that won seven of eight World Series; Yogi for teams that won 10 of 14.

Berra won the American League MVP Award three times, was in the top three in the voting six times, in the top five seven times, and was mentioned in the voting in 15 seasons. Dickey never won the award, was in the top three once, in the top five three times, and was mentioned nine times.

Dickey was a great player. But Berra was better. Yogi was the greatest catcher who ever lived. That can be said with conviction because he was the only one who played every day, batted cleanup, did the job defensively, and never had a bad season. Mike Piazza is a better hitter than Yogi was and never has a bad year, but Piazza's defense is lacking. Dickey was about as good as Berra, but he didn't play every day and he didn't bat cleanup. Roy Campanella was as good as Berra was in his best seasons, maybe better, and so was Bench and maybe Mickey Cochrane, too. Put all three together, and they had about as many great seasons combined as Yogi did by himself.

Josh Gibson was probably a better hitter than Yogi was and about as good a catcher, but it is unnerving to make judgements by relying on poorly documented records against a mix of uneven competition, which is the case with Gibson.

Yogi was a complete player: consistent and productive. If you are choosing a catcher on looks, take Carlton Fisk; on style, your man is Bench. If you want to win the pennant, choose Yogi.

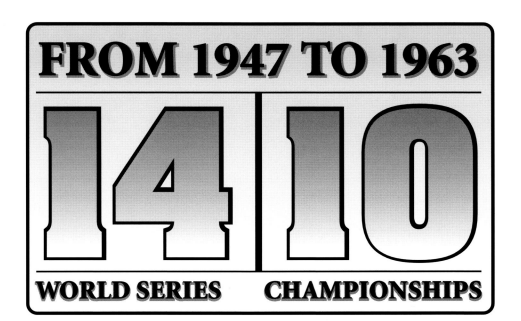

FROM 1947 TO 1963

14 WORLD SERIES

10 CHAMPIONSHIPS

Players in Pinstripes

CATCHER

ELSTON HOWARD

It was a long march for Elston Howard. Almost 80 percent of major league players enjoy their peak three-year period by the age of 32. Howard was 32 before he really got a chance to catch.

Howard had to establish and prove himself in the Negro Leagues. The Yankees signed him, but then he had to spend two years in the Army. Upon his return, Howard had to prove himself in the minor leagues and play his way to the Yankees. By that time he was 26, and three obstacles still loomed large in front of him: He was the first African-American to sign with the Yankees; Yogi Berra; and Yankee Stadium.

Berra had run off Sherm Lollar, Gus Triandos, and other competent catchers, and he was a long way from finished when Howard came along — Berra was just four years older than Howard. Yankee Stadium's spacious dimensions in left field and left center made it difficult for a right-handed bat-

ter like Howard to be successful. Howard didn't run well. He needed to hit home runs to contribute, and they required a prodigious poke if hit to the left side of the outfield.

Howard in 1962 had 18 home runs and 60 RBIs in road games, and three homers and 31 RBIs at Yankee Stadium. For his career, he hit more than two-thirds of his home runs on the road and drove in almost 100 more runs on the road than he did at home. In their road games, Howard had 69 percent more home runs than Bill Dickey did — in 350 fewer at-bats.

Like DiMaggio's numbers, Howard's statistics were adversely affected by his home park, and few have battled tougher competition for work. By 1959, however, Howard had earned enough playing time and was using it well enough to make the American League All-Star team. As Berra conceded that he could no longer catch 145 games a year, Howard more than picked up the slack.

It was noted earlier that Howard did not run well. He was one of those slow-moving but quick-reacting athletes, in the manner of Brooks Robinson. Howard had quick reflexes behind the plate and a great arm. He also had a way with pitchers; he understood them, and, more importantly, they understood him. By the time he got to play, he was a cagey veteran, more than prepared to thrive. From 1961 through 1964, Howard was the best catcher in the major leagues, a .300 hitter with power, and a defensive standout.

THREE OBSTACLES
loomed large in front Howard:

1 He was the first African-American to play with **THE YANKEES**

2 **YOGI BERRA**

YANKEE STADIUM **3**

Like DiMaggio's numbers, Howard's statistics were adversely affected by his home park, and few have battled tougher competition for work.

75

BILL DICKEY

Bill Dickey was among the first modern catchers who hit well. He came to the major leagues at the end of an era when catchers almost always batted eighth. The practice of batting the pitcher ninth and the catcher eighth was adopted in the 1890s. There were very few catchers from 1895 to 1925 who did not bat eighth, even if they were good hitters, and there were extremely few catchers who were good hitters.

When the live-ball era — that's what it's called, but it's a misnomer — arrived in 1920, bunt attempts (which catchers were expected to chase) and stolen-base attempts dropped sharply. That reduced the defensive responsibilities of the catcher, and soon teams were focused on getting catchers who could contribute with the bat.

By the mid-1920s, catchers like Mickey Cochrane, Gabby Hartnett, and Wally Schang had worked their way into the middle of the batting order, and then Dickey arrived to further the movement. Dickey was not Mike Piazza with the bat, and he was not Ivan Rodriguez behind the plate. He was not lightning-quick on defense, and he did not have the best throwing arm in the American League. He was a good left-handed hitter and could do the job defensively, and he improved steadily as he went along.

That really is what made Dickey special: He got better. For much of the 1930s, Yankees manager Joe McCarthy more or less used Dickey in a platoon. Open platooning was in poor standing with the players at that time. It would have been considered unmanly for, say, a left-handed hitter to acknowledge that he was better off on the bench against a left-handed pitcher. So managers rarely said they were platooning, but they did it all the same, usually in a sneaky fashion. On a day that a left-hander was to pitch against the Yankees, McCarthy would announce that Dickey was nursing a strained wrist, or whatever.

In 1936, Dickey learned how to pull the ball down the right field line and take advantage of Yankee Stadium's short fence. He had never been

much of a power threat previously, hitting five to 15 home runs a season in his first seven years with the Yankees, and with a fairly even split between home and road performance. But in 1936, he hit 22 home runs, 14 at Yankee Stadium, and the following two seasons his home/road splits were among the most disparate in baseball history, at least before there was a team in Colorado.

In 1937, Dickey hit .348 with 21 homers and 85 RBIs at Yankee Stadium, and .315 with 8 and 48 on the road. In 1938, he hit .357 with 23 homers and 83 RBIs at Yankee Stadium, and .274 with 4 and 32 on the road. For the two seasons, Dickey played in 136 games and batted 483 times at Yankee Stadium, and produced a .352 average with 44 homers and 168 RBIs. His RBI rate for the 136 games was considerably better than Hack Wilson's in 1930 when he had 190 RBIs, the major league record. Dickey hit two-thirds of his home runs in Yankee Stadium (135 of 202), although his batting average was seven points higher on the road than it was in New York.

The four-year stretch from 1936 to 1939 was one of the Yankees' greatest eras, and Dickey was right in the thick of the success. For those four years of jerking the ball down the right field line, he was a formidable player — and certainly an excellent player in the other years of his career. Dickey typified the Yankees in the wake of Babe Ruth; a team of men that took great pride in their professionalism, considered themselves the best in the business, and went about beating the opposition in cold, workman-like fashion.

WHITEY FORD

Quick now: Who had a better winning percentage: Whitey Ford or Sandy Koufax? Who had a better ERA: Ford or Koufax? Who had a longer career: Ford or Koufax? Here's a hint: This is not a book about the Dodgers.

Ford had a better ERA (2.75 to 2.76) and a better winning percentage (.690 to .655), and a longer career (438 starts to 314) than Koufax.

Koufax had immense impact on pennant races from 1963 through 1966 because he won 25 games and pitched 320 innings a year. If Ford had pitched 320 innings a year, how many games would he have won? Koufax, in his three Cy Young seasons, won one game for every 12.44 innings on the mound — a tremendous rate. Ford met or exceeded that standard in 1950, 1953, 1956, 1957, 1961, and 1963.

If you project Ford's win-loss records over 300 innings a year, these are his records for the first 14 years of his career: 24-3, 26-9, 23-11, 21-8, 25-8, 26-12, 19-10, 24-15, 19-14, 27-4, 20-9, 27-8, 21-7, and 20-16. Granted, Ford did not pitch 300 innings a season. My point is to illustrate the consistency of excellence with which he did pitch. Ford pitched in the majors for 16 seasons and had an ERA better than the league norm in all 16. Almost every year, he was half a run better than the league norm.

Ford gave up 1,107 runs in his career. A league-average pitcher facing the same number of batters that Ford faced would have allowed 1,528 runs — thus Ford was 421 runs better than average. Koufax was 282 runs better than average.

Ford's record was 236-106, 130 games over .500. No doubt, playing for tremendous teams influenced this phenomenal win-loss log. What would his record have been had he played for average teams? As best as can be esti-

mated, about 214-128, a .626 winning percentage, which would rank among the top 50 since 1900.

Was any other pitcher in history as consistent at such a high level of performance as Ford? Warren Spahn, perhaps? Spahn had five seasons in which he won two-thirds or more of his decisions; Ford had 11. Spahn twice had an ERA a run better than his league's; Ford, eight times. Spahn's winning percentage, ERA, and ERA compared to the league's are impressive, but they really are not in Ford's class.

Yankees manager Casey Stengel used a five-man rotation in an era in which almost every other team used a four-man rotation. He had plenty of pitchers to work with, and you can't argue with his results — but the system kept Ford from being a regular 20-game winner. Koufax retired at age 30; Ford pitched until he was nearly 40. You can't deny that advantage, either — but then, there were pitchers who worked 280 to 300 innings a year, and they didn't flame out after a few good years. We'll never know whether Ford would have been one of those.

Ford always was a star but never was considered a superstar, except perhaps in 1961. Benefiting from new Yankees manager Ralph Houk using a four-man rotation that year, Ford went 25-4 and pitched 14 shutout innings in the World Series. Ford was as consistently good as anyone who ever pitched, but unfortunately history tends to favor the spectacular over the consistent.

Let's do a close comparison of Koufax and Ford

FORD		KOUFAX
16	Years Pitched	**12**
16/16	ERA better than league	**7/12**
15/16	ERA at least a half-run better than league	**7/12**
8/16	ERA a run better than league	**6/12**
5/16	ERA a run and a half better than league	**3/12**

Players in Pinstripes

PITCHER

ALLIE REYNOLDS

Allie Reynolds won 18 games for the Cleveland Indians in 1945, but that accomplishment was written off as a kind of fluke because most of the stars were still in the military service for World War II, and because he led the league in walks.

In 1947, his first season with the Yankees, Reynolds won 19 games and earned another victory in the World Series. He was with the Yankees for eight seasons, and he gave them eight outstanding seasons. His worst win-loss record with the Yankees was 16-12; other than that, he won at least 65 percent of his decisions every year.

Reynolds has almost the same career winning percentage and ERA as two other Yankees stars, Ron Guidry and Lefty Gomez, and all three pitched about the same number of innings. Reynolds' winning percentage is slightly lower than the other two's largely because he pitched four seasons for the Indians, during the war. With the Yankees, his winning percentage (.686) is quite a bit better than Gomez's or Guidry's.

Reynolds' year-by-year record looks different than Guidry's or Gomez's for two closely related reasons:

❶

REYNOLDS MADE FEWER STARTS
and more relief appearances than Guidry or Gomez.

❷

Reynolds was a
20-GAME WINNER
only once.

In his autobiography, Casey Stengel listed Reynolds as the fourth-greatest player he managed, behind Joe DiMaggio, Yogi Berra, and Mickey Mantle (in that order), and ahead of Whitey Ford. Stengel wrote, "Reynolds was my greatest pitcher to start and relieve. He could warm up quick and was amazing in relief, amazing starting." As a reliever with the Yankees, Reynolds made 86 appearances and had a 15-9 record, 41 saves, a 2.87 ERA, and averaged more than two innings per appearance. In 209 starts for the Yankees, he went 116-51 with a 3.35 ERA. Reynolds won 56 percent of his starts for the Yankees. Let's put that in context:

PLAYER	GAMES STARTED	WINS AS A STARTER	WINS PCT.
Walter Johnson	666	371	.557
Allie Reynolds*	209	116	.555
Warren Spahn	665	358	.538
Whitey Ford	438	227	.518
Sandy Koufax	314	159	.506

With Yankees*

Reynolds' numbers are even better if you include the World Series. He was 5-2 in nine starts, 2-0 and four saves in six relief appearances, with a sub-3.00 ERA in each role. Stengel couldn't decide whether he liked Reynolds better as a starter or a reliever, so he used him in both roles. That pattern of work compromised Reynolds' record. He didn't get enough starts to be a frequent 20-game winner, or make enough relief appearances to be remembered in the same vein as Goose Gossage.

Gomez had a better record than Reynolds as a starter, but as a reliever Gomez was 5-12 with a 4.24 ERA. Red Ruffing as a reliever was 9-15 with a 3.65 ERA, and Warren Spahn was 5-18 with a 3.68 ERA. The point is, switching back and forth between starting and relieving is a difficult role, and perhaps no one has done it as well as Reynolds.

RED RUFFING

Red Ruffing's career got off to a rather inauspicious start. He joined the Boston Red Sox in 1924 and by the time he was traded to the Yankees in May 1930, he had a 39-96 record — a .287 winning percentage. He is probably the only pitcher in history to have a record that poor and still have a job in the major leagues. Ruffing had just turned 26 when he joined the Yankees, and baseball fans remained excited about his potential for several reasons:

1 HE WAS A BIG MAN FOR THE ERA, STANDING 6-FOOT-1-INCH AND WEIGHING MORE THAN 200 POUNDS.

2 HE COULD THROW **EXCEPTIONALLY HARD.**

3 HE WAS A TERRIFIC ATHLETE. IN ADDITION TO HIS PITCHING SKILLS, HE RAN WELL, WAS A FINE HITTER, AND AN EXCELLENT FIELDER.

HE WASN'T AFRAID TO PUT THE BALL OVER THE PLATE **AND LET BATTERS HACK AT IT.** **4**

The 1927 Yankees were one of the great teams in history, but that club's rotation unraveled in the subsequent few years. Herb Pennock, 19-8 in 1927, was 35 years old by 1929 and went 9-11 that year. Waite Hoyt, 22-7 in 1927, came up with a sore arm. Urban Shocker, 18-6 in 1927, died a year later. The Yankees, despite an offense that was stronger than ever, were dropping behind the Philadelphia A's and began scrambling for help. The Red Sox needed money, and Ruffing was available.

Ruffing's record with the Yankees over 15 years was 231-124 — a .651 winning percentage. The odd thing about his career is that when he was with a bad team such as the Red Sox, his record was far worse than his team's record; and when he was with a good team such as the Yankees, his record was better than his team's. Or maybe it is not odd at all. In his early years with the Red Sox, Ruffing really should have been in the minor leagues perfecting his craft. By the time he got to the Yankees, he had picked up a thing or two about pitching, including learning how to throw a sharp-breaking curveball.

In the early 1930s, Ruffing began experimenting with

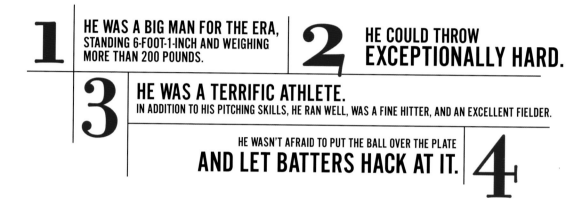

the pitch that now is called "the slider." It had various names at that time: sailer, tailing fastball, nickel curve. Whatever it was called, it was a good pitch if thrown properly, and Ruffing threw it probably better than anyone else of his time, in part because he was one of the few who threw it.

By the late 1930s, Ruffing was a perennial 20-game winner. As a bonus, he was one of the league's most reliable pinch-hitters, batting .364 in 1930, .330 in 1931, .306 in 1932, .339 in 1935, .307 in 1939, and .303 in 1941. He hit 36 home runs and 98 doubles in his career.

Ruffing was drafted into the military for World War II, although he was 39 at the time, and missed two years of baseball. By war's end he was ancient, yet he still could pitch. A sore arm prevented Ruffing from working regularly, but when he was able to take the mound he was highly effective. In 19 starts over 1945 and 1946, he went 12-4 with a 2.43 ERA. He no longer threw hard, but had become a wizened veteran who knew how to get by on guile and pain tablets. Twenty years after his career ended, Ruffing was elected to the Hall of Fame.

Ruffing's record with the Yankees over 15 years was 231-124 — a .651 winning percentage.

RON GUIDRY

Ron Guidry pitched a little bit for the Yankees in 1975, but spent most of the final two months of the season lost in the shadows of the bullpen, as the Yankees commenced the Billy Martin era.

At the winter baseball meetings that December, the Yankees talked with the Pirates about a trade — the discussion led to the Yankees' acquisition of Willie Randolph — and the Pirates asked about Guidry being included in the deal. A few hours later, the Yankees talked with the Angels about a trade, and the Angels brought up Guidry's name. "I don't know who this Ron Guidry is," Billy Martin told the Yankees party as the Angels group left the room, "but we ain't tradin' him to anybody."

as 20-game winners without an overpowering fastball. Guidry spent his entire career with the Yankees; Gomez was with the Yankees for all but one game. Gomez started 320 games and relieved in 48; Guidry started 323 and relieved in 45. They have almost identical career winning percentages and ERAs (Guidry .651, 3.29; Gomez .649, 3.34). Gomez won 20 games four times, 18 once; Guidry won 20 games three times, 18 once. Guidry had seven straight seasons with a winning percentage better than .600; Gomez did that eight times

Three years later, Guidry fashioned a 25-3 record with a 1.74 ERA and 248 strikeouts.

HOW GOOD WAS GUIDRY'S 1978 SEASON? NOTE THE FOLLOWING:

> SINCE 1940, ONLY TWO PITCHERS HAVE FINISHED A SEASON 22 GAMES BETTER THAN .500: GUIDRY AND DENNY McLAIN, WHO WENT 31-6 IN 1968.

> GUIDRY'S .893 WINNING PERCENTAGE IS THE ALL-TIME RECORD FOR A 20-GAME WINNER.

> GUIDRY'S 1.74 ERA WAS EQUALED BY PEDRO MARTINEZ IN 2000. THEY ARE THE LOWEST ERAs IN THE AMERICAN LEAGUE SINCE THE END OF THE 1960s.

Guidry was a small, slender man, but very much a power pitcher, combining a mid-90-mph fastball with as good a slider as anyone has ever thrown. That was a mid-90s fastball on the radar guns used then; on the ones used these days, he probably would register 100 mph. Guidry was late starting his major league career — he turned 27 in his first full season — and within a few years after his monster season he was making the transition to being more of a finesse pitcher.

Guidry's career has much in common with Lefty Gomez's. Both were reed-thin left-handers who had a big season early in their careers — Gomez was 26-5 with a 2.33 ERA in 1934. Both lost something off their fastballs in mid-career, survived a couple of seasons on instinct and guile, then re-emerged

in nine years. Each led the league twice in ERA, wins, and winning percentage. Gomez pitched 28 shutouts; Guidry, 26.

Gomez is in the Hall of Fame; Guidry isn't and probably won't be. Some argue that if Gomez is in, Guidry should be in, too. Both were exceptional pitchers, but neither is on a plateau with the greatest left-handers. Neither reached the brilliance of Sandy Koufax or Randy Johnson except in one season, and neither lasted long enough to afford his career the stature of Whitey Ford, Steve Carlton, or Warren Spahn. Gomez was elected to the Hall of Fame in an era of profligate selections. He is far from being the worst pitcher selected — and Guidry was every bit as good as Gomez.

GOOSE GOSSAGE

In the midst of a run of spectacular seasons as a relief ace, Goose Gossage spent one miserable year as a starting pitcher. That was 1976 with the Chicago White Sox, whose manager was 68-year-old Paul Richards. If you think about it from Richards' perspective, you can understand where he was coming from. He was a major league catcher in the 1930s and 1940s, when pitchers with 97-mph fastballs were in the rotation, and old guys with dinky curveballs and herky-jerky deliveries were in the bullpen. To a man of Richards' generation, it was an article of faith that the best pitchers belonged in the rotation.

Relief pitchers and bullpen strategy have undergone numerous metamorphoses over the years. The way relievers are used now is quite different from the way they were used 10 years ago; and the way they were used 10 years ago was very different from the way they were used 10 years earlier. The bullpen has been an experimental lab since the 1920s, and each generation of managers has mixed the potion differently.

Gossage and the other great closers of his era — Dan Quisenberry, Sparky Lyle, Mike Marshall, John Hiller, Rollie Fingers — were the most valuable relief pitchers of all time. First, they pitched a lot more innings than modern relief aces. Gossage pitched 142 innings for the White Sox in 1975, 133 for Pittsburgh in 1977, and 134 for the Yankees in 1978. Lyle pitched 137 innings for the Yankees in 1977. Dennis Eckersley had an incredible 1990 season, but he pitched only 73 innings in 63 appearances. The top closers now pitch even less than Eckersley did. Second, the closers of the Gossage era worked more in high-impact situations than today's closers do. The modern closer usually works only in the ninth inning of a save situation. Often a save situation is not a high-impact situation — a team with a two- or three-run lead, with an inning to play almost always wins. The highest-impact situation is when the score is tied. Gossage and the other

relief aces of his era often were summoned to work in tie games. That's why save totals then were not as high as they are now — Gossage led the American League in saves with totals of 27 (1978) and 33 (1980) — and why closers then had more decisions — Gossage was 10-11 in 1978 and 13-5 in 1983. In his six years with the Yankees, 1978 to 1983, he had 150 saves and a 41-28 record.

Gossage almost always pitched in the late innings when a game was close or tied. Comparing Gossage and Mariano Rivera, Gossage pitched many more innings, and more critical innings. Thus, his impact had to be higher.

Gossage missed a good portion of the 1979 season because of a broken thumb, and by 1980 the concept of limiting the closer to save situations was sweeping baseball. Thus, Gossage never again worked 100 innings in a season, but he remained an effective pitcher into the early 1990s. He is one of seven pitchers that worked in 1,000 games — and perhaps the best in that group.

How long a pitcher lasts depends mostly on two things: his fastball and his health. Gossage had a great fastball and good health. He was a colorful, original, intimidating star, as memorable and effective a figure as has ever worked from the middle of the diamond in the late innings.

"When I cross the white lines, something clicks in me. I feel like no one can hit me. It's unbelievable how confident I feel. I turn mean. If my wife came out and looked in my eyes, she would say,

'WHO IS THIS GUY?'"

— GOOSE GOSSAGE

LEFTY GOMEZ

Yankee Stadium, built in the early 1920s, was designed to favor left-handed hitters for a reason so obvious that it doesn't need to be mentioned — okay, for Babe Ruth. However, it didn't immediately dawn on the Yankees that the park would also favor left-handed pitchers. The 1923 Yankees, the first to play in the Stadium, had only one left-hander — Herb Pennock — and their record in road games was six games better than their home record.

Gomez (far right) with 1937 World Championship teammates (from left) Frankie Crosetti, Red Rolfe, Joe DiMaggio, Lou Gehrig, Bill Dickey, George Selkirk, Myril Hoag, and Tony Lazzeri.

By 1929, the Yankees had numerous left-handed pitchers, but none of great quality. That same year, 20-year-old left-hander Lefty Gomez led the Pacific Coast League in ERA and won 18 games for the San Francisco Seals. The PCL of that era was stronger than any minor league since, boasting many players who were just as good as many in the major leagues. A 20-year-old leading the PCL in ERA would get your attention. The Yankees took notice and arranged to purchase Gomez's contract for $35,000.

Gomez was a skinny, nervous kid who could just throw hard. Not much

of a curveball, no forkball, no change-up; just "Here it is. Try to hit this." His fastball had great movement as well as velocity. Gomez initially failed with the Yankees, but after picking up a curveball and learning to change speeds, he returned in 1931 and won 21 games, then 24 the next year.

Gomez had his greatest season in 1934, going 26-5 with a 2.33 ERA. This was the same season that Dizzy Dean won 30 games in the National League. Sportswriters of the time liked to sell baseball players as "characters." Lefty — like Dizzy — was all for it. If writers wanted to make him a character, that was

1934

26-5

RECORD

1934

2.33

ERA

money in his pocket, he reasoned. He became "Goofy" Gomez, baseball's most famous and most successful after-dinner speaker. He concocted funny stories about things that supposedly had happened to him, made teammates the foils of his tales, and gabbed away as a guest speaker for 50 years. Literally hundreds of Gomez's anecdotes are part of the literature of baseball.

Gomez was a great deal more complicated than the cartoon character he made himself to be. The fact that he was funny and articulate gave the media much to write about, and masked the fact that among the great stars of that era, Gomez was the most difficult to live with. He was high-strung and had a terrible temper, and like all truly great players he had a low tolerance for defeat.

Gomez endured arm trouble in 1935 and 1936, and his fastball was not quite as fast anymore. He developed an effective slow curve and returned to form in 1937, going 21-11 and leading the league in ERA (2.33). Then he won 18 games in 1938. With apologies to Pennock, Gomez was the Yankees' first great left-hander. Only Whitey Ford has had a better career than Gomez.

MARIANO RIVERA

To put the argument for Mariano Rivera as an all-time great closer in its strongest form, let's begin with a question: How many relief pitchers in history have had six consecutive quality seasons like Rivera had from 1996 through 2001?

Answer: Five or six, including Rivera. Rollie Fingers had seven straight, beginning in 1972, although a couple might have been of lesser quality. Bruce Sutter had seven straight, beginning in 1976; Goose Gossage had six straight, beginning in 1980; Lee Smith had seven straight, beginning in 1982; and Dennis Eckersley had six straight, beginning in 1987.

Hoyt Wilhelm, although he had more good seasons than any other reliever in history, never had more than five in a row. There are other guys you can argue for: Trevor Hoffman, Dan Quisenberry, John Franco, and John Wetteland.

Rivera has two credentials to be considered among the brightest of stars:

1) He is among a handful of closers who has been consistently excellent for several seasons in a row.

2) His performance in postseason play is probably the most brilliant of any reliever in history.

In modern baseball, the closer tends to get credit for what the team accomplishes, regardless of whether he deserves it. We constantly hear that a team cannot win a pennant without a top-notch closer, even though it happens frequently. We often hear that the key to success in postseason play is a strong bullpen, even though there is little evidence that this is true.

There is some connection between a strong bullpen and postseason success. From 1980 through 2001, the team with the best bullpen in the playoffs — based on performance during the season using objective criteria — has won the World Series on seven occasions. The 1984 Tigers, 1985 Royals, 1986 Mets, 1988 Dodgers, 1989 Athletics, 1990 Reds, and 1996 Yankees each entered postseason play with the best bullpen and won the World Series. In that same span, six teams that had the best bullpen didn't make it to the World Series: 1980 Yankees, 1982 Braves, 1991 Blue Jays, 1992 Athletics, 1997 Orioles, and 1999 Mets.

It is true, of course, that successful teams tend to have good bullpens — just as they tend to have good second basemen, good left fielders, good catchers, etc. The upshot of all this? Rivera is a terrific pitcher, and he certainly deserves a measure of the credit for the Yankees' run of good seasons — but no more than Derek Jeter, Bernie Williams, Jorge Posada, and Tino Martinez deserve. The Yankees have won a lot since the mid-1990s, and there is plenty of credit to go around.

GRAIG NETTLES

Perhaps the most intriguing question about Graig Nettles is why he never got credit for his defensive brilliance. You had to see him play third base to believe it. He could catch a line drive two feet into foul territory. He could knock down a ball several feet behind third, pick it up, and throw out the runner. A team that depends on left-handed pitching depends on its third baseman — and Billy Martin's Yankees had one of the best.

There are two reasons why Nettles wasn't fully recognized as a defensive master craftsman. First, the American League was ankle-deep in Gold Glove–caliber third basemen: Nettles, Aurelio Rodriguez, Buddy Bell, Brooks Robinson, Sal Bando, Don Money. All were better defensively than any AL third baseman since. If someone raved about Nettles' defense, someone else could make a compelling argument for any other guy on the list. Second, Brooks Robinson. Although Clete Boyer was probably just as good a defensive player as Robinson, Brooks had established himself as the definitive glove man at third base by 1961 and had cemented that reputation with his spectacular play in the 1970 World Series. Furthermore, Robinson had parlayed his defensive reputation into a position as the league's most beloved star, the one player at that time who was cheered loudly in every park. Many were reluctant to accept that Nettles was as good a third baseman as God ever made, because . . . what about our beloved ole Brooks Robinson?

The failure to accept Nettles' excellence as a hitter is not hard to understand. It has to do with the misperception of statistics. The public was weaned on batting averages. For many people, a .250 hitter can never be the equal of a .300 hitter. Well, yes he can. A home run is a lot different from a single, and the batting average gives no credit for a walk, even though walks lead frequently to runs scored. Nettles hit .248 for his career, and for each 100 hits he had 57 runs scored and 59 RBIs. Rod Carew hit .328, and for each 100 hits he had 47 runs scored and 33 RBIs. If Nettles got 150 hits and Carew got 200, who was more valuable? Do the math: Nettles was going to score 80 runs and drive in 88; Carew 93 and 66.

Occasionally someone suggests Nettles for the Hall of Fame, and a chorus of catcalls is sure to follow: What was his batting average? How many Gold Gloves did he win? Suffice it to say that Nettles might have been the best .248 hitter who ever lived.

"I expect every ball to be hit to me. When I do that, **I'M NEVER SURPRISED.**"

— GRAIG NETTLES

PHIL RIZZUTO

Phil Rizzuto was probably quicker on the double play than any other shortstop in history. We think a lot about a second baseman's ability to turn the double play; less about a shortstop's. In fact, the shortstop is the pivot man on the double play 82 percent as often as is the second baseman. If the shortstop isn't the pivot man, he often is the player who has to feed the ball to the second baseman, which means that his quickness and the timing of his throws is just as critical.

PARTICIPATED IN
1,217
DOUBLE PLAYS
89 PER 1,000 INNINGS, THE HIGHEST RATE IN HISTORY

Turning the double play is a big part of a shortstop's role, and Rizzuto did that better than anyone else who ever played major league baseball. Playing shortstop in about 13,614 innings in his career, he participated in 1,217 double plays — 89 per 1,000 innings, the highest rate in history.

Baseball statistical analysts have complicated ways to estimate a team's "expected double plays" and thus determine whether an infielder turned a lot of double plays because he had many chances, or simply because he was good at turning the double play. Rizzuto was just good at turning the double play. Rizzuto and Joe Gordon probably were the best combination. But Rizzuto and Billy Martin were good, as were Rizzuto and Jerry Coleman, and Rizzuto and Gil McDougald.

Setting aside his double-play ability, Rizzuto still was a fine shortstop. He was quick and had a good arm when it was healthy, and his fielding percentages were extremely good. In his first two seasons in the major leagues, Rizzuto hit .307 and .284, averages that projected over a full career likely would have led to 2,500 hits. Rizzuto was in the army for three years after that, and when he returned to the Yankees it took him five years to get his average back to .280. He hit .280 or better in only three seasons: the first two and his 1950 MVP year.

Rizzuto, who is in the Hall of Fame, had the subtle skills of a winning player. He was fast, a high percentage base-stealer, an accomplished bunter, and a terrific fielder. When he got on base, he kept moving. Rizzuto and Willie Randolph would have been an ideal double-play combination, except that they were almost too much alike.

Upon retiring, Rizzuto assumed an even more prominent role in the Yankees family, entering the homes of the team's fans as a broadcaster and becoming an emotional part of their attachment to the Yankees.

By most accounts, Rizzuto is low on the list of the great shortstops in baseball history. This, perhaps, should be the bottom line on him: He was the anchor of great, great teams.

DON MATTINGLY

When Don Mattingly joined the Yankees for the first time in 1982, there was little indication that he was going to be the first homegrown star in their everyday lineup since Thurman Munson. (The Yankees had two formidable pitchers at that time: Ron Guidry and Dave Righetti, who were products of the team's player development program.)

By the standards of modern athletes, the 6-foot, 175-pound Mattingly was scrawny, and he did not run well. He had hit .300 everywhere he had played, but with single-digit home run totals and stolen-base numbers. The scouts, however, liked his defense.

Mattingly became the Yankees' regular first baseman in 1984, and he won the batting title that year with a .343 average. More surprisingly, he hit 23 home runs. That hardly is a significant number by today's standards, but in 1984 only eight American League players hit 30 home runs, and six batted less than the league average that year. Players who could hit .300 with power were scarcer than saints. Mattingly led the league in doubles, was near the league lead in extra-base hits, and drove in 110 runs.

In the following two years, Mattingly was often mentioned when discussion cropped up concerning who was the best player in the game. His 145 RBIs in 1985 were by far the highest total in the major leagues in the 1980s. In 1986 he became the first major league player in 25 years to hit .350 with 30 home

runs. He drove in 100 runs five times in the six seasons from 1984 through 1989, and led the major leagues in RBIs during that period by more than 50. Mattingly had 684 RBIs; second-place George Bell had 625.

As the 1990s dawned, Mattingly was essentially finished as one of the major league's biggest stars, done in by a chronic back problem. He played until 1995, but never again approached his achievement of the 1980s.

New Yorkers revered Mattingly. A native of Indiana, he was not urbane, sophisticated, or hip, but Yankees fans grew to appreciate his values and work ethic, and put him on the pedestal reserved for the storied franchise's true greats.

Mattingly played in an era when the press almost made a sport of baiting the Yankees, yet he was able to walk through controversy like a ghost through fire. Controversy and madness never touched him. He was neither a back-stabber nor a target of it. Rather, Mattingly maintained a sense of decorum that had seemingly been passed down from the other great first baseman in Yankees history, Lou Gehrig.

MATTINGLY HAD THE HIGHEST SINGLE-SEASON RBI TOTAL OF THE 1980s.

1985

145

RBIs

"In big games, the action slows down for him where it speeds up for others. I've told him, **'I'LL TRADE MY PAST FOR YOUR FUTURE.'**"

— REGGIE JACKSON, on Derek Jeter

DEREK JETER

Guessing where Derek Jeter's career will wind up is kind of like guessing whether an arrow in flight will hit the target. Or to use the base-ball version of that analogy: It's like guessing whether a high fly will clear the fence. We really don't know. But we can avoid the pitfalls of history by not focusing on the destination of Jeter's career, and instead asking objective questions about his career thus far. Such as:

HOW MANY SHORTSTOPS HAVE PLAYED THIS WELL OVER A FIVE-YEAR PERIOD? About 10. Two shortstops have played at a distinctly higher level for a five-year period: Honus Wagner and Arky Vaughn. Eight others have played that long at a comparable level: Luke Appling, Ernie Banks, Lou Boudreau, Joe Cronin, Hughie Jennings, Cal Ripken Jr., Alex Rodriguez, and Robin Yount. Some shortstops in the Hall of Fame — Pee Wee Reese, Phil Rizzuto, Ozzie Smith, Luis Aparicio, Joe Sewell, and Dave Bancroft — never played as well for a five-year period as Jeter played from 1998 through 2002.

HOW MANY SHORTSTOPS HAVE HAD CAREERS COMPARABLE TO JETER'S AT THE SAME AGE?
Five to eight, depending on how far you stretch "comparable." The certain five are Vaughn, Ripken Jr., Rodriguez, Yount, and George Davis. If you want to stretch "comparable" a bit, add Cronin, Vern Stephens, and Jim Fregosi.

IN FIVE CONSECUTIVE YEARS

	MOST HITS BY A SHORTSTOP				MOST RUNS BY A SHORTSTOP		
1	Derek Jeter	1998–2002	1,005	1	Herman Long	1891–1895	638
2	Harvey Kuenn	1953–1957	969	2	Alex Rodriguez	1998–2002	625
3	Joe Sewell	1923–1927	954	3	Bill Dahlen	1892–1896	619
4	Honus Wagner	1899–1903	945	4	Derek Jeter	1998–2002	614
5	Cal Ripken Jr.	1982–1986	922	5	Frankie Crosetti	1936–1940	570
	Alex Rodriguez	1996–2000	922	6	George Davis	1891–1895	550
7	Al Dark	1950–1954	920	7	Woody English	1928–1932	538
8	Tony Fernandez	1986–1990	907	8	Donie Bush	1909–1913	535
9	Maury Wills	1961–1965	899		Cal Ripken Jr.	1983–1987	535
10	Cecil Travis	1937–1941	898	10	Pee Wee Reese	1949–1953	525

"JETER IS A SIX-TOOL PLAYER.
I've never eaten with him so I can't tell you if he has good
table manners, but I would imagine he has those too."

—JOHNNY OATES, **former major league player and manager**

HOW SHOULD WE EVALUATE JETER'S DEFENSIVE GAME? Everyone has their own take on it. What may be said without fear of contradiction is: His defensive statistics are not good; defensive statistics contain many puzzles, are highly unreliable on an intuitive level, and are not terribly reliable even if you study them morning to night and know more about them than you know about your best friend; and Jeter's defensive reputation is better than his statistics.

WHAT DOES JETER HAVE TO DO TO MAKE THE HALL OF FAME? Not a lot. He has to finish out his career in a fairly normal progression. I have a method (unpublished) that estimates a player's chance of making it into the Hall of Fame, and it shows that Jeter at this point has a 75 percent chance. This differs from idle speculation. Why, exactly? Because it is *organized* speculation, relying on a specific method that says, "Given this set of facts, this outcome will occur 75 percent of the time." Given 100 players who have accomplished this much by this age, 75 will be in the Hall of Fame. Jeter is essentially in the same position that Banks, Fregosi, Joe Medwick, and Willie Keeler were at the same age. All but Fregosi are in the Hall of Fame.

FOUR WORLD CHAMPIONSHIP RINGS
4 FOR 5
IN FIRST FIVE SEASONS

WILLIE RANDOLPH

An appropriate title for a biography of Willie Randolph would be: *A Winning Type of Player.*

Tony Lazzeri is the only Yankees second baseman in the Hall of Fame, but many regard Joe Gordon, whose career was almost a continuation of Lazzeri's, as the best of the Yankees at that position. Others maintain that Randolph was the best second baseman the Yankees have had.

Baseball is a percentage game; Randolph was a percentage player. Lazzeri and Gordon were power guys: athletic, strong, and possessing great arms. They were great players. Randolph rarely hit the ball hard. He didn't have a showy arm; you didn't see him zing the ball to third base and nail someone a foot off the bag,

something Lazzeri could do. Randolph was best at taking what the opposition gave him and not making mistakes.

Lazzeri and Randolph played about the same number of games for the Yankees and had about the same number of at-bats. Randolph never scored 100 runs in a season, never drove in more than 67. Lazzeri scored 100 runs twice, drove in 100 runs seven times, and never drove in fewer than 67, which was his count in 1934 when he missed a month. On what basis could one argue that Randolph was a better player than Lazzeri? Five points:

OFFENSIVE CONTEXT The American League norm in Lazzeri's time was 5.1 runs a game; 4.4 in Randolph's era. If Lazzeri put 100 runs on the scoreboard and Randolph 90, Randolph would be ahead, based on how many wins he could purchase with the runs he created.

PLAYING TIME Randolph didn't score 100 runs because he would miss 20 games a year due to injuries, but he scored 99 runs in 138 games in 1980, and 96 runs in 120 games in 1987. If you focus on runs scored per game rather than per season, Randolph is ahead of Lazzeri. He scored 75 runs more with the Yankees than Lazzeri did in about the same number of games.

CONTROL OF THE STRIKE ZONE Lazzeri struck out as much as he walked, which in his time gave him one of the poorer strikeout/walk ratios. Randolph played in an era when there were fewer walks and more strikeouts, yet he walked twice as often as he struck out, which gave him nearly the best strikeout/walk ratio of his generation. The only contemporary who had a better ratio was Wade Boggs, and not by much.

BASERUNNING Randolph stole 100 bases more than Lazzeri did, and was caught stealing almost the same number of times. That adds about 20 runs to Randolph's value, which isn't a lot. But there is a certain amount of base-running value that isn't documented in statistics.

DEFENSE Make no doubt, Lazzeri was a better hitter than Randolph was. So was Gordon, for that matter. But as he was when at-bat, Randolph in the field was quicker than Lazzeri and a better percentage player, too. Lazzeri turned 797 double plays with the Yankees and made 246 errors; Randolph had 1,233 and 183. By the standards of his time, Lazzeri was a fine second baseman. Until about 1930, second basemen were hitters first, defensive players second. That was true of Lazzeri, who came along at the end of that era. If he had come to the major leagues 10 years later, he would have been a third baseman. Randolph played at a time when the double play was more common, and therefore the ability to turn the double play was more important. Randolph had a larger defensive assignment — and he handled it.

The 1970s Yankees jelled in 1976, the year they added Randolph, and they ceased to be a winning team for several seasons when they let him go. Look at these win-loss records for the Yankees:

Five years before acquiring Randolph:
413-388 .516

First five years with Randolph:
489-317 .607

Last five years with Randolph:
445-364 .550

First five years without Randolph:
376-433 .464

At both ends of Randolph's career, the Yankees were 14 games a year better with him than without him. Yes, there are a million other factors that go into that; one player doesn't make a team. I'm not arguing that this proves Randolph was a winner, but these facts are irrefutable: The Yankees got better when they had Randolph; they got worse when they lost him.

ROY WHITE

Roy White was as valuable to the Yankees in 1972 as some Most Valuable Players — 19, to be exact — were to their teams. White in 1972 was as valuable as the 1987 MVPs in both leagues, George Bell and Andre Dawson. White in 1972 was more valuable than the 1995 AL MVP winner, Mo Vaughn.

White in 1970 was as good as or better than 60 percent of the players who have won MVP awards, including the AL MVP that season, Boog Powell.

White never hit .300, never hit 25 home runs, never drove in 100 runs. How can a player who didn't accomplish any of that in a season be rated for his career ahead of players such as Heinie Manush, Joe Carter, George Foster, Greg Luzinski, Kirk Gibson, and Don Baylor?

Statistics can be interpreted intuitively, or they can be interpreted by careful logic. The logical interpretation of baseball statistics depends on finding the answers to two questions: How many runs did the player create?; and in his era and home park, How many runs did it take to win a game?

White created a large number of runs because he did a lot of things well. Let's compare him with Manush, who is in the Hall of Fame. Manush hit more singles, doubles, and triples than White, but White hit more homers, drew more walks, and stole more bases. Comparing White with Carter, Carter hit more doubles and homers, but White hit for a higher average, hit more triples, drew more walks, stole more bases, and was a better defensive player.

When you add everything together, White didn't create as many runs as Manush or Carter, but he doesn't trail them by much, either. What made White a better player than those men, in addition to his defense, is that he created a lot of runs in an environment where runs were scarce: in a pitcher's park in a pitcher's era. When runs are scarce, each run has more impact on a team's win-loss record. The runs White created, relative to the context in which he played, had more impact in terms of winning games

than the runs created by Manush or Carter.

The problem is, no one remembers White as being an MVP-type of player. For that matter, no one thought of him in that light when he was playing. In 1970, when White had a better season than the AL MVP, Powell, he finished 15th in the voting.

Memory contributes immensely to our impression of players. Without a memory of White, or Mickey Mantle, for that matter, no one would care what their statistics were.

The problem with relying on memory when evaluating players is that memory doesn't always stand up under extensive questioning. If you saw White play, no doubt you gained an impression of him. But how many times did you see him play? 100 times? 200 times? Do you know? Did you see him play 10 percent of his games, or five percent? What did he hit when you saw him play? How many runs did you see him score, after he had worked the pitcher for a walk? How many subtle, nearly invisible contributions to victory did he make — when you saw him and when you didn't? If you are comparing White with Manush, you have to answer the same questions about Manush — and the truth is, you don't know most of the answers.

White was a better player than Jim Rice. If you put them in the same park in the same season, most people would be able to see that. The impression that Rice was a fearsome, mighty slugger, and White was a quiet complementary player is not based on logical interpretation of their records. It is based on a generalized impression of their relative greatness as hitters, which really is based on a casual interpretation of batting statistics. A careful, logical interpretation leads to the truth, even if you don't want to believe that a team with White in its lineup was better off than a team with Rice in its lineup.

TONY LAZZERI

Tony Lazzeri grew up in San Francisco during the years of World War I. The kids in his neighborhood played baseball in Golden Gate Park about 350 days a year, and the games became quite competitive. The neighborhood kids included Joe Cronin, Wally Berger, Ernie Lombardi, Lefty O'Doul, Mark Koenig, and, later on, Frankie Crosetti. All made it to the major leagues; Lazzeri, Cronin, and Lombardi made it to the Hall of Fame. Lazzeri was the star of those neighborhood teams. He was a year or two older than most of the others, bigger, stronger, the best hitter, and the best pitcher.

60 Home Runs

222 RBIs

202 Runs Scored

Pacific Coast League

1925

ALL WERE RECORDS FOR A PROFESSIONAL BASEBALL SEASON AT THE TIME.

Lazzeri entered pro ball in 1922 and within three years was playing shortstop for Salt Lake City of the Pacific Coast League, the major leagues of the West, so to speak. He hit 60 home runs, drove in 222 runs, and scored 202 runs in 1925 — all records for a professional baseball season at the time. Lazzeri had the benefit of a 200-game season and the high altitude of Salt Lake City, but a lot of people had played long seasons and in great hitter's parks, too, yet no one previously had had a year quite like Lazzeri's in 1925. He committed 85 errors, but that hardly deterred the Yankees, who were rebuilding their infield after a mid-1920s swoon.

Lazzeri joined the Yankees in 1926 and was their regular second baseman for 12 years. Though he hardly had the physique of a slugger at 5-feet-11-inches and 170 pounds, Lazzeri was a prominent member of the "Murderers' Row" line-up of the late 1920s. He reached 100 RBIs seven times and 18 home runs four times. Italian-Americans who followed baseball took quickly to Lazzeri; he was their first superstar.

"He spoke seldom," author Frank Graham wrote of Lazzeri, "and when he did, his voice had an angry quality, although he was seldom angry." In 1936, Joe DiMaggio went east to join the Yankees, riding in a car across the country, with Lazzeri and Crosetti doing the driving. During the long trip, DiMaggio asked Lazzeri if he had any advice. "Keep your mouth shut and play baseball," Lazzeri responded. Another year, Lefty Gomez made the cross-country drive with Lazzeri. A reporter asked Gomez if Lazzeri had said anything on the trip. "Just outside of Albuquerque," Gomez said, "I asked him if he wanted to stop for a hamburger. He said 'No.'"

These stories could give the impression that Lazzeri was a dour man, which was anything but the case. He was quiet and intense, but he also had a great sense of humor and a warm smile — and was a notorious practical joker. A preacher used to visit the Yankees' clubhouse once a year and hand out copies of the Bible. On one occasion, a Lazzeri crony invited the preacher out onto the field to play catch. When the preacher returned to the clubhouse, he reached into his satchel for Bibles — only to find that the satchel now was filled with risqué French novels. Lazzeri had made the switch.

Lazzeri didn't have much time left after he retired from baseball. An epileptic since childhood, he had a seizure on the stairs in his home in 1946, and suffered a broken neck that ended his life at age 42.

Frank Crosetti, Tony Lazzeri, and Joe DiMaggio (left to right).

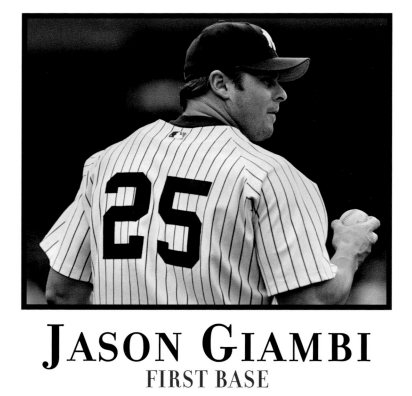

JASON GIAMBI
FIRST BASE

Giambi's achievement for the 2002 season, his first with the Yankees, set him on a path to become the second-best first baseman in Yankees history. That honor belongs to Don Mattingly, yet he takes a back seat to Giambi in career slugging percentage (.552 to .473) and on-base percentage (.416 to .363). Projecting Giambi's statistics through 2006 — the final year of the contract he signed with the Yankees before the 2002 season — he will have drawn 609 walks as a Yankee (more than Mattingly had in his career) and hit 204 home runs (18 less than Mattingly hit in 14 seasons). Additionally, Giambi will have scored 571 runs and driven in 627 runs — both more than half of Mattingly's career totals.

	YR	BA	H	R	2B	3B	HR	RBI	SB
ALFONSO SORIANO	2002	.300	209	128	51	2	39	102	41
TONY LAZZERI	1929	.354	193	101	37	11	18	106	9
JOE GORDON	1940	.281	173	112	32	10	30	103	18
WILLIE RANDOLPH	1987	.305	137	96	24	2	7	67	11

ALFONSO SORIANO
SECOND BASE

Soriano accomplished things in 2002 that rarely are associated with a second baseman. With 381 total bases, he became the second player in history at his position to exceed 360. (Rogers Hornsby did it five times, including 450 in 1922.) Soriano had 39 home runs and 41 stolen bases — one homer short of becoming the fourth 40-40 man in history. His 2002 season compares favorably with the best seasons of former Yankees second basemen Tony Lazzeri, Joe Gordon, and Willie Randolph. If Soriano can become a more disciplined hitter — his 23 walks in 2002 were about one-third the total of an average player — he could become the best second baseman in Yankees history.

128-70

CAREER RECORD

ANDY PETTITTE
PITCHER

If Pettitte pitches as well in his 30s as Whitey Ford did, Pettitte will take a place among the elite left-handers in Yankees history. Pettitte, who turned 30 during the 2002 season, entered 2003 with a superb career record of 128-70. Ford at that age was 105-40, and Ron Guidry was 76-29. Ford pitched for nine more seasons, winning another 131 games before retiring. Guidry had 94 victories after turning 30. Should Pettitte finish his career in the manner of Guidry, he would be one of the two best Yankees pitchers since 1981. Durable and reliable for most of his career, Pettitte had averaged 31 starts a year prior to 2002, when injuries limited him to 22 starts.

ROGER CLEMENS
PITCHER

Clemens joined the Yankees in 1999, at age 36, after 15 seasons and 233 victories with Boston and Toronto. Though clearly on the backslope of his career, he fashioned a 60-27 record in his first four seasons with the Yankees, adding to his status as one of the greatest pitchers in major league history. In 2001, Clemens became the first 20-game winner in history without a complete game, a testament to his ability to pitch well despite diminishing physical skills and to the Yankees' extraordinary bullpen. His 20-3 record that year merited him his sixth American League Cy Young Award.

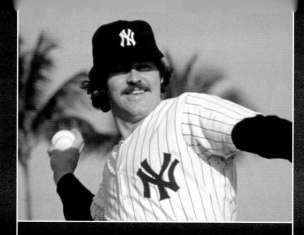

Jim "Catfish" Hunter
PITCHER

Hunter had most of his best years with the Oakland Athletics, but in 1975 he justified George Steinbrenner's free-agent investment in him by having one of the best seasons ever by a Yankees pitcher. Hunter's 328 innings that year — the first of his five seasons with the Yankees — was exceeded during the rest of the century only by Phil Niekro, who did it three times. Hunter made 75 starts over the 1975 and 1976 seasons, a two-year total that was surpassed only once — by Niekro — during the rest of the century. Hunter's 30 complete games in 1975 has not been topped, because no team has had that many since 1989.

Mike Mussina
PITCHER

Mussina joined the Yankees in 2001, after a decade with the Baltimore Orioles, for whom he was one of the most reliable pitchers in the major leagues. Mussina had an exceptional first season with the Yankees, winning 17 games and posting a 3.15 ERA that ranked second in the American League. He was not as consistent in 2002, when his ERA rose by nearly a run, although he won 18 games. His two-year winning percentage of .625 was slightly lower than his winning percentage for the Orioles, who never had a team as formidable during his tenure as either the 2001 or 2002 Yankees.

Mussina is among the elite class of pitchers who can rely on both power and control. He throws a fastball in the mid-90-mph range, and his knuckle-curveball has long been recognized as one of the hardest pitches to hit in the major leagues. Mussina can throw five pitches with uncanny control, leaving hitters off-balance. Not surprisingly, he has taken a no-hitter into the eighth inning on four occasions — including a game against Boston in 2001. Mussina is an exceptional athlete, and he has won five Gold Gloves for his fielding.

Thurman Munson
— CATCHER —

Munson joined the Yankees during their lost years of the early 1970s and became an integral part of their revival. He was the American League MVP in 1976, when the Yankees made the World Series for the first time in 12 years. Munson was anything but a pretty player — a squat, grumpy-faced man usually in need of a shave. But he was the best catcher in the major leagues in his era not named Bench or Fisk, a hitter who produced runs with line-drive power and a receiver who had the respect of his pitchers and the other team's base-runners. Munson died in a plane crash in 1979, during his 11th season with the Yankees.

MEL STOTTLEMYRE >>
PITCHER

The Yankees were in third place when Stottlemyre joined the team in August 1964. He won nine games in six weeks, leading the Yankees to the pennant, the only time the team made the World Series in his 11 seasons. Stottlemyre won 20 games in three of the next five seasons, despite the degeneration of the team around him. He started at least 35 games for nine consecutive seasons, a feat matched in the 20th century only by Gaylord Perry, who did it 10 times. Elston Howard said Stottlemyre threw the best slider he ever saw. Stottlemyre's sinker was equally famous, and he was adept at changing speeds on all of his pitches. Stottlemyre became the Yankees pitching coach in 1995.

<< DAVE RIGHETTI
PITCHER

Righetti was a successful starter for the Yankees for three years, going 33-22, including a no-hitter in 1983. When the team needed a replacement for closer Goose Gossage in 1984, Righetti accepted the assignment and flourished in the role for seven years, averaging more than 30 saves. He had 46 saves in 1986, a major league record until 1990. When he went to the bullpen, Righetti was able to pare his repertoire to his two above-average pitches, a lively fastball and a hard-bending curve. Righetti is the Yankees all-time leader in appearances by a pitcher with 522.

WALLY PIPP >>
FIRST BASE

Pipp is most famous for losing his job to Lou Gehrig, but he was a good player in his own right, comparable to someone like Bill Buckner or Chris Chambliss in the 1970s and 1980s. Pipp, the Yankees' regular first baseman for 10 years, twice led the American League in home runs and had a four-year run in which he drove in from 90 to 114 runs. Pipp played defense better than any first baseman in the major leagues except for another man in his town, George Kelly of the Giants.

<< BOBBY MURCER
CENTER FIELDER

From Earle Combs to Joe DiMaggio to Mickey Mantle, the man in center field for the Yankees was destined for the Hall of Fame. Murcer was next in that link, and he turned out to be merely a very good player. He was a solid No. 3 hitter in the lineup and a reliable center fielder. The media never gave Murcer his due, largely because the Yankees were also-rans most of the time he was with them; the best players on a bad team usually get the most blame. By the time the Yankees started winning again, Murcer had been traded to San Francisco. He returned to the Yankees in 1979 and completed his career as a part-time player. In 1983, Murcer returned to the team as a broadcaster.

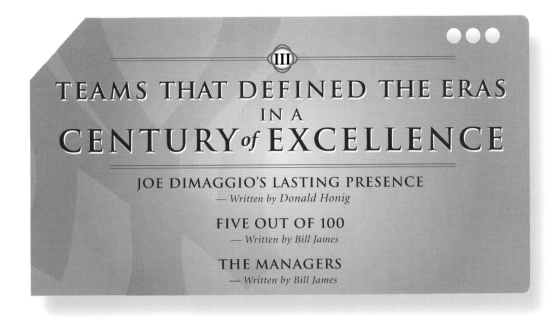

TEAMS THAT DEFINED THE ERAS
IN A
CENTURY *of* EXCELLENCE

JOE DIMAGGIO'S LASTING PRESENCE
— *Written by Donald Honig*

FIVE OUT OF 100
— *Written by Bill James*

THE MANAGERS
— *Written by Bill James*

Any attempt to select or define the greatest individual team in baseball history starts with the New York

Yankees. For most of the 20th century the debate rested with the 1927 Yankees of Babe Ruth and Lou

Gehrig. More recently the case has been made for Joe DiMaggio's 1939 team. Bill James looks at five

Yankee teams and makes a case for each, including Mickey Mantle's in 1961, Reggie Jackson's in 1978,

and the 1998 team of Derek Jeter and Bernie Williams. In the opening essay, noted author Donald

Honig sets the stage by revisiting DiMaggio and a legend that has never gone out of style.

JOE DiMAGGIO

Written by Donald Honig

In March 1998, *Time* magazine observed the 75th anniversary of its founding. To mark the occasion, Time, Inc., arranged a dinner and invited some 1,200 of the world's most notable personalities. The guests, many of whom had graced the cover of *Time*, included the most renowned names from the spheres of arts and letters, politics, medicine, science, athletics, and entertainment. No less a venue than Radio City Music Hall was procured to accommodate the gathering.

The guest list included then President Clinton, Henry Kissinger, Mikhail Gorbachev, Muhammad Ali, Bill Gates, Sophia Loren, Tom Cruise, Steven Spielberg, Walter Cronkite, an array of Nobel Prize winners, and just about anyone else whose achievement had illuminated some corner of the globe. Never before had such an assemblage of glamour, glitter, and accomplishment been gathered under one roof. Toasts were made as luminary upon luminary of the earthly firmament rose to honor one another.

It fell on actor Kevin Costner to toast a man who had done little of note for nearly a half-century, yet Costner had no trouble hitting the mark with his introduction:

"Men like Joe DiMaggio," Costner said, "are not just of their own time. They are men for the ages. And as the century comes to a close, and debates heat about who is the man or woman of the century, I know the list will be impressive. But it will not be complete unless Joe DiMaggio's name is on it. So I'd like you to raise a glass to Joe DiMaggio, for showing us the way."

And more than a thousand of the world's elite rose to their feet and accorded an 83-year-old long-retired baseball player the evening's "longest and most thunderous ovation," newspapers reported the following day. It is doubtful that, except for his 56-game hitting streak in 1941, many of the august crowd at Radio City Music Hall could have recited the statistics that had brought the frail, silver-haired old slugger to eminence in the first place. Not his .381 batting title in 1939 (unmatched by any right-handed hitter since); not his 167 RBIs in 1937; not his .325 lifetime batting average; not his astonishingly meager 13 strikeouts in 1941 (about one for every 42 at-bats). The truth was that the man, the persona, had long-since transcended his celebrated statistics and grown into the perfect fit for the nation's image of a hero.

In reference to that remarkable paucity of strikeouts, Yankees pitcher Vic Raschi once made a statement that unwittingly served as a metaphor for DiMaggio himself. "For a power hitter," Raschi said, "Joe had an incredible eye. He had an uncanny talent for making contact."

In DiMaggio's case the "uncanny talent" for making contact extended far beyond the pitched ball, beyond the observable exploits, beyond the playing days. It went on and on, in the public mind forever undiminished and untarnished. In the retired baseball player, the national imagination sensed something that it wanted, perhaps felt it needed, and elevated him to a plateau where the ovations would always be the "longest and most thunderous."

The irony lies in the fact that the man who was able to make "contact" with and evoke such adulation among legions of admirers for decade after decade was someone with a remote, undemonstrative personality. His seedbed was baseball, of course, the national game. But there are few truly legendary baseball figures, and diamond heroics alone will not insure a place in the country's mythology.

Among baseball's enduring legends, personalities vary. There is no prototype. The grandest of all is Babe Ruth, the man DiMaggio came to replace in the skies over Yankee Stadium. Ruth was a noisy extrovert, crude and lovable. He has been described as "Moby Dick in a goldfish bowl." He roared through life with the orgiastic appetites of a Roman emperor. There was no mystery to Ruth. Set him to music and he was "The 1812 Overture."

No less loved and idolized, Ruth and his successor could not have been more unalike. DiMaggio was different from all other diamond legends. Ty Cobb was a taut wire of snarls and ferocity. Honus Wagner was modest and folksy. Walter Johnson was the humble epitome of American virtues. Dizzy Dean was cornball witty and boastful. With all his mighty power, Lou Gehrig lacked electricity — he immediately was overshadowed in 1936 by the rookie DiMaggio —and gained legendary status through tragedy. Willie Mays was a bubbly personality who seemed to embody the game's spirit of eternal youth. The near-flawless hitter Ted Williams was known during his career for his explosive temper. Mickey Mantle was a Hercules of baseball talent.

All of them part of our folklore, yet the essential renown of each was gained solely through their baseball careers. It was DiMaggio who took his fame further, doing it without noise, wit, theatrics, or discernible "personality." DiMaggio alone seemed to fit an ideal and have a status conferred upon him. He came as close to royalty as a democratic nation allows.

How did he do this? "He did it by doing nothing," sportswriter Red Smith said. "By that I mean nothing except be Joe DiMaggio. He simply perpetuated that plain fact. I'm afraid you have to resort to hyperbole to describe the impact he had on people." Smith recalled a walk he took with DiMaggio from a New York nightclub to a hotel where yet another testimonial dinner awaited. "The gawking and the gasping he evoked in a cynical, seen-it-all city had to be experienced to be believed," Smith said. "Cab drivers yelled to him and almost drove into the plateglass windows because they couldn't take their eyes off him. People just stopped dead in their tracks and stared at him. It was a modest whiff of what the Second Coming might be like. I never felt more invisible than when I was in Joe's company."

On the field, DiMaggio was as zealously competitive as Cobb was at his most ferocious self. But the man who came to stylize baseball, as it had never been before, did it with a quiet intensity that kept all eyes riveted on him. What inner demons possessed him were not for public display, to the extent that his lone display of emotion on a baseball field was considered notable and is often replayed on highlight reels.

The display occurred at Yankee Stadium in the sixth game of the 1947 World Series, Yankees versus Dodgers. DiMaggio tore into a pitch and sent a throbbing drive to deep left field that looked for sure to be a game-tying three-run home run. He certainly believed the ball had sufficient carry. But Dodgers left fielder Al Gionfriddo, in the breathless words of announcer Red Barber,

but he never put himself up on a pedestal. He was always approachable. If you needed a favor, like tickets for a hit Broadway show, he'd get them for you. Joe knew all the big shots in town."

They all said he was the perfect teammate, one who never considered himself different from anyone else. He asked only one thing of his fellow Yankees: professionalism. For DiMaggio that meant playing to win, all the time.

"If he didn't think you were bearing down on the field," Chandler said, "God help you."

DiMaggio's rancor was in character. "He wouldn't say anything," Chandler said. "But you'd get into the dugout and find him frowning at you. Believe me, it made you shrivel."

★ World Series ★
APPEARANCES
10

★ World Series ★
CHAMPIONSHIPS
9

went "back, back, back, back, back" and made a spectacular grab at the wall. DiMaggio was approaching second base when he saw the catch being made. It was then that he allowed his memorable, uncharacteristic display of emotion: a brief, frustrated kick at the ground. For many people this slight fissure in an otherwise wall of stoic resolve remains as graphic as Gionfriddo's catch.

DiMaggio's reticence impressed itself upon his teammates more than any exclamatory outbursts would have.

"Joe was a good teammate," said pitcher Spud Chandler. "He was quiet but not silent, if you know what I mean. You knew when he was around. I always said I could have walked into the Yankees clubhouse blindfolded and told you whether Joe was there or not. That's what he did: create an atmosphere. The mood was different, the talk was different. We were in awe of him,

"He played with a streak of fire in him," Vic Raschi said. "It was pride. I think he took more pride in his game than any player I ever saw."

When asked why he played with such unremitting fervor, even at times when the score did not demand it, DiMaggio's oft-quoted answer was: "Because there might be somebody out there who's never seen me play before."

The answer is an insight into the man: The impression he left on the mind of every nameless stranger who was watching him was important. The leader's responsibility was unceasing. He remained faithful to this creed for all his days.

DiMaggio brought his star qualities to New York in 1936. The most acclaimed player in the minor leagues, he had excelled with his hometown San

Francisco Seals, for whom he achieved a harbinger streak of hitting safely in 61 consecutive games in 1933. A knee injury in 1934 made him suspect, and major league teams backed away from the heavy price tag Seals ownership had placed on him. The Yankees, however, took a gamble and obtained DiMaggio's contract in exchange for $25,000 — no small sum in those Depression years — and five players. A proviso in the deal was that the 20-year-old center fielder remain with the Seals for the 1935 season. Playing in the elongated Pacific Coast League season — Joe appeared in 172 games — he collected 270 hits and batted .398. On that wave he rode into New York, proclaimed by an anticipatory New York press as the heir to Ruth, who had left the Yankees two years earlier.

No rookie had ever entered the major leagues faced with such expectations, and no rookie had so instantly and lavishly fulfilled them. By 1939, DiMaggio had attained iconic status. The shy, at times almost wary son of an immigrant Sicilian fisherman came to feel at home in the most dynamic and sophisticated city in America. From the time he arrived in New York, when baseball was still almost exclusively a daylight game, the new man chose to spend his evenings in places like Toot Shor's restaurant or the high-profile Stork Club, in the company of the city's most popular, colorful, and powerful politicians, entertainers, journalists, columnists (most especially the influential Walter Winchell), Broadway characters, and an amorphous species known in those days as "sportsmen."

The apotheosis of Joe DiMaggio began on those long, smoky nights, far from the

1936 SAN FRANCISCO SEALS

MOST VALUABLE PLAYER SEASON TOTALS

Games	At Bats	Hits	Runs
172	679	270	173

Doubles	Triples	Home Runs	RBI	Average
48	18	34	154	.398*

Led the League   *Missing the batting title by a point to Oscar Eckhardt

San Francisco wharves of his childhood, far from the Sicilian culture brought across the Atlantic and then transcontinentally by his fisherman father, who by some genetic quirk raised a trio of baseball players from among his nine children (Joe's brothers Dominic and Vince would follow him to the major leagues). Ironically, the man born to become the sleekest ship of state ever to make passage across the green grass of America's outfields was subject to bouts of sea sickness when working aboard his father's boat, an early, telltale sign of where the young man's destiny lay.

DiMaggio's range of associations grew exponentially. He was a brilliant young star who possessed a special magic on the field and off, and the famous, always drawn to their kind, vied to sit in his reflected glory. Sportswriters sensed something unique had entered the tent and found in the reserved young ballplayer a fascinating subject, one whose self-protective screen made him even more intriguing.

"He was quiet, almost inarticulate in those years," Red Smith said. "He sat among a lot of the lions of the day, but looking back I don't think Joe was ever awed by anybody. That shoe was on the other foot. Joe created his own magnetic field right from the beginning. He saw how people reacted to him and he just built his own sense of who he was, and that it was more than just being a ballplayer. With some kids — and that's what he was then, remember — this sort of fawning and outright sycophancy increases the head size by quantum leaps. But with Joe you got the feeling he was absorbing it very carefully.

Outside of what he did when he had spikes on his feet you couldn't really define him. Successful young men tend to transparency, but not this one.

"Joe had what you might describe as a 'shrewd silence.' I wouldn't call him a student of human nature. Something else perhaps. A student of fame and the famous. I think he knew he was in it for the long haul and was learning how to conduct himself."

This makes the young DiMaggio sound somewhat calculating, but more likely he was following natural instincts, focusing on self-involvement with the same diligence that he focused on the ballfield. Yankees pitcher Eddie Lopat recalled being the beneficiary of DiMaggio's brand of concentration.

"What made me realize just how great DiMaggio was," Lopat said, "was something that happened during a game I was pitching in New York against Cleveland in 1948, my first year with the Yankees. We were winning by either 2-1 or 3-2. I had two men on and two out and Lou Boudreau was up. In spots like that I would sometimes turn my back on the hitter and do a little thinking about how to start him off. I noticed Joe out there, playing straightaway in center. Then I turned around, got my sign, and threw the first pitch. It was a ball. When I got the ball back I turned around again, mumbling to myself, and there's Joe out in dead center. The next pitch was ball two. Now I was really upset with myself and didn't turn around.

"I threw the next pitch and Boudreau stepped in and creamed it. He sent a line drive over Rizzuto's head. One of those vicious long line drives. The moment that ball left the bat I knew it was ticketed. Right into the left-center slot. A sure triple and two runs. When I turned around Joe was standing there, catching the ball without ever having moved. I was shocked, frankly.

"When we got into the dugout after the inning I sat down next to him. 'Joe,' I said, 'I noticed you were in dead center on the first couple of pitches.

Lou Gehrig and Joe DiMaggio (left to right).

But then he hits the ball flush into the gap and you're standing right there.'

" 'Well,' he said, 'I've seen you pitch enough times now to know how you work. I knew that as long as you stayed ahead of him or were even you wouldn't let him pull the ball. But when you went behind two balls and no strikes, I knew you had to get the next one over and that he knew it too and would probably pull it.'

"Do you know how far over he moved before I threw that pitch? About 80 feet.

"So I said to him, 'That was great thinking, Joe.' And do you know what? He just turned away from me with kind of a scowl. He didn't want to be complimented. I guess he just thought it was his job to do the right thing, that that was what was expected of him."

The specialness that was DiMaggio was immediately apparent to his Yankees teammates. Although he was often open and congenial with them, he also could be aloof and private, sitting alone in an enigmatic silence. The latter moods disturbed no one.

"He was revered in that clubhouse," Spud Chandler said. "He was so dedicated and splendid a player that we all recognized the fact that he was different, and it got to the point where we wanted him to be different. So if he was moody now and then and didn't always hang around with the boys, that was all right. We expected it. He was different, you see."

As .406 is to the legend of Ted Williams, so the 56-game hitting streak is to DiMaggio. The streak is the perfect metaphor for the man: a pressure-ridden run of high-caliber consistency. It is DiMaggio's career vibrantly encapsulated. As the streak gradually extended into headline-making proportions, the daily pressure must have been excruciating.

"You'd watch him before one of those games and you couldn't help won-

DATE	HITS	TEAM
May 15	1-for-4	Chicago
May 16	2-for-4	Chicago
May 17	1-for-3	Chicago
May 18	3-for-3	St. Louis
May 19	1-for-3	St. Louis
May 20	1-for-5	St. Louis
May 21	2-for-5	Detroit
May 22	1-for-4	Detroit
May 23	1-for-5	Boston
May 24	1-for-4	Boston
May 25	1-for-4	Boston
May 27	4-for-5	Washington
May 28	1-for-4	Washington
May 29	1-for-3	Washington
May 30	1-for-3	Boston
May 30	1-for-4	Boston
June 1	1-for-4	Cleveland
June 1	1-for-4	Cleveland
June 2	2-for-4	Cleveland
June 3	1-for-4	Detroit
June 5	1-for-5	Detroit
June 7	3-for-5	St. Louis
June 8	2-for-4	St. Louis
June 8	2-for-4	St. Louis
June 10	1-for-5	Chicago
June 12	2-for-4	Chicago
June 14	1-for-2	Cleveland
June 15	1-for-3	Cleveland
June 16	1-for-5	Cleveland
June 17	1-for-4	Chicago
June 18	1-for-3	Chicago
June 19	3-for-3	Chicago
June 20	4-for-5	Detroit
June 21	1-for-4	Detroit
June 22	2-for-5	Detroit
June 24	1-for-4	St. Louis
June 25	1-for-4	St. Louis
June 26	1-for-4	St. Louis
June 27	2-for-3	Philadelphia
June 28	2-for-5	Philadelphia
June 29	1-for-4	Washington
June 29	1-for-5	Washington
July 1	2-for-4	Boston
July 1	1-for-3	Boston
July 2	1-for-5	Boston
July 5	1-for-4	Philadelphia
July 6	4-for-5	Philadelphia
July 6	2-for-4	Philadelphia
July 10	1-for-2	St. Louis
July 11	4-for-5	St. Louis
July 12	2-for-5	St. Louis
July 13	3-for-4	Chicago
July 13	1-for-4	Chicago
July 14	1-for-4	Chicago
July 15	2-for-4	Chicago
July 16	3-for-4	Cleveland
July 16	3-for-4	Cleveland
July 16	3-for-4	Cleveland

TOTALS	AB	R	H	2B	3B	HR	RBI
	223	56	91	16	4	15	55

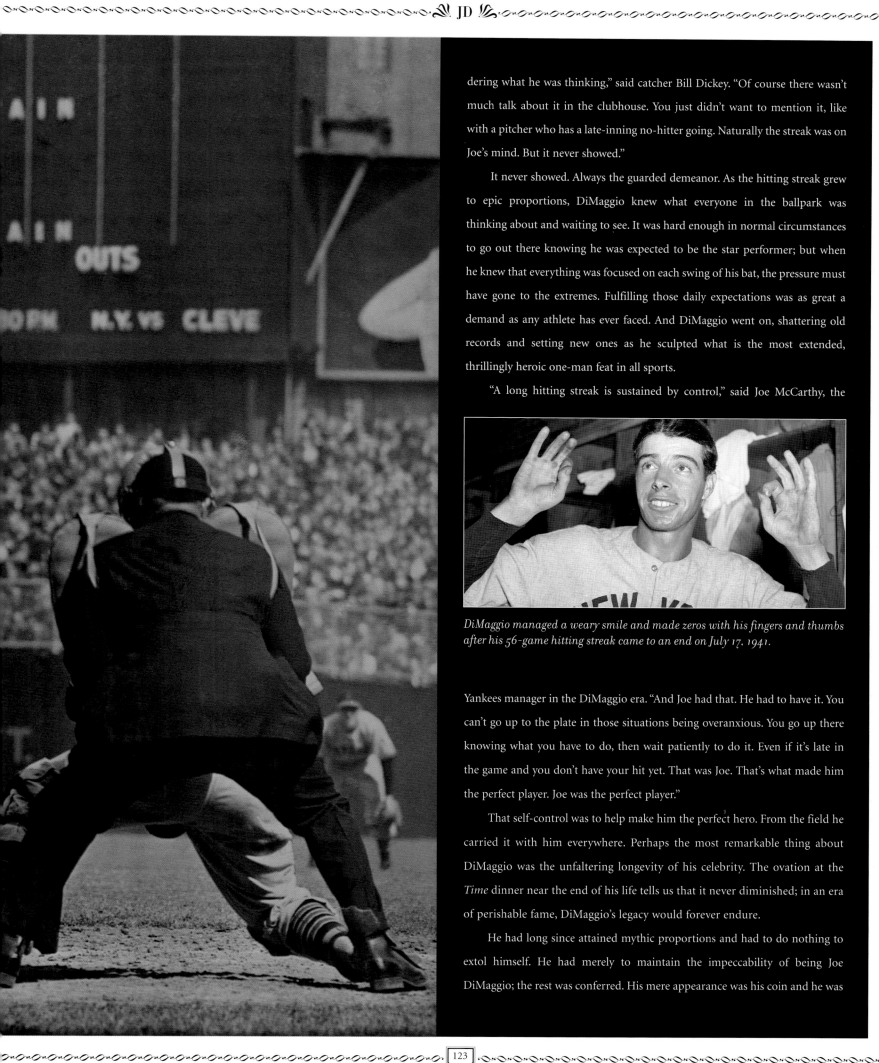

dering what he was thinking," said catcher Bill Dickey. "Of course there wasn't much talk about it in the clubhouse. You just didn't want to mention it, like with a pitcher who has a late-inning no-hitter going. Naturally the streak was on Joe's mind. But it never showed."

It never showed. Always the guarded demeanor. As the hitting streak grew to epic proportions, DiMaggio knew what everyone in the ballpark was thinking about and waiting to see. It was hard enough in normal circumstances to go out there knowing he was expected to be the star performer; but when he knew that everything was focused on each swing of his bat, the pressure must have gone to the extremes. Fulfilling those daily expectations was as great a demand as any athlete has ever faced. And DiMaggio went on, shattering old records and setting new ones as he sculpted what is the most extended, thrillingly heroic one-man feat in all sports.

"A long hitting streak is sustained by control," said Joe McCarthy, the

DiMaggio managed a weary smile and made zeros with his fingers and thumbs after his 56-game hitting streak came to an end on July 17, 1941.

Yankees manager in the DiMaggio era. "And Joe had that. He had to have it. You can't go up to the plate in those situations being overanxious. You go up there knowing what you have to do, then wait patiently to do it. Even if it's late in the game and you don't have your hit yet. That was Joe. That's what made him the perfect player. Joe was the perfect player."

That self-control was to help make him the perfect hero. From the field he carried it with him everywhere. Perhaps the most remarkable thing about DiMaggio was the unfaltering longevity of his celebrity. The ovation at the *Time* dinner near the end of his life tells us that it never diminished; in an era of perishable fame, DiMaggio's legacy would forever endure.

He had long since attained mythic proportions and had to do nothing to extol himself. He had merely to maintain the impeccability of being Joe DiMaggio; the rest was conferred. His mere appearance was his coin and he was

"Heroes are people who are all good with no bad in them. That's the way I always saw Joe DiMaggio. He was beyond question one of the greatest players of the century."

— MICKEY MANTLE

conscious of it, always outfitted in custom-made suits and overcoats. If the public had an image of him, he made sure not to blur it. He remained the embodiment of old glories tailored in grace, style, dignity — the flesh and blood representation of the American hero.

The genuine and unending esteem of millions, for decades, is a recipe for swollen ego. If DiMaggio fell victim to this human failing it was never apparent to those who came to fete him. He seemed to have effortlessly adapted himself to cheers, applause, beaming faces, to have absorbed it all rather than allow it to resonate within him. His responses were studies in long-honed instinct. There was no excess of humility, just the magic name, the familiar trimly tailored figure, raising his hand and sending out a greeting with a slight twirl of his fingers. (Whether Joe knew it or not, the gesture was similar to that offered crowds from the balcony of Buckingham Palace by Great Britain's wartime King George VI.)

But there was another DiMaggio, one all too sensitive to his man-on-a-pedestal stature, a condition that now and then could nag at him. On one occasion he had accepted an invitation to attend a testimonial dinner on the West Coast. Delegated to meet him at the airport and shepherd him to his accommodations was Bobby Bragan, former major league player and future major league manager, then managing the Hollywood Stars of the Pacific Coast League.

"Somebody else had booked the motel," Bragan said, "and had screwed up royally. When we got there I was appalled. It was a third-rate place off the highway. You know, one of those places with a blinking neon sign with one of the letters crashed out. I was embarrassed, and I apologized to Joe and offered to take him to a more upscale place. But he said, 'For Christ's sake, Bobby, all I want is a bed to sleep in. What the hell's the dif-

Ruth, sportswriter Bill Corum, and DiMaggio.

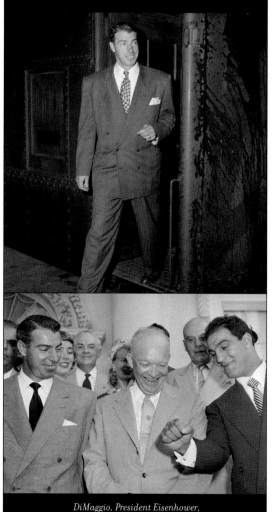

DiMaggio, President Eisenhower,
and boxing champion Rocky Marciano.

ference?' When we walked in to register, the clerk almost fell over. Joe gave him an autograph and went to sleep. That's the Joe I knew."

On another occasion — this was in the 1970s — DiMaggio was one of the celebrities at a Jimmy Fund golf tournament at a course outside Hartford, Connecticut. To help publicize the event, he agreed to an interview with Arnold Dean, the area's widely admired sports talk show host. Dean was broadcasting from a makeshift studio set up in the upstairs of a small building at the edge of the course.

"Joe showed up just before the top of the hour," Dean said, "which meant we had about a 10-minute wait until the news had been read. He said that was fine with him and he took a seat. The next thing I knew some people were calling his name and making a fuss outside. There was a sliding door that opened onto a portico and I went out to have a look. About 15 or 20 people had gathered below and were calling for him.

"I knew Joe was very shy, especially when it came to the unexpected. When I came back in and told him what was going on down there, he got up and went outside and waved to the people and posed for pictures, all very good-naturedly.

"I guess word had got around that Joe DiMaggio was there and was posing for pictures, because when we finally finished the interview there was quite a hubbub outside. When I looked out again I was taken aback — there must have been well over 100 people gathered, all shouting for Joe. I guess I was kind of embarrassed; I'd gotten the poor guy into more than he'd bargained for. He asked me how many people were down there, and I gave him my estimate.

" 'Look,' he said, 'I'm not going to go out there again. It makes me very uncomfortable to be standing somewhere looking down at people. Hell, I'm not the Pope.'

"What he did," Dean said, "was go downstairs and plunge right into that crowd, shaking hands, signing autographs, posing for pictures. I don't know if he enjoyed it or not. I doubt it. But he did it, and graciously. Because he felt uncomfortable looking down at them."

This was the same man who as a ballplayer would sometimes sit for hours in the Yankees clubhouse after a game until he knew the crowds waiting outside for him had broken up and gone away, the same man who could freeze intrusive strangers with a glare and who had a natural predisposition for privacy.

Contradictory? Perhaps, but understandably, for throughout his long years of fame the man faced many varied, and sometimes whimsically unexpected, things.

DiMaggio would now and then attend the annual induction ceremonies at the Baseball Hall of Fame in Cooperstown, New York. On one of those occasions, seeking a few hours' respite, he and a companion went for a drive through the countryside. The two men soon found themselves lost on a remote country road. Seeing a farmer riding his tractor in a nearby field, they

stopped and signaled the man over to ask for directions.

"The guy was very obliging," the companion said. "He climbed down from the tractor and came over to the car and leaned his elbow on the window and found himself face to face with Joe DiMaggio. I asked him for directions and he gave them, never taking his eyes off Joe the whole time. I thanked him, but he wasn't finished. He had a favor to ask: Would Joe mind stepping out and autographing his tractor? Joe looked at me with that poker face of his, then got out and followed the guy across the field. I'll never forget the sight of Joe, in his beautifully tailored suit, following that guy in overalls and floppy hat across the field, where he autographed the tractor. They shook hands and Joe came back to the car. When he had settled himself in, he said, 'I've autographed pictures, bats, balls, gloves, menus, you name it . . .' He didn't have to finish the sentence. But somewhere in upstate New York there's a guy driving around on a tractor autographed by Joe DiMaggio."

When Ted Williams, DiMaggio's lone contemporary rival for diamond supremacy, died in July 2002, the admiring tributes mentioned Williams having missed nearly five prime seasons to military service,

"There is always some kid who may be seeing me for the first or last time, I owe him my best."

— JOE DIMAGGIO

with dreamy speculation about what his record might have looked like had he played in those years. DiMaggio likewise lost prime years — from 1943 through 1945 — to military service, but baseball fantasists seldom try to fill them in. DiMaggio, it seems, always has been seen as complete, in need of no enhancements, no what-ifs, because his record needs no embellishment.

The man to whom DiMaggio's Yankees torch was passed also possessed extraordinary post-career charisma. Within the hierarchy of retired athletes, Mickey Mantle was indeed a close rival of DiMaggio's in popularity. Some fans, in fact, saw Mantle as the superior player, citing his greater power (from both sides of the plate) and blinding foot speed. The debates could be fervent, but as far as the long-term public consciousness was concerned, they were irrelevant, because immense though Mantle's accomplishments had been, they had been built upon perishables: power and speed. They left behind awe and magical memories, but what Mantle always evoked was baseball — baseball of Ruthian might, yes, but only baseball — whereas DiMaggio had excelled at championship baseball and then carried on through decades of tumultuous social change like a talisman of the old and the good. The eminent

Yankee had been anointed as the connection between past and present, the repository of standards and ideals whose decline many felt had a negative effect on the national health.

What flaws and shortcomings DiMaggio might have had did not matter; they were mere scratches on a sculpture, from a distance invisible. He could be brusque, aloof, demanding — the perfect hero could be at times all too human. That he also could be generous, loyal, and giving were likewise of no relevance, for these too were human qualities and of little interest to an adoring public. An idealization had occurred, and that was that.

DiMaggio was to be raised even higher in the public imagination by his second marriage, to Marilyn Monroe, who was to undergo her own apotheosis. The short-lived marriage — it lasted about a year — was to be woven forever into the tapestry of the DiMaggio mystique. It was more a collision of headlines than a marriage, a hard bumping of two distinct and ultimately incompatible legends. Two antithetical personalities: she insecure and flashy, he a study in self-control. Whatever the initial expectations they brought to the union, whatever love, affection, and need, it was doomed. She could not

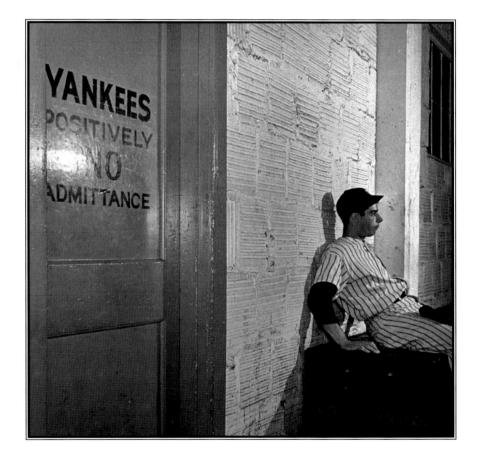

"Joe was the loneliest man I ever knew. He couldn't even eat a meal in a hotel restaurant, the fans just wouldn't let him. He led the league in room service."

— EDDIE LOPAT, DiMaggio teammate, 1948–1951

change; he would not.

He accepted her untimely death with a soundless mourning that ceased only with the moment of his own passing. Never did the inner man come more to the surface than with Marilyn's death. Her name was not to be mentioned in his presence, except by himself, and then only to intimate friends.

"He would occasionally mention her," one of those friends said. "It was usually in bitter, resentful terms about those whom he felt had betrayed and exploited her, like the Kennedys or Sinatra. Those conversations were always one-sided; you knew enough not to ask questions. He just had to let it out now and then."

When the editor-in-chief of a large New York publishing house met DiMaggio on a social occasion and offered him "a blank check" for his autobiography, DiMaggio, knowing what revelations such a book must include, declined.

"He was polite," the editor said, "but in a way that told me it would be futile to pursue it."

Asked if he was disappointed, the editor indicated his own fascination with the DiMaggio image. "I was disappointed that he said no," the editor said, "but I think I might have been more disappointed had he said yes."

That DiMaggio was willing to forgo seven-figure publishing deals if accepting them meant he had to drop the veils of his privacy and that of his fabled ex-wife is an insight into the man and the code he lived by. In an age of lurid and shameless tell-all, his was the rare principled silence.

His fame had reached an apogee and there it remained, never to decline. At Old-Timers games all introductions ended with "The Man They Saved for Last," when his appearance and the roaring ovation it evoked seemed to place an official stamp on the event. He was named "The Greatest Living Player," but even that impressive accolade defined him only partially. Years ago, Yankees pitcher and close DiMaggio friend Lefty Gomez whimsically described his teammate as "mysterious." And mysterious DiMaggio remained, and that the mystery was never solved did not seem to matter.

Presidents fawned over him. He attended the big prizefights with Ernest

Hemingway (who had referred to "the great DiMaggio" in his novella *The Old Man and the Sea*). Henry Kissinger couldn't believe that one day "I would be friends with DiMaggio."

Why DiMaggio, and not Mays or Williams, players of equal stature? Maybe because DiMaggio was "mysterious." To the public eye he had begun that way and had never changed. Trying to put him in larger context, one writer wrote that DiMaggio had become "a symbol to hang on to and cherish, a man from the old, strong, flawless America when Franklin Roosevelt was president and Joe Louis was heavyweight champion and Clark Gable was the king of Hollywood and Ernest Hemingway was shooting lions in Africa."

How would DiMaggio be seen if he were playing today, subjected to a more prying, less deferential media? One has to wonder at his reaction to ceaseless barrages of microphones, tape recorders, camcorders, pointed questions by insistent writers. It is unlikely that this guarded man would have been any different. He would be cooperative to a point, and beyond that the media would have to adapt, accepting his supreme talents as the ultimate point of contact.

Among today's often excessively exuberant, high-fiving heroes, DiMaggio would appear, as he always did, unique. And perhaps his would be the style, the uncompromising professionalism, that young players would seek to emulate, that the man who had set not only records but standards years ago would have done so today.

As time went on and DiMaggio aged, the feeling that we weren't going to see his kind again become more pervasive. The accolades grew more heartfelt, the applause more fervent, as though we were seeing off the man and what he represented. DiMaggio was going to take it all with him, as well he might, for there was no one to replace him.

Yankees pitcher Spud Chandler once recalled, "Just before the first pitch of every game I would turn around and look out to center field. I liked the feeling of seeing him out there. You don't know what a good feeling that was."

1927

In October 1927, longtime Brooklyn Dodgers manager Wilbert Robinson expressed the opinion that the 1927 Yankees were the greatest baseball team of all time. Hearing this, longtime New York Giants manager John McGraw yelped and jumped about three feet into the air.

Written by Bill James

A little background: Robinson and McGraw were teammates on the Baltimore Orioles in the 1890s and best of friends for years after that. McGraw became manager of the Giants in 1902. When Robinson in 1914 was hired to manage the Dodgers, the two men began to quarrel and feud.

By 1927, McGraw had spent 10 years trying to convince baseball writers that the 1894 Baltimore Orioles were the greatest baseball team ever put together. When Robinson expressed the opinion that the 1927 Yankees were the greatest team ever, perhaps he truly believed it, or perhaps it was an attempt to undermine McGraw's campaign for the 1894 Orioles. Sportswriters dwelt on the topic for a month or so, and after that, the idea that the 1927 Yankees were the greatest team ever was well established in the public's mind. The Yankees went 110-44, won the pennant by 19 games, and won the World Series in four games.

But were they really the best ever? One method of considering this issue is to break the large, general question into smaller, more specific questions that might be more conducive to objective study.

1) Has there ever been a team, aside from the 1927 Yankees, that has had two stars of the magnitude of Babe Ruth and Lou Gehrig, both with big seasons?

Yes. In the 19th century there were several teams that had two pitchers who would win about 35 games each and play the outfield when they weren't pitching. The 1886 St. Louis Browns had Bob Caruthers, who went 30-14 as a pitcher and played the outfield the rest of the time and batted .334. His teammate Dave Foutz went 41-16 as a pitcher and also played the outfield and batted .280. Caruthers and Foutz had more impact on the league than Ruth and Gehrig did because the game was very different in their era.

Since 1900, one team has had two players have bigger seasons than Ruth and Gehrig did in 1927. The 1912 Boston Red Sox got a 34-5 record and 1.91 ERA from Smokey Joe Wood, and

THE REGULARS

		G	R	H	HR	RBI	BA	OBP
C	Pat Collins	92	38	69	7	36	.275	.407
1B	Lou Gehrig	155	149	218	47	175	.373	.474
2B	Tony Lazzeri	153	92	176	18	102	.309	.383
3B	Joe Dugan	112	44	104	2	43	.269	.321
SS	Mark Koenig	123	99	150	3	62	.285	.320
OF	Earle Combs	152	137	231	6	64	.356	.414
OF	Babe Ruth	151	158	192	60	164	.356	.486
OF	Bob Meusel	135	75	174	8	103	.337	.393
Team		155	975	1,644	158	908	.307	.381
AL rank			1	1	1	1	1	1

THE ROTATION

	G	ERA	W	L	SV	IP	SO
Waite Hoyt	36	2.63	22	7	1	256	86
Herb Pennock	34	3.00	19	8	2	210	51
Urban Shocker	31	2.84	18	6	0	200	35
Dutch Ruether	27	3.38	13	6	0	184	45
George Pipgras	29	4.11	10	3	0	166	81

THE TOP RELIEVERS

	G	ERA	W	L	SV	IP	SO
Wilcy Moore	50	2.28	19	7	13	213	75
Bob Shawkey	19	2.89	2	3	4	44	23
Team	155	3.20	110	44	20	1,389	431
AL rank			1	1	3	2	3

he wasn't the most valuable player on the team. That honor belonged to Tris Speaker, who batted .383 with 53 doubles. Wood-Speaker in 1912 were the best one-two combination any team has ever had.

2) Has there ever been another team that had two hitters like Ruth and Gehrig?

Never, and no team is close. Ruth and Gehrig were by far the best hitters in the major leagues in 1927. One team has had the two most productive hitters on eight occasions:

YEAR	HITTERS	TEAM
1880	George Gorem, Abner Dalrymple	Chicago Cubs
1884	Charley Jones, John Reilly	Cincinnati Reds
1927	Babe Ruth, Lou Gehrig	New York Yankees
1928	Babe Ruth, Lou Gehrig	New York Yankees
1930	Babe Ruth, Lou Gehrig	New York Yankees
1931	Babe Ruth, Lou Gehrig	New York Yankees
1959	Hank Aaron, Eddie Mathews	Milwaukee Braves
1989	Will Clark, Kevin Mitchell	San Francisco Giants

of those other seven cases, the only ones that approach Ruth-Gehrig in 1927 are the other Ruth-Gehrig combinations. Think of it this way: Ruth and Gehrig batting third and fourth would be like a team today having

BARRY BONDS AND SAMMY SOSA
BATTING THIRD AND FOURTH.

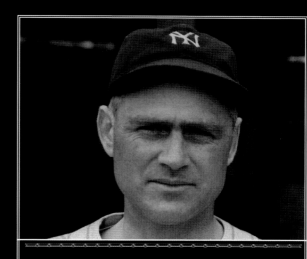

EARLE COMBS
Center Fielder

Combs, the Yankees center fielder during the Babe Ruth era, was a left-handed leadoff hitter who slapped the ball to all fields, was a skillful bunter, and ran exceptionally well. He was adept at fielding his position, but didn't have much of an arm. Combs, a career .325 hitter, generally was regarded as the best leadoff hitter of his era. He is in the Hall of Fame.

WAITE HOYT
Pitcher

Hoyt reached the majors as a teenager and stayed as a player and then a broadcaster for almost 60 years. He learned to pitch in Boston, where he was a teammate of Babe Ruth's, then joined Ruth and the Yankees in 1921. Hoyt took a regular turn in the Yankees rotation and won 17 to 20 games a year like clockwork through most of the 1920s. His most famous quote is: "The secret of success in pitching lies in getting a job with the Yankees." Hoyt is in the Hall of Fame.

Lou Gehrig, Earle Combs, Tony Lazzeri, and Babe Ruth (left to right).

3) Did the 1927 Yankees have the greatest offense ever?

Probably not. It depends on whether you mean the Yankees of 1927 specifically, or the Yankees of that era. If you mean the 1927 team, the answer is no. The 1931 and 1932 Yankees offenses were every bit as good, probably a little better, and other teams have had offenses just as good, including the 1975 and 1976 Cincinnati Reds, and the 1982 Milwaukee Brewers (Harvey's Wallbangers). If you mean the Yankees of that era, yes, it was the greatest offense ever put together.

4) How good was the pitching staff?

It was the best staff in the major leagues in 1927 because it was the deepest staff and the only one that had an effective relief ace. However, it is not among the 100 best staffs of all

er Earle Combs had very good range but couldn't throw. Ruth in right field and Bob Meusel in left had terrific arms but not a lot of speed. All of the other great Yankees teams were better defensively than the 1927 team.

6) How many of the 1927 Yankees were the best players in the league at their position?

Five: Gehrig, Ruth, Lazzeri, Combs, and Moore. One National League center fielder, Hack Wilson, was as good as Combs that season, but no better. Two NL second basemen, Rogers Hornsby and Frankie Frisch, had better seasons than Lazzeri did. Koenig was the second-best shortstop in the league, and Meusel the third- or fourth-best left fielder. The other two regulars, Dugan and catcher Pat Collins, were about average. Moore had the best season ever by a reliever up to that point.

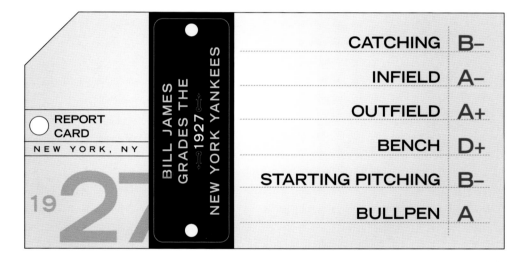

REPORT CARD	BILL JAMES GRADES THE 1927 NEW YORK YANKEES		
NEW YORK, NY		CATCHING	B–
		INFIELD	A–
1927		OUTFIELD	A+
		BENCH	D+
		STARTING PITCHING	B–
		BULLPEN	A

time. The four starters — Waite Hoyt, Herb Pennock, Urban Shocker, and Dutch Ruether — had been around for years and knew how to pitch, but none was a Randy Johnson. The ace reliever, Wilcy Moore, had a good sinker and a deceptive motion, and turned in, by far, his best season.

5) How good was the defense?

It was spotty. Gehrig was okay, but not Gold Glove–caliber. Tony Lazzeri was a decent second baseman by the standards of the time. Shortstop Mark Koenig had a fantastic arm but was an erratic fielder. Third baseman Joe Dugan had sure hands but had lost a step. Center field-

7) Setting aside Ruth and Gehrig, how good was this team?

If the 1927 Yankees had a .240 hitter without power instead of Ruth, it still is likely they would have won the pennant. If they had the worst first baseman in the league instead of Gehrig, they likely still would have won.

If they had neither Gehrig nor Ruth and been unable to replace them with quality players, the 1927 Yankees probably still would have had a record better than .500 and finished in third or fourth place.

1939

For fans of that era, the dominant story of the 1939 Yankees was the illness and retirement of Lou Gehrig. Yes, the team had a 106-45 record, won the pennant by 17 games, and won the World Series in four games — but the Yankees had won the pennant in each of the previous three years by an average of 14 games and had won all three World Series with comparative ease. It would have seemed strange to everyone at the time to have marked 1939 as one of the Yankees' greatest seasons, given the pall that hung over the season.

Years later, after the publication of baseball encyclopedias, after people began to try to organize baseball history, the case for the 1939 Yankees began to gather steam. Rob Neyer and Eddie Epstein wrote a book, *Baseball Dynasties*, in which they carefully weighed and measured the top candidates and concluded that the 1939 Yankees were the greatest team ever. And Richard J. Tofel wrote an excellent book just about the 1939 Yankees, *A Legend in the Making*.

With all due respect to Mr. Tofel's title, the 1939 Yankees are not defined by legend, but by logic. They have — or had for many years — very little legend, but awfully good credentials. They averaged more runs a game than the 1927 Yankees and yielded fewer — the 1927 Yankees led in runs, 975 to 967, but played three more games than the 1939 Yankees.

THE REGULARS

		G	R	H	HR	RBI	BA	OBP
C	Bill Dickey	128	98	145	24	105	.302	.403
1B	Babe Dahlgren	144	71	125	15	89	.235	.312
2B	Joe Gordon	151	92	161	28	111	.284	.370
3B	Red Rolfe	152	139	213	14	80	.329	.404
SS	Frank Crosetti	152	109	153	10	56	.233	.315
OF	George Selkirk	128	103	128	21	101	.306	.452
OF	Joe DiMaggio	120	108	176	30	126	.381	.448
OF	Charlie Keller	111	87	133	11	83	.334	.447
	Tommy Henrich	99	64	96	9	57	.277	.371
Team		152	967	1,521	166	903	.287	.370
AL rank			1	2	1	1	2	1

THE ROTATION

	G	ERA	W	L	SV	IP	SO
Red Ruffing	28	2.93	21	7	0	233	95
Atley Donald	24	3.71	13	3	1	153	55
Bump Hadley	26	2.98	12	6	2	154	65
Lefty Gomez	26	3.41	12	8	0	198	102
Monte Pearson	22	4.49	12	5	0	146	76
Oral Hildebrand	21	3.06	10	4	2	127	50
Marius Russo	21	2.41	8	3	2	116	55

THE TOP RELIEVERS

	G	ERA	W	L	SV	IP	SO
Johnny Murphy	38	4.40	3	6	19	61	30
Steve Sundra	24	2.76	11	1	0	121	27
Team	152	3.31	106	45	26	1,349	565
AL rank		1	1	1	1	7	3

The success of the 1927 Yankees rested heavily on the exploits of Lou Gehrig and Babe Ruth, while the 1939 team drew from a much broader base of support.

THIS CHART IS A COMPARISON OF THE 1927 AND THE 1939 TEAMS, POSITION BY POSITION:

	1927	1939	COMMENT
C	Pat Collins	Bill Dickey	big edge 1939
1B	Lou Gehrig	Babe Dahlgren	huge edge 1927
2B	Tony Lazzeri	Joe Gordon	basically even
3B	Joe Dugan	Red Rolfe	big edge 1939
SS	Mark Koenig	Frank Crosetti	slim edge 1939
LF	Bob Meusel	George Selkirk	about even
CF	Earle Combs	Joe DiMaggio	big edge 1939
RF	Babe Ruth	Charlie Keller/ Tommy Henrich	you guess

The 1939 team had the advantage at five of eight positions, and the teams had comparable pitching. The 1939 Yankees had the best catcher in the major leagues (Bill Dickey), the best second baseman (Joe Gordon), the best third baseman (Rad Rolfe), and the best player in baseball in center field (Joe DiMaggio), plus a good shortstop, and three extremely productive players (Selkirk, Keller, and Henrich) filling out the outfield.

Another standard of greatness: a team's accomplishments over a period of years. The Yankees won pennants in 1926, 1927, and 1928, and two World Series. Starting in 1936, the Yankees won four consecutive pennants, four consecutive World Championships, and seven pennants in eight seasons.

Another, more subtle argument on behalf of the 1939 team: Baseball matured significantly between 1927 and 1939. If you liken baseball history to a life cycle, the baseball of the 19th century may be seen as an infant, and the dead-ball era (1901 to 1919) may be viewed as baseball's adolescence. The game in 1915 was loosely organized. Efforts to identify the best players and get them into the major leagues were haphazard at best. Players often reached the major leagues for no apparent reason other than that someone liked them, while more-skilled players remained in the minor leagues simply because the system to recognize and promote talent was in its rudimentary stage. This was less the case by 1927, but still true. Baseball in 1927 can be likened to a 21-year-old player — grown up but green as a ball field — while baseball in 1939 was much more mature. The Yankees in 1927 dominated an immature game with talent they had purchased from other teams. By 1939 they had a highly organized scouting and development operation that produced ballplayers.

Yet baseball cannot be viewed as a fully mature game until it admitted African-Americans in 1947, or maybe not until a few years after that. While the Yankees had a sophisticated farm system by 1939, some of the teams had nothing of the kind.

If you put the 1939 Yankees and the 1927 Yankees in a pennant race, the 1939 team probably would win.

One of the questions to ask about a great team is: What makes this team special? If you ask that question about the 1927 Yankees, you have an answer: They

JOE GORDON
Second Base

Gordon was an acrobatic second baseman and a power hitter — a rare combination for a player at his position in the 1940s. He replaced Tony Lazzeri in 1938 and was virtually the same player as Lazzeri, although Lazzeri was not as smooth as Gordon in the field. Gordon averaged 25 homers and 100 RBIs in his first five seasons, and he won the American League Most Valuable Player award in 1942, getting more votes than Ted Williams, who had led the league in batting, home runs, and RBIs.

REPORT CARD	BILL JAMES GRADES THE 1939 NEW YORK YANKEES	CATCHING	A
NEW YORK, NY		INFIELD	B+
1939		OUTFIELD	A+
		BENCH	C
		STARTING PITCHING	C+
		BULLPEN	A+

Charlie Keller, Joe DiMaggio, and George Selkirk (left to right) carried big bats for the 1939 Yankees.

had the greatest one-two punch in baseball history and exceptional hitters surrounding them. It is also very easy to get an answer, if you ask that question about the 1961 Yankees, the 1998 Yankees, the 1911 Philadelphia Athletics, or the 1974 Oakland A's. But it is not so easy to answer that question about the 1939 Yankees. What made that team special? A cold, mechanical efficiency? A farm system that was ahead of everyone else's? An exceptional ratio of runs scored to runs allowed? Those aren't very satisfactory answers, are they?

The 1939 Yankees were not greater than the 1927 Yankees — they were technically superior. The 1939 Yankees coped with and overcame tragedy. Maybe that should have elevated them to the status of legend — but the reality is, it didn't. Gehrig spent his life in the shadow of Babe Ruth. And perhaps the greatest team that Gehrig was part of was obscured for a long time by the shadow of his illness.

1961

In the spring of 1961, it was like baseball was reborn. Casey Stengel, manager of the Yankees seemingly forever, had been fired. His undoing came the previous fall, in the wonderful and exciting 1960 World Series that ended with Bill Mazeroski's home run. And the American League had expanded, for the first time ever, from eight to 10 teams.

Baseball still was the national game in 1961; football didn't explode in popularity until about three years later. Also, baseball fans had yet to develop the suspicion that club owners were ruining the game. That notion was hatched in 1969, when baseball split its leagues into divisions, and mushroomed in the 1970s, with the coming of the designated hitter and free agency. When AL expansion was announced in late 1960, a lot of people liked the idea, and probably just as many didn't — but there wasn't the "Oh, God, they're ruining the game again" reaction that tends to follow every change nowadays.

Baseball never went to sleep in the winter between the 1960 and 1961 seasons. A constant rumble echoed through the snow-covered months as discussion persisted about expansion and how it would affect the game. The 1961 season opened to an almost unparalleled level of interest.

The Yankees began the post-Stengel era by undoing a lot of what he had instituted. New manager Ralph Houk went from a five-man to a four-man pitching rotation, which gave Whitey Ford 10 more starts than in 1960 and enabled him to win 25 games. Houk also drastically scaled back Stengel's practice of platooning. Six Yankees got at least 500 at-bats in 1961; in the 12 Stengel years, only 33 players got 500 at-bats in a season.

The 1927, 1939, and 1998 Yankees led the league in runs scored and in fewest runs allowed, as did several other Yankees teams. The 1961 Yankees didn't lead the league in either category. They didn't lead in runs scored because, while they had phenomenal power, they had nothing except power. They didn't hit for a high average, didn't draw a lot of walks, didn't have a lot of speed, and didn't manufacture runs. Their power was awesome, but their leadoff hitters were mediocre. It was a Mark McGwire offense: nothing except home runs.

The Yankees went 109-53, won the pennant by eight games — Detroit, with hugely productive years from Norm Cash and Rocky Colavito, won 101 games — and beat the Reds in the World Series in five games. Yet we need to take into account that it was an expansion year, and that the 1961 Reds were perhaps the weakest champions in National League history.

The Yankees pitching staff didn't lead the league in ERA because they had only about three good pitchers: Ford and Ralph Terry in the rotation, and Luis Arroyo in the bullpen. The rest of the staff was composed of kids who were good enough to win under the circumstances, those circumstances including a superb defense.

The 1961 Yankees catching corps — Elston Howard and Johnny Blanchard, and Yogi Berra for 15 games — was the best in major league his-

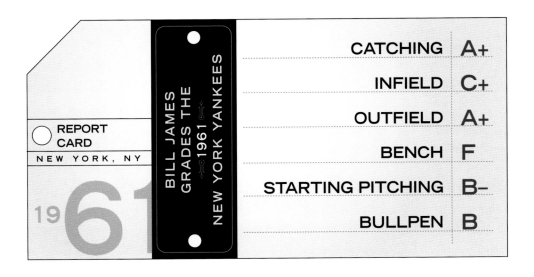

REPORT CARD
NEW YORK, NY

BILL JAMES GRADES THE 1961 NEW YORK YANKEES

19**61**

CATCHING	A+
INFIELD	C+
OUTFIELD	A+
BENCH	F
STARTING PITCHING	B–
BULLPEN	B

John Blanchard, Bill Skowron, Bob Hale (left to right, back),
Whitey Ford, and Roger Maris (left to right, front).

ROGER MARIS
Right Field

Maris was an unassuming, workman-type player who was thrust into an unwelcome spotlight in 1960 and 1961, when he kept hitting home runs. The Yankees right fielder for the first seven years of the 1960s, Maris was a career .260 hitter and often maligned as a one-dimensional player, but that was far from the truth. In addition to his home-run power, he was a superb fielder with a fine arm, and rarely made a mistake on the bases. A common belief that Maris hit 61 home runs in 1961 largely because he was a left-handed hitter taking advantage of the short distance to Yankee Stadium's right field fence is not supported by fact. Maris hit more home runs in road games in 1961 and for his career with the Yankees than he did in home games.

tory. Howard batting .348, backed by Blanchard hitting 21 homers, backed by Berra — that's better than Johnny Bench backed by Pat Corrales, Roy Campanella backed by Rube Walker, or any other combination you can name.

The 1961 Yankees bench gets a failing grade because:

1) It is among the weakest benches in history, even if you count Blanchard as part of the bench.

2) If you don't count Blanchard as part of the bench, it contributed virtually nothing.

The underrated part of the 1961 Yankees was the defense. The infield — Bill Skowron, Bobby Richardson, Tony Kubek, and Clete Boyer — was phenomenal, all Gold Glove quality. Yet as hitters they had a combined on-base percentage of .306, about 20 points below what is marginally acceptable.

Four Yankees were the best in the major leagues at their positions in 1961: Howard, Arroyo (15-5, 29 saves), Roger Maris in right field, and Mickey Mantle in center. Ford and Kubek, while not clearly better than their competitors, were as good as anyone at their positions. At the other positions, the 1961 Yankees were more or less an average team.

Bill Skowron, Roger Maris, Bud Daley, Elston Howard, and Mickey Mantle (left to right)

If we ask, What makes this team special?
WE GET A CLEAR ANSWER:
POWER.

If you put the 1961 Yankees in a pennant race with other great teams in history, they probably would get buried. In an eight-team league with the 1927 Yankees, 1939 Yankees, 1978 Yankees, 1998 Yankees, 1953 Dodgers, 1975 Reds, and 1970 Orioles, the 1961 Yankees would finish last. But there are other tests of greatness for a team: What did it accomplish over a period of years? In postseason play? Answer: A lot. The Yankees of this era won five straight pennants, and in both 1961 and 1963 won more than 100 games. The five-year run included two World Championships.

If we ask, What makes this team special? we get a clear answer: Power. The 1961 Yankees hit 240 home runs, a major league record that was not broken until 1996. Maris hit 61, a record that stood for 37 years. Maris and Mantle combined for 115, the most ever by two teammates. There was a lot of history in the making. The 1961 team, flawed as it might have been, was among the best in Yankees history.

THE REGULARS

		G	R	H	HR	RBI	BA	OBP
C	Elston Howard	129	64	155	21	77	.348	.387
1B	Bill Skowron	150	76	150	28	89	.267	.318
2B	Bobby Richardson	162	80	173	3	49	.261	.295
3B	Clete Boyer	148	61	113	11	55	.224	.308
SS	Tony Kubek	153	84	170	8	46	.276	.306
OF	Roger Maris	161	132	159	61	142	.269	.372
OF	Mickey Mantle	153	132	163	54	128	.317	.448
OF	Yogi Berra	119	62	107	22	61	.271	.330
	John Blanchard	93	38	74	21	54	.305	.382
	Hector Lopez	93	27	54	3	22	.222	.292
	Bob Cerv	57	17	32	6	20	.271	.344
Team		163	827	1,461	240	782	.263	.328
AL rank			2	4	1	1	4	5

THE ROTATION

	G	ERA	W	L	SV	IP	SO
Whitey Ford	39	3.21	25	4	0	283	209
Ralph Terry	31	3.15	16	3	0	188	86
Bill Stafford	36	2.68	14	9	2	195	101
Rollie Sheldon	35	3.60	11	5	0	163	84
Bud Daley	23	3.96	8	9	0	130	83

THE TOP RELIEVERS

Luis Arroyo	65	2.19	15	5	29	119	87
Jim Coates	43	3.44	11	5	5	141	80
Team	163	3.46	109	53	39	1,451	866
AL rank		2	1	10	1	3	4

THE REGULARS

		G	R	H	HR	RBI	BA	OBP
C	Thurman Munson	154	73	183	6	71	.297	.332
1B	Chris Chambliss	162	81	171	12	90	.274	.321
2B	Willie Randolph	134	87	139	3	42	.279	.381
3B	Graig Nettles	159	81	162	27	93	.276	.343
SS	Bucky Dent	123	40	92	5	40	.243	.286
OF	Mickey Rivers	141	78	148	11	48	.265	.302
OF	Reggie Jackson	139	82	140	27	97	.274	.356
OF	Lou Piniella	130	67	148	6	69	.314	.361
DH	Cliff Johnson	76	20	32	6	19	.184	.307
	Roy White	103	44	93	8	43	.269	.349
	Fred Stanley	81	14	35	1	9	.219	.324
Team		163	735	1,489	125	693	.267	.328
AL rank			4	4	6	4	4	7

THE ROTATION

	G	ERA	W	L	SV	IP	SO
Ron Guidry	35	1.74	25	3	0	274	248
Ed Figueroa	35	2.99	20	9	0	253	92
Catfish Hunter	21	3.58	12	6	0	118	56
Dick Tidrow	31	3.84	7	11	0	185	73
Jim Beattie	25	3.73	6	9	0	128	65

THE TOP RELIEVERS

	G	ERA	W	L	SV	IP	SO
Rich Gossage	63	2.01	10	11	27	134	122
Sparky Lyle	59	3.47	9	3	9	112	33
Ken Clay	28	4.28	3	4	0	76	32
Team	163	3.18	100	63	36	1,460	817
AL rank		1	1	1	1	2	2

1978

From 1921 through 1964, the longest the Yankees went without winning the American League pennant was three years. In those 44 years, the team had a losing record only once (69-85 in 1925), finished 20 games out of first place only once (in 1925), and had a winning percentage of less than .600 only 13 times.

T hen came the dark period in Yankees history. From 1965 through 1975, the team had losing records five times, finished 20 games out of first place six times, and had a winning percentage as high as .550 only once. The Yankees of that era certainly were not as hapless as the Boston Braves of the 1920s or the San Diego Padres of the 1970s, yet they no longer were entertaining their fans in the manner to which those fans had become accustomed.

That changed for the better starting in 1976, when the Yankees won the first of three successive AL pennants. In 1977 they won the World Championship for the first time in 15 years, and a year later the team was even better, one of the best in Yankees history. The 1978 team went 100-63, including a dramatic win in Boston in a playoff for the AL East title, and beat the Los Angeles Dodgers in six games in the World Series.

The story of the 1978 Yankees, as it played out at the time, was the saga of a team winning its second successive World Championship despite a clubhouse rocked by dissension. In 1977 the big addition to the team was Reggie Jackson. He was the straw that constantly stirred something. In 1978 the big addition was Goose Gossage, who was brought in to be the closer, even

though the 1977 closer, Sparky Lyle, had performed so well that he won the AL Cy Young Award.

Jackson and Thurman Munson clearly resented each other, Lyle had a chip on his shoulder, and Cliff Johnson was a smoldering powder keg. The veterans Lou Piniella, Graig Nettles, and Dick Tidrow, though not exactly controversial figures, were quick to speak up if they felt someone was stepping on their toes. And the man in the manager's seat, Billy Martin, was the most volatile personality in the clubhouse, at least until he resigned under pressure in late July and was replaced by the mellow Bob Lemon.

From the high ground of retrospect, it seems evident that the 1978 Yankees probably didn't have any more internal conflict than most teams. It just seemed that way because the Yankees were followed by a large press corps, and the sports media, in the wake of Watergate, had moved off a cooperative, go-along, and get-along approach and into a more aggressive mode. No doubt there was conflict among the 1958 Yankees and the 1928 Yankees, too; it just never made the newspapers, so the public was unaware of it.

The 1978 Yankees came together at the onset of the free-agent era. The great teams that preceded the 1978 Yankees largely were populated by players who went through the minor leagues together and had played together for years. The 1978 Yankees were a group of players thrown together in mid-career, veterans who were set in their ways and had to figure out how to get along to go along. "Clubhouse chemistry" is perhaps the most misunderstood term in sports. It doesn't mean that everyone likes each other and gets along famously. It means that a team has a lot of players that do not deal well with losing. This team had many of those guys — the type that wouldn't stand for losing, was miserable when it happened, and didn't care if he made everyone around him miserable, too.

How good were the 1978 Yankees? Let's consider their key players. Munson was the AL MVP in 1976, although he was not as good a player in 1978. Jackson was the AL MVP in 1973 and now is in the Hall of Fame. Lyle and Gossage were among the top closers of their era. Nettles at third base and Willie Randolph at second base were two of the best players the Yankees ever had at those positions. Ron Guidry went 25-3 and had a 1.74 ERA, the best season by a Yankees pitcher since Lefty Gomez went 26-5 with a 2.33 ERA in 1934.

No one element of the team, other than the bullpen, was truly outstanding. Every other factor of the team was very good — and that is quite unusual.

SPARKY LYLE
Pitcher

Lyle's seven seasons with the Yankees were by far the best of his 16-year career. His achievement for the Yankees —141 saves, 57 victories — makes him the top left-handed reliever in club history and the third-best reliever overall, behind Mariano Rivera and Goose Gossage. Lyle's best season was in 1977, when he led the American League in appearances with 72, won 13 games and saved 26, had a 2.13 ERA, and became the first reliever to win the AL Cy Young Award. Lyle pitched 137 innings in 1977, a total that was exceeded only six times through the rest of the century by pitchers with at least 20 saves.

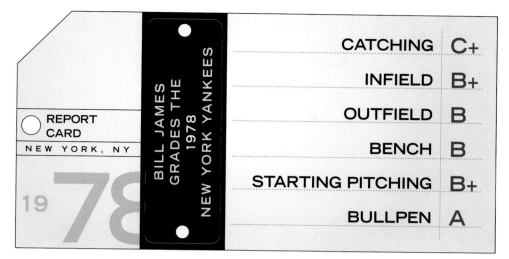

REPORT CARD	
NEW YORK, NY	
BILL JAMES GRADES THE 1978 NEW YORK YANKEES	
CATCHING	C+
INFIELD	B+
OUTFIELD	B
BENCH	B
STARTING PITCHING	B+
BULLPEN	A

Almost every team has a weakness.

What makes the 1978 Yankees special? Two things:

1) They succeeded through turmoil that played out daily in the news media.

2) They wrote the manual for success in the free-agent era.

And perhaps there is a third reason: They had many stars. Jackson, Gossage, Munson, Nettles, Piniella, Randolph, Guidry, Chris Chambliss, Mickey Rivers — these guys were really good players. Tony Lazzeri played second base and Earle Combs center field for the 1927 Yankees, and both are in the Hall of Fame. Randolph was a better player than Lazzeri, and Rivers was much the same player as Combs, though not quite as good. Guidry was every bit as good as Herb Pennock, the star lefthander on the 1927 team. Continuing the matchup of the 1978 Yankees and the 1928 Yankees, Jackson certainly was not Babe Ruth and Chambliss was not Lou Gehrig, but Munson and Nettles were far better than Pat Collins and Joe Dugan. Virtually everyone in the 1978 lineup except shortstop Bucky Dent could be called a star — and he certainly lived at that level when his home run over the Green Monster in the playoff game beat the Red Sox and set in motion the Yankees' march to another World Championship.

1998

In the summer and fall of 1998, as the Yankees marched to 114 wins and decisive victories over three postseason opponents, many people asked: Is this the greatest team of all time? Where does this team rank among the best ever? Those questions could not be answered, for there was much about the 1998 Yankees that could not have been known in 1998. It takes time to understand what has happened.

F ive years is not long enough for all the truth to emerge, but it is sufficient to allow the drivel to drain off. Accordingly, it is not irresponsible to conclude after five years that the 1998 Yankees were the greatest baseball team of all time. Why? Let us begin with the question: What are the standards of a great team?

1) It should dominate its competition.

The 1998 Yankees won the American League East by 22 games and went 11-2 in three levels of postseason play. That is about as thoroughly as any team has ever dominated its competition.

2) It needs to be successful over a period of years.

This team won three successive World Series and four in five years in an era when winning the World Championship required three straight series conquests over high quality teams. No other team in history has accomplished that much in postseason play.

3) It should have — at the least — a good offense, good defense, and good pitching staff.

The 1998 Yankees had an incredible offense, getting about 100 runs created from every position except left field. They had five good starting pitchers, backed up by five good relievers — an absolutely astonishing staff. Their defense, while not as strong as the other two elements, was competent.

PAUL O'NEILL
Right Field

O'Neill was traded to the Yankees after a modestly successful six-year career with the Cincinnati Reds, and he thrived in pinstripes. O'Neill kept getting better, batting better than .300 almost every year, becoming a more disciplined hitter, and hitting with increased power. Perhaps the most telling fact about O'Neill is that he had his best season as a base-stealer — successful on 22 of 25 attempts — at age 38, in his final year in the major leagues. The man just never quit improving his game, and that is why he was a cornerstone of the great Yankees teams of the late 1990s and early 2000s.

THE REGULARS

		G	R	H	HR	RBI	BA	OBP
C	Jorge Posada	111	56	96	17	63	.268	.350
1B	Tino Martinez	142	92	149	28	123	.281	.355
2B	Chuck Knoblauch	150	117	160	17	64	.265	.361
3B	Scott Brosius	152	86	159	19	98	.300	.371
SS	Derek Jeter	149	127	203	19	84	.324	.384
LF	Chad Curtis	151	79	111	10	56	.243	.355
CF	Bernie Williams	128	101	169	26	97	.339	.422
RF	Paul O'Neill	152	95	191	24	116	.317	.372
DH	Darryl Strawberry	101	44	73	24	57	.247	.354
	Tim Raines	109	53	93	5	47	.290	.395
	Joe Girardi	78	31	70	3	31	.276	.317
Team		162	965	1,625	207	907	.288	.362
AL rank			1	2	4	1	2	1

THE ROTATION

	G	ERA	W	L	SV	IP	SO
David Cone	31	3.55	20	7	0	208	209
David Wells	30	3.49	18	4	0	214	163
Andy Pettitte	33	4.24	16	11	0	216	146
Hideki Irabu	29	4.06	13	9	0	173	126
Orlando Hernandez	21	3.13	12	4	0	141	131

THE TOP RELIEVERS

Mariano Rivera	54	1.91	3	0	36	61	36
Graeme Lloyd	50	1.67	3	0	0	38	20
Ramiro Mendoza	41	3.25	10	2	1	130	56
Darren Holmes	34	3.33	0	3	2	51	31
Jeff Nelson	45	3.79	5	3	3	40	35
Mike Stanton	67	5.47	4	1	6	79	69
Team	162	3.82	114	48	48	1,456	1,080
AL rank		1	1	1	3	3	4

4) It should have great players having great years.

The 1998 Yankees do not score as well here as in the other areas. Derek Jeter and Bernie Williams both had outstanding seasons, and both could have Hall of Fame credentials by the end of their careers. Yet there was no Babe Ruth, no Joe DiMaggio, no Mickey Mantle on this team. The top three stars of the 1950s Yankees teams — Mantle, Yogi Berra, Whitey Ford — all would have ranked ahead of anyone on the 1998 team.

5) It should be deep in truly talented players.

A truly talented player is one who has had more than one good season. A truly great team is not composed of six guys having career years. On this standard, the 1998 Yankees rank far, far ahead of any other team in history. Of the 10 players on the team who had 300 or more plate appearances, nine could be considered truly talented. We have mentioned Jeter and Williams. Here are the others:

- Jorge Posada, who was having his first good season, has become one of the best catchers of his era.

- First baseman Tino Martinez, who drove in 123 runs, has had five other 100-RBI seasons.

- Second baseman Chuck Knoblauch scored 100 or more runs six times, and was in position to make a run at 3,000 hits until his fielding work betrayed him and his reputation collapsed along with his defense in 1999.

- Third baseman Scott Brosius, although he didn't hit as well the rest of his career as he did in 1998 (.300, 98 RBIs) was a fine defensive player and had more than 1,000 hits in his career.

- Outfielder Tim Raines, who hit .290 with a .395 on-base percentage, was a Hall of Fame–caliber player over the course of his career, although the press never reorganized it.

A few teams in history have had a stronger eight-man lineup than the 1998 Yankees, namely the 1953 Brooklyn Dodgers, the 1962 San Francisco Giants, the 1975 Cincinnati Reds, and the 1976 Reds.
YET NONE HAD THE DEPTH OF QUALITY ON THEIR PITCHING STAFF
TO MATCH THAT OF THE 1998 YANKEES.

REPORT CARD

NEW YORK, NY

1998

BILL JAMES GRADES THE 1998 NEW YORK YANKEES

CATCHING	B+
INFIELD	A+
OUTFIELD	A
BENCH	B
STARTING PITCHING	A
BULLPEN	A

"... the greatest team in baseball history."

— BILL JAMES

Bernie Williams, Derek Jeter, and Scott Brosius (left to right).

- Darryl Strawberry, who hit 24 homers as a half-time player in 1998, was a feared power hitter for many years.
- Right fielder Paul O'Neill hit .300 or better in each of his first six seasons with the Yankees, had at least 100 RBIs in four successive seasons, and was a player who did everything well.

Literally every player the Yankees put on the field, except left fielder Chad Curtis, meets the standard of a player of substance. And Curtis, while he did not hit enough to be a high-quality outfielder, had more than 1,000 hits, more than 100 home runs, and more than 200 stolen bases in his career.

A few teams in history have had a stronger eight-man lineup than the 1998 Yankees, namely the 1953 Brooklyn Dodgers, the 1962 San Francisco Giants, the 1975 Cincinnati Reds, and the 1976 Reds. Yet none had the depth of quality on their pitching staff to match that of the 1998 Yankees. The top three starters that year — Andy Pettitte, David Wells, and David Cone — have more than 500 victories among them. Orlando Hernandez, the fourth starter, has been a star for many years, although most were in Cuba. Relievers Mariano Rivera, Ramiro Mendoza, Mike Stanton, Jeff Nelson, and Darren Holmes are genuinely fine pitchers, and there were others that were pretty effective.

No other team in baseball history has ever had as many truly talented players having good to great seasons as the 1998 Yankees.

The 1998 Yankees infield was far better than those of the four other great Yankees teams, but not the best in team history. Here are the top five infields in Yankees history (players are listed in order at first base, second base, third base, and shortstop):

1) 2002 (Jason Giambi, Alfonso Soriano, Robin Ventura, Derek Jeter)

2) 1936 (Lou Gehrig, Tony Lazzeri, Red Rolfe, Frankie Crosetti)

3) 1998 (Tino Martinez, Chuck Knoblauch, Scott Brosius, Derek Jeter)

4) 1932 (Lou Gehrig, Tony Lazzeri, Joe Sewell, Frankie Crosetti)

5) 1999 (Tino Martinez, Chuck Knoblauch, Scott Brosius, Derek Jeter)

One test of a great team is its ability to thrive under any circumstances. Envision a super league, in which the great teams of all time compete against one another. Could the 1998 Yankees travel to 1906 and compete against the Chicago Cubs in a dead-ball-era game? Could the 1998 Yankees travel to 1975 and compete against the Reds in Cincinnati on an artificial turf field where any ball that hit the ground was likely to scoot to the wall?

The answers lie in the completeness of the 1998 Yankees. They hit 207 home runs (a huge number), and also had a .288 batting average, 153 stolen bases in 216 attempts (an excellent success ratio), and 653 walks. With Jeter, Knoblauch, Williams, Curtis, and Raines in the lineup, they could have stolen 250 bases easily if they had reason to do it. With quality right-handed and left-handed pitchers both in the rotation and the bullpen, excellent right-handed and left-handed hitters, power, speed, a high batting average, and good defense, the 1998 Yankees could march into any city in any era and win more frequently than any of their opponents. That makes it the greatest team in baseball history.

	YRS.	W	L	PCT.	WHAT THEY WON
Miller Huggins					
Yankees	12	1,067	719	.597	6 pennants, 3 World Championships
Other Teams	5	346	415	.455	Nothing
Joe McCarthy					
Yankees	16	1,460	867	.627	8 pennants, 7 World Championships
Other Teams	8	665	466	.588	1 pennant
Casey Stengel					
Yankees	12	1,149	696	.623	10 pennants, 7 World Championships
Other Teams	13	756	1,146	.397	Nothing
Ralph Houk					
Yankees	11	944	806	.539	3 pennants, 2 World Championships
Other Teams	16	1,157	1,135	.505	Nothing
Billy Martin					
Yankees	8	556	385	.591	2 divisions, 2 pennants, 1 World Championship
Other Teams	11	697	628	.526	3 divisions
Joe Torre					
Yankees	7	685	445	.606	6 divisions, 5 pennants, 4 World Championships
Other Teams	14	894	1,003	.471	1 division

THE MANAGERS

Casey Stengel undoubtedly was the most popular manager in Yankees history, but he was not the team's greatest manager. That honor goes to Joe McCarthy, who well might be the greatest manager in history among all teams.

McCarthy's record is much better than Stengel's. Both McCarthy and Stengel managed other teams before and after the Yankees. McCarthy was tremendously successful before he joined the Yankees, tremendously successful with the Yankees, and he had a .604 winning percentage after he left the Yankees. Stengel, too, was very successful with the Yankees, but his teams never won more than 77 games in a season before he joined the Yankees, and he had a .302 winning percentage after he left the Yankees. Among the Yankees who played for both McCarthy and Stengel, most were asked many times to compare the two. Virtually all of them said McCarthy was the better manager.

However, two things should be noted:

1) Stengel's record, when he managed poor teams, has nothing to do with how well he managed the Yankees.

2) How good is a specific manager? The question cannot be answered objectively. Whether a manager's record is good or bad depends on the talent of his players and his ability to get the most out of them — a relationship that no one really can measure. Why waste time debating questions that have no objective answer? It is more worthwhile to try and understand how managers differ from one another; how they take different paths but try to get to the same place. The Yankees have had tremendously successful teams under five different managers — or six, if you count the Billy Martin/Bob Lemon/Gene Michael/Dick Howser shuffle, which we will label *Martin* for space considerations. The six, in the order of eras: Miller Huggins, McCarthy, Stengel, Ralph Houk, Martin, and Joe Torre. Following are discussions of each man.

1) Huggins represented a type of manager — the scrappy, contentious former middle infielder — that is so common now that one might assume it always has been the dominant model of a manager. In fact, it was uncommon in Huggins' era.

2) Huggins managed the Yankees during their successful conversion from an early John McGraw–style organization to a modern Branch Rickey–style organization.

Discussing the second point first, when Huggins was hired to manage the Yankees in 1918, teams did not have front offices, as they do now. The manager was more or less responsible for the composition of his team's roster, much as a college basketball coach is today. The manager personally signed and trained young players that he liked. Drawing on his network of acquaintances in the game and on a few scouts who reported to him, the manager made the decision to purchase players from minor league operations, and he made trades with other managers.

Thus, Huggins' success in his early seasons as a manager was based largely on his judgment of talent. He had an advantage in that the Yankees had owners who were willing and able to put money into a deal to get the players they wanted. But as we have seen many times, spending alone doesn't lead to success. Huggins recognized the type of player who could help him win, and in his early years as the Yankees manager he was the leading force in acquiring those players.

Within three years of Huggins becoming the Yankees manager, teams began to hire front office executives who took responsibility for acquiring talent, and

MILLER HUGGINS
1918–1929

scouts whose role it was to locate promising players and sign them. At the same time, teams began to form farm systems to feed talent to the major league team.

Huggins was the only manager to run his team successfully through this transition. John McGraw continued to run the New York Giants the old-school way until the end of his career in 1932, and Connie Mack tried to do everything himself until it became apparent that a one-man show just couldn't compete with the increasingly organized and sophisticated baseball operations. While many organizations were thrashing around trying to sort out this new relationship between manager and front office, Huggins backed off gracefully and allowed the Yankees to develop a state-of-the-art operation. Thus, to a certain extent the achievements of later Yankees teams can be traced back to Huggins.

As for the first point: Huggins as a player led the National League in walks four times, even though nobody was aware of it back then. At that time, a walk was considered a non-event for the batter. Huggins took all those walks not because he got paid for it, but because that was the type of player he was; he knew that getting on base helped the team win, and he did it, even though nobody was counting.

As a player with virtually no talent — he was slow as well as tiny — Huggins had to scrap for every edge he could find. He took the same mindset into managing. Huggins was detail-oriented, understood the game, understood why some teams won and others didn't.

The biggest, strongest, and loudest players tended to evolve into managers in the 1800s and through the first 25 years of the 20th century. Huggins was a departure from the norm, a 135-pound second baseman who became a manager and succeeded on his wits.

❖

1) McCarthy understood how an offense works better than any other manager in history.

2) McCarthy had great confidence in his ability to judge talent — and thus no fear of his players.

If you make a list of the highest-scoring teams in

JOE McCARTHY
1931–1946

easier to get a single, a walk, and a homer than it is to get three solo homers. That was true then, and it is true now.

A book written a few years ago included a passage about how McCarthy did not like to use rookies. This is historical ignorance on the same scale as saying that Tony La Russa does not like left-handed relievers. McCarthy had no trepidation about putting a rookie into the starting lineup or into the rotation, and thus no fear of telling veteran players exactly what he expected them to do and exactly how he expected them to do it. In that regard, he was unique among managers of his time.

McCarthy played and managed in the minor leagues, but he

major league history between 1900 and 1996, McCarthy's teams dominate it. You think: Gehrig and Ruth, sure; they scored more runs than anyone else did. But of the four highest-scoring non-Yankees teams in that period, three were McCarthy's teams: the 1929 and 1930 Chicago Cubs, and the 1950 Boston Red Sox, who were built by McCarthy, although he resigned as manager in midseason.

McCarthy was virtually a genius at putting together an offense. Long before anyone else, he grasped the importance of hitters taking pitches and running long counts to put pressure on the pitcher. McCarthy understood something that isn't well understood today: A combination of little guys who punch the ball and try to get on base and big guys who look for a pitch they can drive to the moon is much more effective than either type by itself. Today, we have phenomenal individual batting numbers, and we also have some teams on which everyone tries to be a home run hitter. McCarthy realized that it's a lot

never played in the major leagues. His view of the baseball world — accurate at that time — was that there were a lot of guys in the minor leagues who were every bit as good as the guys in the majors. McCarthy believed a major league manager needed to establish good rapport with players of exceptional ability, but otherwise the talent was fungible. If a lesser player didn't want to go along with the manager's program, to hell with him, there were many who could take his place.

One more point on McCarthy: He was the first to divide a pitching staff into starters and relievers. At the onset of baseball history, there were only starters. By 1925 a fair percentage of games involved the use of relief pitchers, but there really was no such thing as a pure starter or a pure reliever. Literally every pitcher in the 1925 to 1935 era was used both as a starter and a reliever, as the occasion demanded. McCarthy in 1936 gave his pitchers definitive roles in the rotation or in the bullpen. The Yankees won four straight pennants, and the idea caught on.

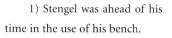

1) Stengel was ahead of his time in the use of his bench.

2) The sources of advantage for Stengel's teams were double plays and home runs.

When professional baseball was first played, it was dominated by a few exceptional athletes. Teams attempted to gather as many of those athletes as possible and filled the rest of the roster in ad hoc fashion. As the game became popular, the talent base grew and became better trained, and the difference between the best players and those at the bottom of the roster narrowed dramatically. Stengel was among the first managers to

CASEY STENGEL
1949–1960

are reluctant to make changes. If a second baseman has a good season, almost any manager will pencil that second baseman into his lineup the next season and stick with him. Not Stengel. His second baseman was Jerry Coleman one year, Billy Martin the next, Gil McDougald the year after that, then Martin again, then Jerry Lumpe, then Bobby Richardson. It wasn't that these guys were not good players. But if one was in a slump, he had about a week to get his bat going before Stengel turned to someone else.

On a bad team, this chronic impatience can be destructive. How can you develop a talent core with an impatient manager? But on a good team, it works well. Stengel didn't allow a second baseman to

recognize this and use it to his team's advantage. By platooning, by revising his lineup daily, Stengel got 200, 300, even 400 at-bats a year for his bench players — in a time when many managers were perfectly content to write out a lineup in April and ride it through September.

A statistical measure called Bench Value Percentage shows how well Stengel used his reserve players. In Stengel's first season as a manager, his 1934 Brooklyn Dodgers had the highest Bench Value Percentage in the major leagues. They led again in 1935 and were third in 1936. Stengel's 1940 and 1941 Boston Braves each had the highest Bench Value Percentage in the majors. With the Yankees, he had the highest percentage in the majors in 1949, 1951, and 1954. Even with the awful New York Mets in 1962 and 1963, he had the highest Bench Value Percentage in the major leagues. When Stengel's teams didn't lead in this category, they were close to the top.

When Stengel managed poor teams, this didn't help him at all. But when he managed the Yankees and had a regular and predictable flow of talent, it helped him a lot. Most managers commit themselves to certain players and

play 150 games and hit .232 with 4 homers and 38 RBIs. He recognized the strengths and weaknesses of his players and used them accordingly. Stengel liked to rotate four or five outfielders, giving each 350 to 450 at-bats. If one stopped hitting and dropped out of the rotation, someone else went into the slot. And it was usually a good player, because the Yankees had more good players than any other team in those days.

Concerning the second point, Stengel's Yankees teams had huge advantages over their opponents in only two areas: double plays and home runs. In 1948, the year before Stengel became manager, the Yankees turned 161 double plays and their hitters grounded into 136. In 1949 the double plays increased to 195, and the hitters grounded into 141. That's a plus 54; the league average was plus 39. In 1950 the Yankees were plus 66, by 1952 they were plus 106, in 1954 they were plus 104, and in 1956 plus 112. You might imagine that these advantages are common for a good team — but they are not. Good teams have more runners on base than their opponents do, thus they often have little or no advantage in double plays.

The Wisdom of
CASEY STENGEL

✳ "Been in this game 100 years, but I see new ways to lose 'em I never knew existed before."

✳ "Being with a woman all night never hurt no professional baseball player. It's staying up all night looking for a woman that does him in."

✳ "Good pitching will always stop good hitting and vice versa."

✳ "Yogi Berra could fall in a sewer and come up with a gold watch."

✳ "Mickey Mantle has it in his body to be great."

✳ "I couldna done it without my players."

✳ "I feel greatly honored to have a ballpark named after me, especially since I've been thrown out of so many."

✳ "If we're going to win the pennant, we've got to start thinking we're not as good as we think we are."

✳ "I got players with bad watches; they can't tell midnight from noon."

✳ "It's wonderful to meet so many friends that I didn't used to like."

✳ "Managing is getting paid for home runs someone else hits."

✳ "Son, we'd like to keep you around this season, but we're going to try and win a pennant."

✳ "The secret of managing is to keep the guys who hate you away from the guys who are undecided."

✳ "The Yankees don't pay me to win every day, just two out of three."

✳ "They say some of my stars drink whiskey, but I have found that ones who drink milkshakes don't win many ball games."

✳ "They told me my services were no longer desired because they wanted to put in a youth program as an advance way of keeping the club going. I'll never make the mistake of being 70 again."

✳ "You have to go broke three times to learn how to make a living."

Stengel worked at maximizing his team's double play advantage. He tried to avoid putting two right-handed sluggers back-to-back in the lineup because that type of hitter is susceptible to the double play. He preferred ground-ball pitchers, and he liked hitters who put the ball in the air; one induced double plays, the other avoided them. The primary reasons the Yankees traded for Roger Maris in December 1959 were that Maris batted left-handed and hit the ball in the air. He batted only .240 in 1958, but hit 28 homers and grounded into only two double plays — Stengel's type of player.

RALPH HOUK
1961–1963, 1966–1973

used Ford in Boston, for example, and, if the Yankees were playing the Senators and then the Indians, he would hold back Ford to pitch against the Indians, figuring the Yankees probably could beat the Senators with Duke Maas or the like. While this strategy was effective, it limited Ford to 25 to 29 starts a year. Houk went to a four-man rotation and it paid off quickly for Ford, who got 39 starts in 1961 and went 25-4.

Houk also scaled back considerably Stengel's practice of platooning, which certainly placated those chosen to play regularly. In 1961 second baseman Bobby Richardson and third baseman Clete Boyer each got more than 500 at-bats for the first time and proved to be championship-caliber players.

———❖———

The Yankees in their first three seasons under Houk won 309 games and two World Championships. He succeeded essentially for two reasons:

1) He worked exceptionally well with young pitchers.

2) He wasn't Casey Stengel.

Houk in his first three years as Yankees manager put Bill Stafford, Rollie Sheldon, Jim Bouton, and Al Downing in the rotation, and all were effective starters for a while. Every spring Houk surveyed the young pitchers in his camp, found a couple who weren't far away, simplified and focused their approach to pitching, and put them in the rotation. Talented 22-, 23-year-old kids who go into a rotation usually pitch well for a year or two, then hurt their arms. But for the short run, this strategy works fine if you have good kids to work with and know how to teach them, and that certainly was the case with the Yankees and Houk, who had been a backup catcher in his playing career.

After 12 years under Stengel, the Yankees were ready for a change in 1961, and Houk got the job. Probably no one was more grateful than Whitey Ford. Stengel, at the suggestion of pitching coach Jim Turner, used a five-man rotation 20 years before anyone else did. Stengel not only used a five-man rotation, but also held back pitchers to get more favorable matchups. Stengel almost never

So much has been written about Martin that it is difficult to offer original observations, or even trite ones that can be disguised as original. However, with respect to Martin's well-known affection for Casey Stengel, we can note these two points:

1) Martin was very much like Stengel as an offensive manager.

2) Martin was very different from Stengel as a defensive manager.

Martin had many bench players — like Oscar Gamble, Jim Spencer, and Fred Stanley — who were typical of Stengel's bench players. All had limitations as regulars, but were very productive in well-defined roles. Like Stengel, Martin did not have a lot of patience with players who stopped producing.

Martin also learned from Stengel the value of players who didn't hit into a lot of double plays. Martin liked left-handed hitters who hit the ball in the air. The players he had who hit the ball on the ground were mostly quick enough to stay out of double plays, like Mickey Rivers and Willie Randolph.

BILLY MARTIN
1975–1978, 1979, 1983, 1985, 1988

Martin compensated for a right-handed hitter who was a threat to hit into a double play, like Bucky Dent, by often calling for a bunt or having base-runners moving with the pitch.

Unlike Stengel's teams, Martin's teams did not turn a lot of double plays. Martin did not focus on procuring ground-ball pitchers, as Stengel did. And whereas Stengel's ideal pitching staff was eight starters, five of whom could also work in relief, Martin's ideal staff was four guys who could pitch 325 innings each. Like Ralph Houk had done, Martin in his own way reacted against his mentor, doing some things the exact opposite of how Stengel did.

JOE TORRE
1996–

Yankees hired both when they were at a relatively advanced age, in their late 50s, and each launched the Yankees into a series of enormously successful seasons.

Their personalities could not have been more different — Stengel was a clown; Torre is a reflective, mature leader — yet each became a master at dealing with the New York media, a challenge that many a manager hasn't met successfully.

Like Stengel, Torre has been successful with the Yankees because his managerial style works better with a good team than with a poor team. Like Stengel, Torre likes to use a lot of pitchers; if he opened spring training with 14 proven pitchers, Torre would be looking for a 15th. When a manager has scarce resources, he should determine his three best pitchers and figure out how to get the most from them. But with a team that can bring in the likes of Dwight Gooden or Jeff Weaver and add him to an already well-stocked staff, Torre's style is well-suited to the cause.

It seems that the parallels between Torre and Casey Stengel are both broad and profound. Both began their managerial careers with poor New York teams in the National League, and both had managed several National League teams with limited success before getting to the Yankees. The

What have we learned from this discourse? Well, while Casey Stengel may not have been the greatest of Yankees managers, he certainly is the pivotal figure among the greats. Ralph Houk made a conscious effort to avoid being like Stengel. Billy Martin was both like and unlike Stengel. Joe Torre, except for his personality, almost seems like the second coming of Stengel. Joe McCarthy won many championships. Stengel also won many championships, in addition to many friends who greatly admired him. If you combine management skills and style, it is easy to understand why Stengel is so beloved and usually mentioned ahead of McCarthy in the hierarchy of great Yankees managers.

How would our Yankees have done back then? I think our guys would have been just as good as they are now.

MY YANKEES CLUBS HAVE BEEN AS SOLID AS THERE EVER HAVE BEEN.

— JOE TORRE

On the wall in my office, I have a picture that a policeman made — it's me with Miller Huggins, Joe McCarthy, Casey Stengel, and Billy Martin. That's pretty good company for me. What would be even more flattering is if the "Major," Ralph Houk, also was in the picture. Every time I achieve a milestone now, it seems to put me in the same company as Houk.

I came to New York in 1996 to manage the Yankees, certainly feeling like, You're walking on sacred ground. You don't belong here. Because of the deep tradition of the Yankees, the idea of being somewhere special has passed from generation to generation. With what has happened in the years since I arrived, at least now I feel comfortable walking in here and feeling like I belong.

How I match up against other managers or how my teams match up against other teams is for historians to decide. Huggins and McCarthy were in a class of their own, obviously, and Martin was excellent at getting a lot of mileage out of players.

Stengel was unique. His clubs were dynamite, always based on power. Well, power and pitching. Casey's teams did a lot of things that scared people. They had guys like Enos Slaughter, who really was more of a line-drive hitter than a traditional power hitter. John Blanchard, who was primarily a pinch-hitter because they didn't have the DH rule back then, hit 21 home runs in 1961. He did that as a second-string catcher. The Yankees brought in a person that had led the league in homers, Johnny Mize. Then you had the Mantles and Yogis.

I think a Stengel team would fare just fine in today's game. Even though Casey's teams hit a huge number of home runs, they didn't strike out anywhere near what we tolerate now. I watched those teams from the time I was a 10-year-old kid into my teenage years. To me, Stengel's Yankees were like a machine: They were efficient, and they rarely lost.

Even more so than offensively, Casey's teams would do well today because his pitchers would have thrived in any era. Starting pitchers in those days typically would work 250 innings and more, and they would throw batting practice on the day before their scheduled start. That was a starter's in-between workout: tossing BP. You can't even comprehend such a thing now, considering how we protect pitchers. If you matched Casey's rotation against today's hitters, I suspect the pitchers would do very well.

How would our Yankees have done back then? I think our guys would have been just as good as they are now. My Yankees clubs have been as solid as there ever have been. It's not like we were a fluke one season, or that our payroll put us far above the competition. We've done things right for an extended period, and as a result we have achieved success. In that sense, neither baseball nor the Yankees has changed.

Just having marquee players, back then or now, is not enough. You need to have a team that can play as a unit. You build a seven-run lead now, and you can kiss it good-bye in many cases. You still need good pitching, as Casey's teams had and as ours have had, or you have no chance. The good teams then and now have the best pitching. Good pitchers have consistently intimidated the opposition across all eras, more so than an imposing offense.

— Joe Torre

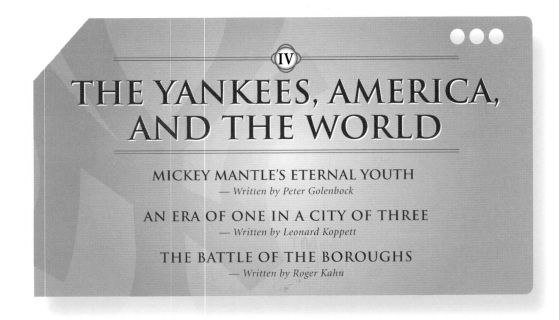

THE YANKEES, AMERICA, AND THE WORLD

MICKEY MANTLE'S ETERNAL YOUTH
— *Written by Peter Golenbock*

AN ERA OF ONE IN A CITY OF THREE
— *Written by Leonard Koppett*

THE BATTLE OF THE BOROUGHS
— *Written by Roger Kahn*

In the America that emerged from World War II, New York City became the center of a country

that had very clearly become the center of the globe. And in the middle of massive cultural and socioeconomic

change was baseball, or, more precisely, the New York Yankees. In a climate not likely to ever be repeated,

New York had three great baseball teams in the Giants, the Brooklyn Dodgers, and the Yankees. But for all

the success that had come before, nothing matched the Yankees of the late 1940s and 1950s. In a 10-year

stretch, the Yankees went to the World Series nine times and won it seven times. There were three Hall of

Fame centerfielders in the same town, and one of them, Mickey Mantle, replaced Joe DiMaggio. Peter

Golenbock recalls Mantle's enduring aura while Hall of Fame writer-reporter Leonard Koppett revisits the

era when America became America and the New York Yankees were a living, breathing example of power,

pride, and dominance. The great Roger Kahn, who covered the Dodgers and the Yankees as a young beat

reporter, revisits their World Series battles.

52
HR

.353
AVG

130
RBI

AMERICAN LEAGUE

19 56

TRIPLE CROWN

Commerce Comet

MICKEY MANTLE

Written by Peter Golenbock

I live with Mickey Mantle every day of my life. A large painting of his 1955 Bowman baseball card hangs on my office wall. It is spring training, exactly where, I do not know. The Mick is in his mid-20s, eternally young, the way he always looked when I was a youngster. He stands facing the camera, his muscles bulging, swinging a bat as he stares unsmiling straight ahead. He wears the Yankees' gray uniform, their road apparel. If the photographer's intention was to make Mantle look like a Greek god, then surely he succeeded.

I was nine years old in 1955. Eisenhower was president in an age of suburban tranquility, cars with big fins, and the rise of Elvis. We lived in southern Connecticut, which was prime Yankees country. I came to idolize Mantle by listening to Mel Allen on my transistor radio at night, under the covers. In the den sat a boxy Dumont console, one of the first color TV sets. It looked just like the border of the 1955 Mantle baseball card. On that TV, I first saw the broad back, the muscular arms, and the powerful swing. It was from watching Mantle that I decided on my life's goal: to succeed him as the center fielder of the New York Yankees.

Whenever I played hit-the-bat or home run derby, I switch-hit like Mantle did, and I ran the bases imitating Mickey's powerful lope. Against the Early Wynns of the neighborhood, I banged tennis balls out of my yard like I imagined Mantle would have. After hitting one far over the pine trees and through a neighbor's second-floor window to the accompaniment of the tinkle of broken glass, to win a one-o-cat game in the bottom of the ninth, I ran the bases with dignity, refusing to indulge in a flashy orgy of celebration, because Mickey never did.

When I woke up in the morning, I knew it was going to be a great day because the odds were heavy that the Yankees were going to win and that Mickey was going to do something memorable, whether it was to hit a towering home run or make a running catch or throw a runner out at home or even lay down a bunt and beat it out with his surprising speed.

For my generation of Yankees fans, to call Mickey Mantle a hero would be to understate reality. Mantle wasn't just a star ballplayer. He was an integral part of our lives, like my Aunt Eva, who brought me silver dollars from Las Vegas every time she visited. Mickey was almost a religious figure, because for the length and breadth of my childhood he was one person who never let me down and often gave me more joy

The young Mantle with his father, Mutt.

"I always wished my dad could be somebody else than a miner."

— MICKEY MANTLE

"When he took BP everybody would kind of stop
what they were doing and watch."
—JIM KAAT, former pitcher

than any human being had a right to experience.

Off the top of my head I can remember a few of the Mick's most glorious moments:

• The home run he hit off Chuck Stobbs in Griffith Stadium in Washington, D.C., that soared out of the stadium and landed — according to legend — some 565 feet from home plate.

• The running catch he made of a Gil Hodges' drive in the fifth game of the 1956 World Series that saved Don Larsen's perfect game.

• The ball he hit against Pedro Ramos of the Washington Senators in May

his center fielder, Duke Snider, was a better player than the Mick. "Duke has to play in Ebbets Field, which is death to left-handed hitters," Pauly would say, "and look at all the home runs Duke hits."

I would respond, "But Mickey plays in Yankee Stadium, where it is 467 feet to centerfield, and look how many home runs he hits."

Another friend, Bobby Nemiroff, would tout the skills of his favorite New York center fielder, Willie Mays of the Giants. "Mays can hit better than Mantle, and he can field better than Mantle, and he can throw better than Mantle," Bobby would say, and soon I would want to grab him by the throat

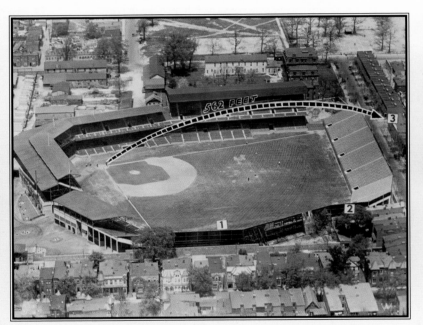

Mickey Mantle's home run at Griffith Stadium travelled 565 feet before it landed in a backyard (3) beyond the left field wall. Jimmy Foxx and Joe DiMaggio had hit balls in the same direction, but they wound up in the bleachers. Other titanic smashes were by Larry Doby (1) and Babe Ruth (2). Each measured about 450 feet.

Mickey Mantle's Longest HOME

04|17|53	09|10|60	09|18|56
565 FEET	**560** FEET	**550** FEET
vs. SENATORS *Griffith Stadium*	vs. TIGERS *Briggs Stadium*	vs. WHITE SOX *Comiskey Park*
Batting right-handed, off Chuck Stobbs; ball cleared 60-foot-high scoreboard in left center field.	Batting left-handed, off Paul Foytack; ball cleared right field roof and landed across Trumbull Avenue.	Batting right-handed, off Billy Pierce; ball cleared left field roof.

1956 that banged against the upper facade of Yankee Stadium, three feet short of becoming the first fair ball hit out of the Stadium.

• The home run he hit against Barney Schultz in the bottom of the ninth to beat the St. Louis Cardinals in the third game of the 1964 World Series.

• His two home runs and five RBIs in Game 2 of the 1960 World Series against the Pittsburgh Pirates. He would hit 18 home runs in his 12 World Series, a record that I consider the most significant of all baseball records.

Not everyone in my neighborhood was a Yankees fan. Pauly Housman rooted for the Dodgers — the Brooklyn Dodgers — and he would argue that

and choke him until he stopped breathing.

But I never did because on some level I knew that if Snider and Mays were Peter Lorre and Edward G. Robinson, Mantle was Clark Gable, a superstar whose fame transcended the game. Dodgers fans loved Snider; Giants fans loved Willie. But around the country, fans from California to Maine, Florida to North Dakota, loved Mantle. One reason was that every fall when the nation tuned in to the World Series, the Yankees almost always were in it, and the star of the production almost inevitably was Mantle. If you lived in Oklahoma or Kentucky or any place that didn't have a major league team, there really was only one hero for you, and that was Mantle. Kids across America wanted to hit like him, tried to run like him, even delighted in striking out like him. As the medium of television grew, the legend of Mickey Mantle grew with it. Mantle's stature hardly wilted in retirement. Rather, it continued to grow and reached iconic proportions. No major league ballplayer since has held greater sway with the public. And with his death in 1995, he became a saint in some quarters. My office, practically a shrine to the Mick, is evidence of that.

As a kid, whenever I argued with Dodgers and Giants fans over the relative merits of our stars, I had verbal ammunition to shut up everyone. If noting that Mantle had won the American League's Most Valuable Player trophy three times wasn't enough, I would make my recitation in sort of a mocking sing-song, and by the time I was 18 it went like this: "1951, 1952, 1953, 1955, 1956, 1957, 1958, 1960, 1961, 1962, 1963, 1964."

Those were the years Mantle led the Yankees to the pennant. You think the Yankees have a lock on the American League today? Joe Torre's boys still have a long way to go to match the Mantle years.

But all dynasties come to an end, and for the final five years of his career Mantle played on bad teams. No one lasts forever, not even the Mick. His legs grew tired and his swing slowed, and on June 8, 1969, proclaimed by New York City mayor John V. Lindsay as "Mickey Mantle Day," Mantle came to Yankee Stadium to say goodbye. I went. So did 65,000 of my closest friends.

After being introduced by the Voice of the Yankees, Mel Allen, Mantle left the dugout and started onto the field, and everyone began clapping with great fervor. I couldn't help thinking that maybe if we clapped long and loud enough, he would come back and play again.

He received a nine-minute standing ovation, the longest ever heard at the Stadium. The fans were asked to stop. Mantle, wearing a conservative dark suit, stood in front of a bank of microphones and soaked up the love from his teammates and fans as his hallowed uniform number 7 was retired.

He told the throng, "Playing 18 years before you folks is the greatest thing that ever happened to a ballplayer. It's been a great honor. I'll never forget it. Thank you very much." It was simple and heartfelt.

Pat Summerall, the master of ceremonies that day, said, "Happiness is Mickey."

Mantle then slowly rode around the perimeter of the field in a white golf

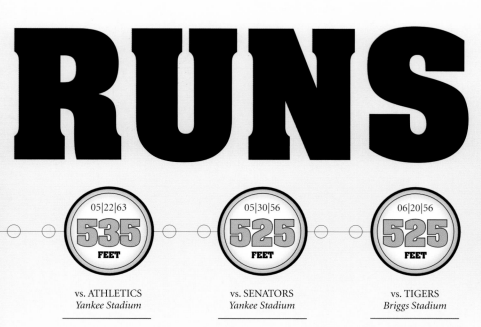

RUNS

05|22|63	05|30|56	06|20|56
535 FEET	**525** FEET	**525** FEET
vs. ATHLETICS *Yankee Stadium*	vs. SENATORS *Yankee Stadium*	vs. TIGERS *Briggs Stadium*
Batting left-handed, off Kansas City's Bill Fischer; ball hit upper deck facade in right field while still rising.	Batting left-handed, off Washington's Pedro Ramos; ball hit upper deck facade in right field on downward arc.	Batting right-handed, off Billy Hoeft; ball cleared center field fence at 440-foot mark, landed four rows from top of bleachers.

Converging arrows show the spot where Mickey Mantle's home run landed, during the first game of the Yanks-Senators twin-bill at Yankee Stadium on May 30. The towering shot traveled 370 feet and struck the facade of the right field roof, just a few feet from going out of the Stadium. No one has ever hit a fair ball out of this ballpark.

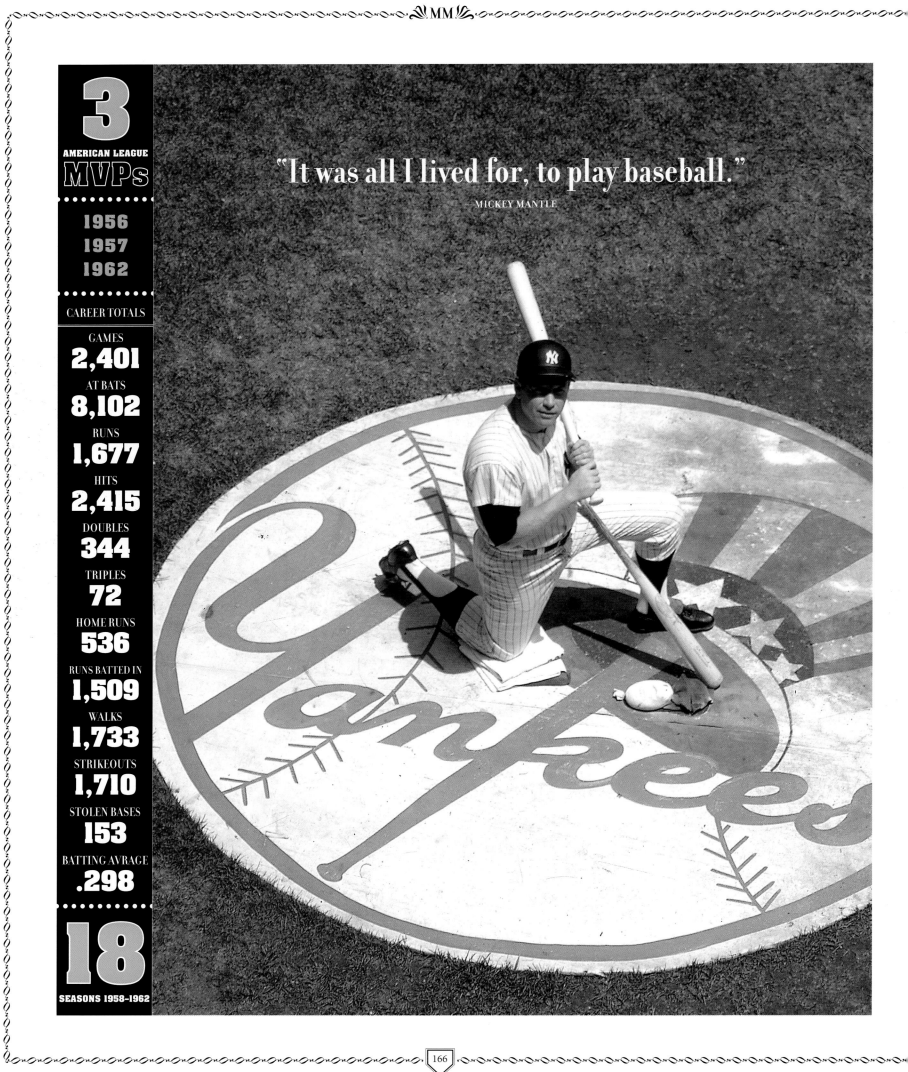

3

AMERICAN LEAGUE
MVPs

1956
1957
1962

CAREER TOTALS

GAMES
2,401

AT BATS
8,102

RUNS
1,677

HITS
2,415

DOUBLES
344

TRIPLES
72

HOME RUNS
536

RUNS BATTED IN
1,509

WALKS
1,733

STRIKEOUTS
1,710

STOLEN BASES
153

BATTING AVRAGE
.298

18

SEASONS 1958-1962

"It was all I lived for, to play baseball."

— MICKEY MANTLE

cart and waved. An entire generation of Yankees fans — Mickey fans — waved back and became teary-eyed as we said our thanks for 18 years of thrills and excitement. We also were crying because his retirement marked the official end to a Yankees dynasty. And to our youth. Where had that nine-year-old boy gone? He had gone to law school. I never did succeed Mantle in center field, of course. Bobby Murcer did. At age 13 I discovered what most other kids find out: Mere mortals cannot hit the curveball.

In the summer of 1972 I was hired by the Prentice-Hall publishing company in New York to be an editor in their legal publications department. After two months I was bored, and so I walked down to the company's trade book division and talked myself into a contract to write a book on my Yankees. If I had picked any other subject, I am convinced I would have been unceremoniously shown the door. I had never written a book. What made me think I could do it? My love of the Yankees, that's what.

I knocked on the door of the editor of the trade books division. He ushered me in. "I have an idea for a book," I said. It turned out he was almost as rabid a Yankees fan as I was. We shook hands on a contract. A career was born.

The Yankees at the time were owned by CBS and run by Michael Burke, a man who promoted the arts. Team officials were kind enough to let me hang out in the bowels of Yankee Stadium throughout the 1972 season and do my research, which included pouring through their vast archive of newspaper articles. During that time, I got a chance to meet Mantle a couple of times when he came to the Stadium for Old-Timers games and special appearances.

One time Mantle, several teammates, and I were in the Stadium Club at about 11 in the morning before an Old-Timers game. What I noticed most about Mantle was that he was uncomfortable being treated as a celebrity. Fame was an enemy. He shied from the limelight and refused to allow others to treat him as someone who was special. Away from the demands of reporters and fans, Mantle appeared relaxed and charming, and at home with former teammates, who clearly loved him. Whenever he laughed, the entire room laughed with him.

After a year of reading newspaper articles, I decided I had no better idea of who these ballplayers were as men than when I began. The articles I had read about Mantle gave no hint of his charm, warmth, and love of laughter. I decided that to write my book, I would need to interview them, a decision that would change my life. It's 30 years later, and interviewing athletes continues to be one of the great pleasures of my life.

I traveled from coast to coast, seeking out the heroes of my childhood. Almost always, the talk would come around to Mantle. As I had observed, his teammates loved him dearly, despite his insecurities. Being his friend was important to them. When they talked about him, it was always with a twinkle in their eyes. It was clear that he had been their hero as well as mine.

I went to see Tom Sturdivant, who had pitched for the Yankees from 1955 through June 1959, when he was traded to Kansas City. When I interviewed him at his home in Oklahoma City, he made it clear how much he loved playing for the Yankees and being friends with Mantle.

"To me, Mickey Mantle was the Yankees," Sturdivant said. "You know the people came out to see the Yankees, but the people really came out to see Mantle. Mantle was the greatest ballplayer walking.

"I'll tell you a funny story. It was in Yankee Stadium after I had been traded to the Athletics. The night before the game Mickey and I go out for dinner, and he says, 'You know, Tom, you're the only right-handed pitcher who has enough control that I'd hit righty off of, and I believe off of you I could hit one completely out of Yankee Stadium.'

"Actually, that got to me a little, putting it to me the way he was. So I said, 'I'll tell you what, Mickey. If the ballgame's not at stake, now I'm not going to take anything off of it, but if you walk up there right-handed, I'll reach back and let you have the best fastball I've got, letter-high, and right down the middle. We'll just find out whether you're a better hitter or I'm a better pitcher.' And he said, 'You're on.'

"Well, the next day we get way behind and sure enough, here comes ole mopup man Sturdivant in to pitch for the Athletics, and Mickey steps into the batter's box as a right-handed hitter. Our manager, Eddie Lopat, he whistles, which is the curveball sign. Lopat at that time had an automatic fine if he called a pitch from the bench and you didn't throw it. I was shaking my head trying to tell Lopat my shoulder hurt. He whistles again and sticks up some money in the air like he's going to fine me. So the first pitch I throw Mickey is a big ole roundhouse curveball, and Mickey, he runs clear out of the batter's box. And he is some kind of mad sombitch.

"He gets up there again, and Lopat whistles again. Well, instead of throwing him a curveball, I throw him a slider, which is a halfway fastball. He hits a line drive, and our center fielder, Bobby Del Greco, runs out to the monuments and catches it. Remember, he has to hit the ball clear out of the ballpark to win the bet. But anyway, it's caught. And he runs to first and makes a circle and comes runnin' back at me.

"I had already given him the mound. I wasn't going to stand on that mound and let that freight train run over me. Aw, he was mad, and everybody was giggling on our bench because they knew what was going on.

"Later on, he said this was one of the funniest experiences of his career, me throwing him the big ole curveball. Crossing him up, you know. Good ole Tom. Ole buddy Tom. Really, I didn't have enough curveball that he couldn't hit it anyway. In fact after that first one, what he said to me was, 'Throw that damned curve again and I'll kill you with it.' And he tried to. Only thing, he hit it too high." And Sturdivant let out a hearty laugh.

Mantle's teammates recalled how he played in pain late in his career, as his injuries took a toll. But he never complained, they all said. He just went out every day and did his job to the best of his ability.

In doing the research for the book, I decided to travel to Commerce, Oklahoma, where Mickey grew up. I wanted to see his hometown with my own eyes. The solitude of the barren town was eerie. The buildings were one

September 16, 1951, New York. Yankee outfielder Mickey Mantle, the first man to face Bob Feller in the first inning. Mantle, the 19-year-old switch-hitting rookie, flied out on the play, but the Yankees outscored the Cleveland Indians 6-1, putting themselves back in first place in the American League.

"During my 18 years I came to bat almost 10,000 times. I struck out about 1,700 times and walked maybe 1,800 times. You figure a ballplayer will average about 500 at-bats a season. That means I played 7 years without ever hitting the ball."

— MICKEY MANTLE

story, and only the leafy green elm trees prevented you from seeing forever. A young boy in tattered blue jeans rode by on a too-small bicycle. He was carrying his fishing pole. No cars passed by the gasoline station.

Mantle's childhood home was only a stone's throw from the hulking gray power plant that once sent energy into the Blue Goose Mine where the Mantle family had worked. The mine was abandoned, but the awesome pyramids of waste materials stretched as far as the eye could see, giving the area a surreal quality. Deep cavernous quarries, filled with rainwater, were dug as far into the ground as the mounds were high. Only an occasional hearty tree was interspersed among the barrenness. The Mantle home was also abandoned. All the windows were broken. The white paint had peeled. The house was built, it seemed, for dwarves. You had to bend down to go into the kitchen. There was only one bedroom, where Mickey, his older brother, his half-brother, his younger twin brothers, and his sister all slept. Mantle had been a poor kid.

When Mutt Mantle was not in the mines, he was usually making his son into a baseball player. The story has become legend. When Mickey came home from school, he went to work, playing baseball. His father and an uncle who threw left-handed took turns teaching him to switch-hit. The incessant practice paid dividends.

The closest major league teams to northeast Oklahoma, where Mantle grew up, were the Cardinals and the Browns in St. Louis. Cardinals scout Runt Marr decided the 5-foot-7-inch teenager was too small, and a tryout with the Browns was cancelled because of heavy rain. When Mantle graduated from Commerce High, the only scout willing to sign him was Tom Greenwade of

> "If I knew I would live this long, I would have taken better care of myself."
>
> — MICKEY MANTLE

the Yankees. Mantle got $1,000, and Greenwade became famous.

When Mantle first joined the Yankees in 1951, he was a child — timid, self-conscious, and completely overwhelmed. He took one look at the Empire State Building and stood in open-mouthed awe. His world had been poling for catfish on the Neosho River, working in the lead-zinc mine, or walking through a grassy field with a piece of straw between his teeth. That he was able to succeed in New York speaks of his talent. That he was able to replace the legendary Joe DiMaggio in center field does, too. Despite his humble upbringing, Mantle was quickly able to capture the hearts of all of New York City. A generation of Yankees fans cannot only picture his face from the baseball cards, they can also tell you the statistics on the back of the cards. We can all recite the grandest line by heart: .353, 52 home runs, 130 RBIs, 132 runs scored. Those were Mantle's major league–leading statistics in 1956, his greatest season. When he retired, he had 536 home runs, more than all but two other players in major league history.

I had plenty of background information for my book. Now it was time to interview Mantle at length. Bob Fishel, the Yankees' public relations director, made the arrangements for me. I opened the steel-gray door leading into the Yankees clubhouse, and I asked Pete Sheehy, the clubhouse attendant, where I could find Mantle, who was in New York for a commercial endorsement. Sheehy pointed to the far end of the room. Mantle, dressed in buckskin — he lived in Texas — stood by a wall mirror combing his blond hair. All that was left for me to do was introduce myself.

I couldn't do it. Mantle had been my hero in so many ways. I wore number 7 on my Camp Winaukee uniform. When I went to the dentist and suffered through a brutal drilling, I would imagine that Mantle had hit a home run and was running around the bases. Usually by the time he crossed home plate, the drilling was over. How could I approach a man who had saved me so much pain?

I asked Elston Howard, who I had interviewed, to make the introduction. Howard was kind, and he told Mantle about the book I was writing. Mantle asked me about several of his former teammates, whether I had seen them, how they were doing. I asked him if we could chat. He put his arm around my shoulder and with a straight face said, "No."

I was stunned. Then his face broke into a wide grin, and he laughed. "Where do you want to do this?" he asked. We sat on a table at the far end of the Yankees clubhouse.

It was 1973, and Mantle had not yet become a media darling. He still had a reputation for surliness and occasional hostility toward the media. When he first came up, in 1951, he was self-conscious of his Oklahoma twang and his lack of education, and like DiMaggio before him, he was wary of the pushy, garrulous reporters. In an attempt to avoid controversy, he said little or nothing. It was the pre–*Ball Four* era, and reporters talked of his prodigious feats rather than about his boorish behavior. I was keenly aware that Mantle had little patience for interviews or photograph sessions when he was a player. "How much longer is this going to take?" he would bark.

But on this summery May afternoon, Mantle was in a bubbly, effusive mood. He was happy to be back in New York, at Yankee Stadium. I stood in awe as I began asking him about the fabric of his life.

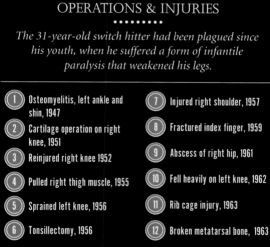

OPERATIONS & INJURIES
· · · · · · · · ·

The 31-year-old switch hitter had been plagued since his youth, when he suffered a form of infantile paralysis that weakened his legs.

1	Osteomyelitis, left ankle and shin, 1947	7	Injured right shoulder, 1957
2	Cartilage operation on right knee, 1951	8	Fractured index finger, 1959
3	Reinjured right knee 1952	9	Abscess of right hip, 1961
4	Pulled right thigh muscle, 1955	10	Fell heavily on left knee, 1962
5	Sprained left knee, 1956	11	Rib cage injury, 1963
6	Tonsillectomy, 1956	12	Broken metatarsal bone, 1963

I knew that his father had worked in the Blue Goose Mine in Commerce, and I began by asking him what his father's job entailed. Mantle talked softly and slowly with a drawl he never did lose. "He started out as a shoveler," Mantle said, explaining that the lead veins were blasted out at night and a crew came along the following day and shoveled the chunks into big cans. "I don't know how big a can is, but it's a very big can. And he was able to shovel, like, 50 cans a day, which was great," said Mantle, his voice welling in pride.

"Did you work with your dad in the mines?" I asked.

"Yeah. I worked in the mines the last two years of high school. In fact, when I joined the Yankees in 1951 I was still working in the mines. I was a screen ape. That's the guy that stands over the boulders that come by that go through a screen, and if they're too big you have to beat them up with a sledgehammer. Everybody thinks I lifted weights or something, because when I first came up I was built good."

I asked him about the knee injury he suffered in the 1951 World Series stepping on a drainage gate in the outfield. "They took me to the hospital, and that's when I found out Dad was sick," Mantle said. "My dad was sitting on the side of me in the cab to the hospital. My knee had swelled up so bad I couldn't move it. Dad got out of the cab first, and I put my arm around his shoulders to jump out of the cab, put my weight on him like this," — and Mickey leaned on me, his strength weighing heavily on my left shoulder — "and he just collapsed on the sidewalk. They call it Hodgkin's Disease. It had eaten up his whole back. My mother told me later that he hadn't slept in bed for a year. But he never would tell me about it. That's the first I ever knew he was sick." Mantle screwed up his face and sighed.

"I got operated on," he said, "and then we went home, and he went back to work, and I could tell he was really sick then. I was told to take him to the Mayo Clinic, so when I got well I took him up there, and they cut him open and sewed him back up, and they said, 'Just let him do whatever he wants to. He doesn't have much longer to live.' He went back to the mines. He worked until about a month before he died, in the spring of 1952."

Mutt Mantle was 39 when he died, and his famous son thereafter carried a fear of early death. An uncle also had died young. Hank Bauer once arrived in the Yankees clubhouse and noticed that Mantle was rather hung over. Bauer suggested to Mantle that he should stay home more and take better care of himself. Mantle looked at Bauer through bloodshot eyes and said, "My father died young. I'm not going to be cheated."

Mantle was 36 when he retired, his body too broken to continue. For the rest of his life he was tormented by the realization that he never again would play the game his father had taught him. He was elected to the Hall of Fame in 1974 and welcomed the honor, but Mantle was never impressed by his accomplishments or any of the rewards, trophies, and honors that came with

"He (my father) had the foresight to realize that someday in baseball that left-handed hitters were going to hit against right-handed pitchers and right-handed hitters were going to hit against left-handed pitchers; and he taught me, he and his father, to switch-hit at a real young age, when I first started to learn how to play ball. And my dad always told me if I could hit both ways

them. He would have traded everything, including his three Most Valuable Player awards, to again be able to cavort with his teammates, to be able to hit long home runs, to hear the adulation of ballpark crowds. When Mantle drank, it was not to cheat death, but to cheat reality.

"I miss baseball," Mantle said softly. "Since I've been away from it, I keep having nightmares. I always dream that I'm trying to make a comeback, and I can't hit the ball, and it pisses me off." Mantle was wringing his hands as we spoke. "Pitchers throw me fastballs, and I just can't hit them anymore.

"There's another nightmare. I'll be outside Yankee Stadium trying to get in, and I can hear them announcing my name on the loudspeaker, for me to hit, and I'm outside and I can't get in. I hear Casey Stengel asking, 'Where's Mickey?' But I can't get in. Those are my two bad dreams."

He had another thought. "I always felt that I was really overpaid. Whitey [Ford] and I figured out that I had 1,700 walks and 1,800 strikeouts. That's a total of 3,500. And if you get up 500 times a year, you figure I spent seven years where I never hit the ball!" Mantle laughed raucously.

"People think that I was always hurt," he said with a sigh, "but I played for 18 years. I played more games as a Yankee than anyone else who ever played

when I got ready to go to the major leagues, that I would have a better chance of playing. And believe it or not, the year that I came to the Yankees is when Casey started platooning everybody. So he did realize that that was going to happen someday, and it did. So I was lucky that they taught me how to switch-hit when I was young."

— MICKEY MANTLE, excerpt from his Hall of Fame induction speech

for them." An overwhelming sense of sadness seemed to engulf Mantle, who was just 41 at the time.

"You know," he said, "I miss playing very much."

That sense of sadness never left him. For the final 25 years of his life, he no longer could play baseball, and to ease the pain he medicated himself with drink. It was only after his son Billy died of alcoholism that Mantle decided to come clean. He not only came to grips with his alcoholism, but he had the grace and hero's dignity to go on TV and talk about the danger of drinking, telling young kids, "Don't be like me." His bravery made us love him even more.

In 1995 we found out that Mantle needed a liver transplant. He got a new liver that June but was dead two months later of cancer, leaving us children of the 1950s and 1960s with a feeling of deep sadness and a lifetime of memories.

When I need to smile, I think back to the summer of 1961, when Mantle and Roger Maris were capturing the hearts of baseball fans all over the country as they pursued the most hallowed of baseball records: Babe Ruth's 60 home runs from 1927. I recall sitting on the white sand at Bradley Beach, New Jersey, listening to my palm-sized Magnavox eight-transistor radio in a brown carrying case. The sun was bright, the water was refreshing, and the Yankees were playing a doubleheader. Mantle and Maris and John Blanchard made mincemeat of the opposition.

What Mantle and those Yankees meant to me is never far away, and I'm sure others just like me feel the same way. Mantle and Maris are an indelible part of my psyche. They are gone now, but my good friend Andy Jurinko painted for me a portrait of the Yankees outfield of my youth. And there on canvas, for all eternity, is the greatest outfield the Yankees ever had, at least in my mind — Mantle, Maris, and yours truly, Peter Golenbock.

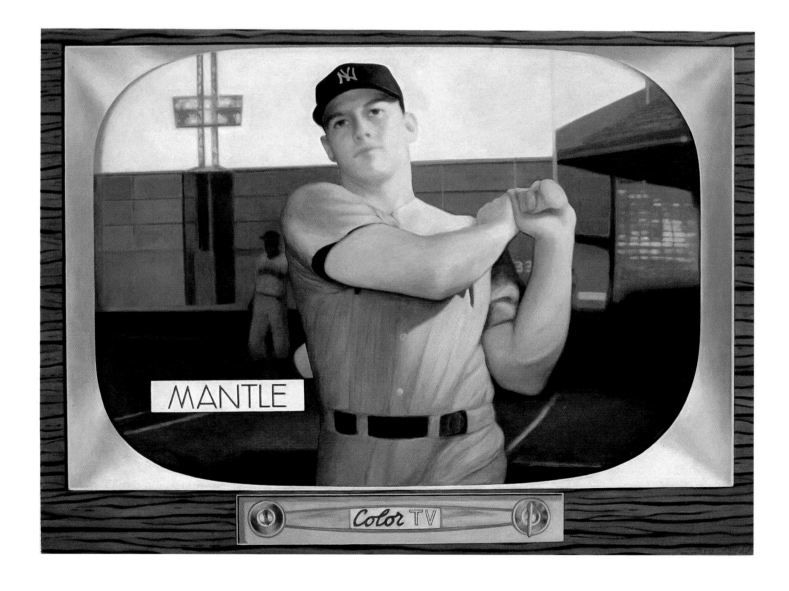

Written by Leonard Koppett

When Joe McCarthy looked out onto the Yankee Stadium field on opening day in 1946, he could see the end of a war. For almost five years, Americans had yearned for the time when the Allies would prevail in the greatest war in human experience. In the microcosm that was baseball, McCarthy looked forward to the day his Yankees would once more appear whole.

Yankees manager Joe McCarthy in 1929.

With the end of the war, the start of a new baseball season was a vivid symbol that America was getting back to normal. Yankee Stadium, as always, was resplendent and awe-inspiring, and the grand ballpark had a new feature: light towers on the roof. Baseball was adjusting its schedule to put the game on the same clock as other forms of entertainment. By June 1948, 15 of the 16 major league teams — all but the Chicago Cubs — would be playing night games.

As fans poured into Yankee Stadium for their first look at the postwar Yankees, there was a feeling that life really could take up where it had left off. During the wartime seasons of 1944 and 1945, the Yankees had failed to reach the World Series for two years in a row — the first time that had happened since 1935. But now McCarthy could look out onto the Stadium grass and see Joe DiMaggio, Joe Gordon, Charlie Keller, Phil Rizzuto, Tommy Henrich, Bill Dickey, and Spud Chandler were back from military service, and the Yankees manager again could field an imposing lineup.

The Yankees finished third in 1946, but a year later they began one of the longest and greatest runs of excellence in the history of sports, winning 11 of 14 American League pennants — a dynasty that paralleled, within its own sphere, the unassailable power that America represented in the world. The Yankees' seamless success alienated almost as many fans as it captured, but their place in the greatest game in the most powerful country could not be overstated. The legendary New York sportswriter, Red Smith, wrote during that era: "Rooting for the Yankees is like rooting for U.S. Steel."

Love 'em or hate 'em, the Yankees were the only sports team known throughout the world. In America, fans flocked in unprecedented numbers to see for themselves the great team. Yankee Stadium, replete with baseball's first stadium club restaurant for affluent customers, was the place to see and be seen. The Yankees' postwar prestige had become even greater than their prewar aura, an incredible testament to their success given all that had come before.

"People ask what makes a Yankee. Part of the answer, at least, is there is that attitude, deeply ingrained in every one of them. Going for the championship of the Bronx, Flatbush, and Jersey City's Journal Square, they expect to win every game. By their reckoning, any World Series is a four-game series. If it takes longer, it's a mistake. If they don't win at all, it's a scandal."

— RED SMITH, *New York Herald Tribune*

When World War II ended in August 1945, New York City emerged as the unquestioned center of the globe. Europe's traditional metropolitan centers had been ravaged by the war. London, Berlin, and Leningrad were physically destroyed; Paris, Rome, Vienna, Moscow, and all the smaller but historic cities that had formed the fabric of Western civilization were economically prostrate and in political turmoil. The greatest cities of Japan and China were even worse off, and Africa, South America, India, and Australia had no comparable relevance to what the postwar world had become.

The atomic bomb, which had signaled a new age, was not yet perceived as a moral issue but rather merely a confirmation of America's supreme power. No Roman legion, no Mongol horde, no overseas empire had ever approached such unchallenged military might over so much of the world as the United States did then. Perhaps even more important was the financial, diplomatic, and productive power America now exerted over the rest of the world.

New York was the dominant center of America to a degree it had never been previously, and in another 20 or 30 years never would be again. All the headquarters of the major press associations, radio networks, book pub-

lishers, advertising agencies — the world's opinion makers — were in New York. So were the greatest financial institutions and most powerful corporations. Washington, D.C., was the official capital of the United States, but New York was the chief influence and locus of political decision making. Rail and air transportation to every other part of the world flowed through New York. Untouched physically by the war, filled with refugees of distinction in every field during the preceding decade, it was the one intact cultural, artistic, and intellectual capital, no longer just one among many.

In that unique setting, New York also was the most important location in the world for spectator sports, and the New York Yankees were at the apex. The Yankees were the perfect symbol of American might and dominance. They were as daunting as any corporation in the land, a powerful machine that seemed to transcend the human condition. When one larger-than-life player was spent, another was poised to take his place. From Babe Ruth and Lou Gehrig to Joe DiMaggio, to Mickey Mantle, the chain was unbroken for more than 40 years. Everything about the Yankees represented success, from their power pinstripes to their ostentatious arena fit for Greek gods. To the rest of the world, America was the land of excess — six percent of the world's population resided in the United States and consumed 33 percent of the world's goods and services — and the Yankees were living proof of it. From 1949

NEW YORK CITY
7.4 million people
Three Major League Baseball Teams

> "There never was a country more fabulous than America. She sits bestride the world like a Colossus; no other power at any time in the world's history has possessed so varied or so great an influence on other nations. . . . Half of the wealth of the world, more than half of the productivity, nearly two-thirds of the world machines are concentrated in American hands; the rest of the world lives in the shadow of American industry. . . ."

— ROBERT PAYNE, British historian after visiting America in the winter of 1948–49

through 1958, the Yankees won every American League pennant except one, and they were World Champions in seven of those 10 years.

Baseball at that time was unchallenged in its position atop of the sports pyramid. Professional and major college football and basketball did not yet compete with baseball's established impact, as television would enable those sports to do. Golf, tennis, soccer, and hockey were marginal activities in American eyes. Only a heavyweight championship fight could command national attention comparable to the World Series. But a boxing match was a one-shot and sporadic affair, while the World Series was the culmination of six months of daily games, followed through newspapers and radio by millions of fans, many of whom never got near a major league ballpark. By the early 1950s, rural America got the Yankees on TV almost every Saturday. In 1953, ABC initiated the Game of the Week — it was later picked up by CBS — but until 1965 the telecasts were blacked out in cities that had major league teams. The Yankees played in the Game of the Week more than two-thirds of the time, extending their legend and becoming America's Team. TV money at that time was divided among the teams according to appearances. The Yankees were smarter than everybody else and now they had another revenue stream to feed the engine.

A long and gradual historical process created the Yankees' rise to unprecedented fame and glory. When John McGraw became manager of the New York Giants in 1902, he created a following that made New York a "Giants town." The team's most important customers were the Wall Street and the Broadway theater crowds, to whom ballgames starting at four o'clock were both

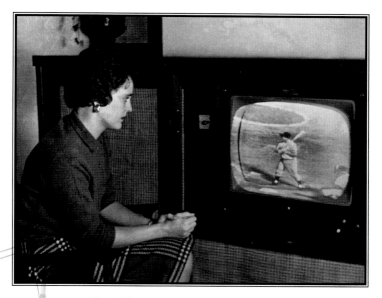

An anxious Patty Maris watches a network monitor at KMBC-TV as her husband, Yankee slugger Roger Maris, fails in his attempt to equal or break the home run record.

accessible and affordable, yet there also was room for many others on this bandwagon. The Giants' fan base soon was citywide and nationally celebrated. Providing a World Series in 1905, 1911, 1912, 1913, 1917, and for four straight years from 1921 to 1924, the Giants and their home at the Polo Grounds were the epitome of sports glamour.

The Yankees, by comparison, entering the upstart American League in 1903, had little success until after World War I. In 1913 they became second-rate tenants of the Giants in the Polo Grounds. The Brooklyn Dodgers, usually a National League also-ran, were no factor outside their own borough. Then Ruth came to the Yankees in 1920, and the sports business changed dramatically. Ruth's home runs and larger-than-life persona set in motion the process of true, full-scale commercialism that to that point had been the province of more traditional entertainment forms. Baseball had always had dedicated fans, but with Ruth it began to reach a broader share of the public.

By 1923 the Yankees had built their own stadium, across the Harlem River from the Polo Grounds, and were out-drawing the Giants. Ruth was the first athlete to transcend his sport and become an international celebrity, and a younger generation of fans gravitated to his Yankees instead of to McGraw's Giants. In the 1921 and 1922 World Series, the Giants defeated the Yankees; in 1923 the Yankees defeated the Giants. The Yankees went to the World Series in 1926, 1927, and 1928, winning the last two, while the Giants began to fall short of the National League pennant.

When the Yankees won the World Series in 1932 and the Giants in 1933, the teams were still on equal

Mickey Mantle being interviewed by CBS sportscaster Frank Gifford in 1966.

footing. But when the Yankees beat the Giants in 1936 and 1937, the Yankees rose to a unique level. The Yankees won pennants in five of the next six years, while the Giants went 13 years without a first-place finish. Meanwhile, the Dodgers introduced New York to night games and daily broadcasts (which the Yankees and Giants had resisted), and captured attention by winning the 1941 pennant under the incendiary Leo Durocher. The Dodgers lost the Series to the Yankees in five games, but just getting there helped them establish a greater presence.

Consider all of the above and you come to this: A 50-year-old baseball fan in 1946 who had grown up in New York had personal memories that ranged from the Giants' supremacy to Ruth's arrival and the onset of the Yankees dynasty, to the Dodgers coming into prominence. The younger fans, too, knew the legends and values of the past. Many had witnessed these events, and everyone had heard and read about them.

After World War II ended, the Yankees and Dodgers resumed their successful ways. The Giants, even with a dramatic pennant in 1951, a stunning World Championship in 1954, and the arrival of Willie Mays, couldn't keep pace. Clearly the third team in town, they planned in 1958 to move to Minneapolis. The Dodgers, meanwhile, were rebuffed in their efforts to get a new ballpark, and they set their sights on Los Angeles.

"Hating the Yankees was as close to defying authority as most Americans came in the 1950s. It served as emotional spring training for feelings and attitudes that were going to be incited and inflamed on a broader and more meaningful scale in the next decade."

— DONALD HONIG, from his book, *Baseball America*

The New York City of 1946 to 1957 was at the forefront of the American Dream. New York was brimming with money in the postwar decade as the center of a booming economy. America's Gross National Product increased 51 percent during the 1950s. Wartime civilians, all employed and usually working overtime, had accumulated tremendous pent-up spending power during rationing and the absence of new products. American companies that had invested heavily in the research and development of wartime technology rushed to convert that knowledge into the production of new and improved consumer goods, creating jobs for the thousands of soldiers returning from overseas. Sleek, modern furniture, automated kitchen appliances, television and hi-fi sets, fancy automobiles, and processed foods were affordable for most consumers. Many of the new or improved products afforded Americans more leisure time, and they had the disposable income to indulge themselves. The restaurant, hotel, and travel industries boomed. Every form of entertainment prospered, including sports.

While the 1950s were a prosperous time in America, they were also a troubled time. Americans welcomed any diversion from the Cold War, which was in full bloom by 1950, the specter of atomic attack, and the McCarthy era of red-baiting, which was felt as deeply in New York as it was in Washington and Hollywood. Spectator sports — baseball especially — provided that respite for New Yorkers. Going to a Yankees game and watching the great, seemingly invincible team perform was seeing America at its best. Babe Ruth's Yankees of the 1920s had made one million in annual attendance the team's norm. In 1946, attendance at Yankee Stadium was 2,265,512, shattering by nearly 800,000 the previous record set by the Chicago Cubs in 1929. The Yankees were the first baseball team to reach two million in home attendance, and they attained that level each year from 1946 through 1950, a period during which major league baseball attendance grew by 61 percent. Every year from 1949 to 1959, the Yankees drew more people to their home games than any of the seven other American League teams did to their parks. New York City's population in 1950 was about 7.9 million; the city's three major league

teams that year drew 4.3 million fans to their ballparks.

In retrospect, two images of New Yorkers of that era were false. One was that they were swellheaded, arrogant, wise guys who thought non–New Yorkers and their institutions were inferior. This was not true. New Yorkers did not think their city was the most important one in the world; they took for granted that it was. Things outside New York weren't less important; their existence simply didn't matter. New Yorkers didn't compare themselves with anyone else because they didn't think there was anything to compare with them and their environment.

The second misconception, an outgrowth of the first, is that New Yorkers reveled in the success of their baseball teams that took 16 of the 20 slots in the World Series from 1947 through 1956, the way fans in other cities imagined *they* would feel in such circumstances. In reality, New Yorkers took this competitive success in stride, as their due. After all, the "real" theater was Broadway. The major radio and television shows originated in New York, the biggest movie houses (Radio City Music Hall, Roxy, Capitol, Paramount) were there. Madison Square Garden housed the biggest fights, basketball games, hockey games, track meets, and the circus. Why wouldn't the World Series be in New York every year? Where else?

The Series turned on the town — but this was a town always turned on. Baseball was one festival among many, special in its own way, but not obscuring everything else New York had to offer year round. For the locals, the Yankees doing well was simply business as usual — a wonderfully attractive and highly visible business — but not so exceptional as to blot out all the other aspects of New York that made it, for them, the only place.

New York life in those days was lived on the street much more than now. Children played stickball, stoopball, and touch football on the side streets, where a play covering "two sewers" was the equivalent of a tape-measure home run or a 100-yard touchdown. Neighborhoods were such a mixture of apartment houses and ground-floor retail shops that residents walked almost everywhere. Most of all, New Yorkers felt safe, at night as well as by day, on subway platforms, walking through Central Park or Riverside Park, on downtown and neighborhood streets. Yankee Stadium at night in the South Bronx beckoned like a shimmering jewel, drawing patrons who never imagined that danger could be lurking on the darkened streets. That feeling of security, to a degree that seems foolhardy now, was routinely accepted in the 1950s.

Ⓐ *Brooklyn's Jackie Robinson slides hard into second base in the first inning of Game 6 at Yankee Stadium in the 1947 Series.*

1949

Ⓥ *Tommy Henrich heads home after his dramatic game-winning home run in the ninth inning gives the Yankees a 1-0 victory in Game 1 of the 1949 Series.*

1950

Ⓐ *Whitey Ford, 21, became the youngest pitcher to win a World Series game when he threw eight shutout innings in a 4-2 victory in the deciding Game 4 in 1950.*

Ⓥ *Joe DiMaggio (right) and pitcher Allie Reynolds embrace after helping the Yankees beat the Giants, 6-2 in Game 4 of the 1951 World Series at the Polo Grounds.*

1951

New Yorkers, more than most, were adaptable and flexible. Institutions flourished and disappeared. The Dodgers and the Giants moved West. If all the change overwhelmed a person at times, he could take solace in one constant that wore as comfortably as an old shoe: The Yankees still were the Yankees, in the same pinstripes as always, winning as regularly as ever.

In that era, every activity had its favorite restaurant hangouts, frequented by those who shared common interests and a similar degree of affluence. Cafeterias were the natural habitat of the working class, especially in the garment district below Times Square. A step up was chains such as Child's and Schrafft's. All were places for doing business as much as for social interaction, much as country clubs have always been.

For the theater crowd, the more successful and wealthier ticket buyers made Sardi's Restaurant on 44th Street their own. Less than a block away, on Eighth Avenue, Downey's was the province of lesser but still solvent patrons, and working theater folk and athletes. Madison Square Garden, on Eighth Avenue between 49th and 50th Street, was winter headquarters for fights, hockey, basketball, and all sorts of special events. Its special restaurant connection was with Mama Leone's on 48th Street, presided over by Gene Leone. Garden patrons also favored Jack Dempsey's Restaurant at Broadway and 49th.

The most important stop for the sports crowd was Toots Shor's, domi-

Gene Woodling's homer got the Yankees off to a flying start in the October 4, 1953, game, which they won 11-7.

nated by its proprietor's outsized personality. From 1940 to 1959, it was at 51 West 51st Street, just east of Sixth Avenue, two long blocks and one short one from the Garden, across the street from Rockefeller Center. Every significant national sports figure dropped in sooner or later. The interaction among sports, media, advertising, and show business people at Shor's was unsurpassed. The Yankees of DiMaggio, Mantle, and Whitey Ford were Shor's intimates, along with Horace Stoneham, owner of the Giants, and his nephew and general manager, Chub Feeney. Baseball commissioner Ford Frick often lunched there. Only the truly elite baseball players frequented Shor's during the offseason; the others needed to supplement their income with winter jobs. The average salary for a major league baseball player in 1951 was $13,000. Hall-of-Famers-to-be Yogi Berra and Phil Rizzuto of the Yankees both sold men's clothing at a Newark store once the baseball season was over.

DiMaggio had become a beyond-baseball celebrity in the 1930s, building on the Italian pride generated before him by Tony Lazzeri, another great Yankees player. DiMaggio was an internationally known figure before World War II broke out, bigger than ever after it, and bigger still when he married Marilyn Monroe. Mantle later took on the same iconic status — a position the greatest players in other sports never attained until Joe Namath came along and took the upstart New York Jets to the 1969 Super Bowl championship.

1952

Ⓐ *Mantle's sixth-inning home run put the Yankees ahead for good in a 4-2 victory over the Dodgers in Game 7 to close out the Yankees' fourth straight World Series title.*

Ⓥ *Mantle holds up four fingers to signify the grand slam he hit in the third inning of an 11-7 Yankees victory in Game 5 of the 1953 Series against the Dodgers.*

1953

1955

Ⓐ *Dodgers second baseman Don Zimmer tries to get the handle on a throw to second base ahead of Yankees catcher Yogi Berra in Game 2 of the 1955 Series.*

Ⓥ *Don Larsen pitched the first perfect game in World Series history in a 2-0 Yankees victory over the Dodgers in Game 5 of the 1956 Series.*

1956

All the enterprises that competed for the New York sports fans' dollars and attention stood in line well behind the Yankees. Success sells, and the Yankees of the late 1940s and 1950s crafted the longest period of success in baseball history. Initially, the war appeared to end the Yankees' dynasty. Joe McCarthy's eight-pennant regime ended when he resigned during the 1946 season, and Bill Dickey took over as player-manager. The team's two-year-old ownership group was off to a shaky start. The raucous regime headed by Larry MacPhail was the polar opposite of the stable and respectable

The older Yankees players, as well as the young ones, responded well to Harris in 1947, and the team won the pennant for the first time in four years and beat the Dodgers in an eventful seven-game World Series. In 1948, however, the Yankees slipped to third behind Cleveland and Boston, although they still had a chance to win the pennant with two days remaining in the season. At least one element of that failure was Weiss' refusal to promote some promising prospects from the farm system soon enough to make a difference. (Weiss had become the Yankees' top executive when MacPhail quit after the 1947 Series and was bought out by the team's other owners.) Never enamored

Yankees manager Casey Stengel.

operation Ed Barrow had insisted on for 25 years. Before the 1946 season ended, Johnny Neun had replaced Dickey as Yankees manager, and MacPhail was talking about hiring Leo Durocher away from the Dodgers.

MacPhail's plans for Durocher fell through and he turned instead to Bucky Harris, who had been hired as the Yankees' general manager. Harris had burst into prominence in 1924 as the 27-year-old manager-second baseman of the World Champion Washington Senators and had been a major league manager for 20 years before joining the Yankees. MacPhail persuaded Harris to go to the dugout, and George Weiss became the team's highest-ranking front office manager, a position that held little sway since he reported to the domineering MacPhail.

of Harris, Weiss used the Yankees' third-place finish as a reason to change managers.

Weiss did what baseball people often do: He selected an old friend, assuring himself of a manager who would be loyal. That manager: Charles Dillon "Casey" Stengel. Casey Stengel? The Yankees? New Yorkers knew Stengel well, and they liked him. He played in six seasons for the Dodgers at the outset of his major league career in 1912, and he spent the 1922 and 1923 seasons with the Giants. But Stengel had been unsuccessful as the Dodgers manager from 1934 to 1936 (sixth-, fifth-, and seventh-place finishes) and even more so as the Boston Braves manager from 1938 to 1943. In those nine seasons, his teams had one winning record. Unable to land another managerial position in the major leagues, Stengel went to the minor leagues. He was the manager of

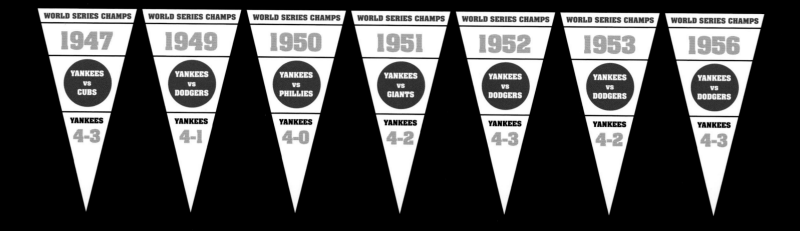

WORLD SERIES CHAMPS	WORLD SERIES CHAMPS	WORLD SERIES CHAMPS	WORLD SERIES CHAMPS	WORLD SERIES CHAMPS	WORLD SERIES CHAMPS	WORLD SERIES CHAMPS
1947	1949	1950	1951	1952	1953	1956
YANKEES vs CUBS	YANKEES vs DODGERS	YANKEES vs PHILLIES	YANKEES vs GIANTS	YANKEES vs DODGERS	YANKEES vs DODGERS	YANKEES vs DODGERS
YANKEES 4-3	YANKEES 4-1	YANKEES 4-0	YANKEES 4-2	YANKEES 4-3	YANKEES 4-2	YANKEES 4-3

the Oakland Oaks of the Pacific Coast League when Weiss called him in 1948. Stengel was considered a lovable clown, but definitely a clown. A funnyman was to carry on the tradition of Miller Huggins (six pennants) and McCarthy (eight) in the Yankees' aristocracy? Most of the Yankees, including DiMaggio, wondered about that.

History, of course, told a different story. Stengel brought the Yankees home in first place in 1949 — they beat the Red Sox in the final two games of the season to do it — and then his team beat the Dodgers in five games in the World Series. Stengel's Yankees also won the Series in 1950, 1951, 1952, and 1953, and made a seamless transition from the DiMaggio era to the Mantle era. Weiss, since his arrival in 1933, had built a farm system that rivaled the Dodgers' as the best in baseball, enabling him to trade promising prospects for

established players. Stengel became the double-talking "Old Perfessor" whose teams won five straight World Championships, a feat unmatched by McCarthy, McGraw, or anyone else in major league baseball history.

In 1957, as the Dodgers finished third and the Giants sixth while playing their final season in New York before bolting for California, the Yankees won their eighth pennant under Stengel. They were first again in 1958 and in 1960 — the end of the Stengel era. He was fired after the Yankees lost the 1960 World Series to Pittsburgh.

New York continued to evolve in the late 1950s. The changes were deeper and broader than what they had been earlier. About 29 million Americans were born in the 1950s, yet New York and other major cities lost population. Many upper- and middle-class families abandoned urban living for the suburbs; by 1960 about 30 percent of Americans lived in suburban areas, a 10-year shift from 20 percent.

At the same time, television was changing the world. Television technology had existed since the late 1920s, but TVs were not mass-produced until after World War II. About 17,000 television sets were in use in 1946, mostly in the East. By 1949, consumers were purchasing 250,000 sets a month. By 1953, two-thirds of American homes had at least one TV. Entertainment of whatever sort now was available in the home. Not only that, it was the same ballgame, drama, or news event that was available at the same moment to everyone in the country. And it was free, except for the price of a television set.

The Yankees won the first five American League pennants of the 1960s, and the Mets — founded in 1962 and managed by the irrepressible Stengel — began carving out their own niche. But the glorious postwar decade was over, and nothing quite like it would exist again.

Written by Roger Kahn

Two profoundly different teams based in distinctly different parts of the same city faced each other in six World Series from 1947 through 1956.

Yogi Berra, Phil Rizzuto, Vic Raschi, Allie Reynolds, and Eddie Lopat (left to right).

The 1947 Yankees were a remarkably competitive team, cobbled together by club president Larry MacPhail, "The Roarin' Redhead," who had built a pennant winner in Brooklyn earlier in the decade. MacPhail went into military service for World War II and upon returning found that his office as Dodgers president was occupied by Branch Rickey.

MacPhail tried to buy the New York Giants, but they were not for sale. He offered $2.8 million for the Yankees in 1945; lawyers for the estate of Jacob Ruppert, the brewer who had long owned the team, were delighted. "Except my father didn't have $2.8 million," said Lee MacPhail, Larry's son. "He never was able to hold on to money. So Dad had this great agreement with the Ruppert

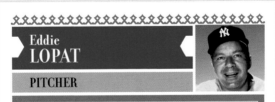

Eddie LOPAT

PITCHER

Lopat, Allie Reynolds, and Vic Raschi were the top starting pitchers on the Yankees teams that won five successive World Championships from 1949 to 1953. Lopat won 80 games in that period, Raschi 92, and Reynolds 83. The left-handed Lopat frustrated batters with an assortment of off-speed pitches, an effective contrast to the other two, both hard throwers. Lopat was particularly effective against the Cleveland Indians, posting a 40-13 career record against them, a major reason why Cleveland usually finished second behind the Yankees in that era. Even in 1954, when Cleveland won a then–American League record 111 games, Lopat went 3-1 against them. Among left-handers in Yankees history, Lopat and Andy Pettitte rate about even, behind Whitey Ford, Lefty Gomez, and Ron Guidry.

estate. All he was lacking was the cash."

MacPhail took his problem to Dan Topping, a sports buff and an heir to Anaconda Copper. Topping agreed to take a third of the deal, and then he called a friend, millionaire Arizona contractor Del Webb, who also took a third. The third share belonged to MacPhail.

The 1947 Yankees had a 97-57 record and won the pennant by 12 games — a year after winning 87 games and finishing 17 games out of first place. "We weren't a very subtle team," said Bobby Brown, a third baseman who batted .439 in four World Series with the Yankees. "We didn't pull a lot of squeeze plays. All we tried to do was hit the ball so hard it broke in half."

The Dodgers, meanwhile, won the

National League pennant, a feat they had achieved only once between 1921 and 1946. The Dodgers had been tied for first place on the last day of the 1946 season, but lost a playoff for the pennant to the St. Louis Cardinals. Rickey brought Jackie Robinson to the major leagues in 1947, and the Dodgers won the pennant by five games.

The World Series opened at Yankee Stadium, and Brooklyn started Ralph Branca, a 21-game winner at age 21. He was just about the best young pitcher in baseball, and for four innings Branca retired the Yankees in order. The Dodgers had a 1-0 lead when Joe DiMaggio opened the Yankees' fifth with a ground ball to deep shortstop. Pee Wee Reese made a backhand stop, but the 32-year-old DiMaggio still had fair speed, and he beat the throw to first base by a step. "I knew I was dominating," Branca said, "but I'm a 21-year-old kid from Westchester [about 10 miles from Yankee Stadium] pitching a World Series shutout at the Stadium. In my youth, I got excited. I've replayed what happened next 500 times."

A more experienced pitcher might have slowed his pace. Branca said, "I just wanted to get the next guy out as quick as I could." He walked George McQuinn and hit Billy Johnson with a pitch, loading the bases. Johnny Lindell's double gave the Yankees a 2-1 lead that had improved to 5-1 before the inning was over. The Yankees held on and won, 5-3.

The next day, cool and hazy, the Yankees rolled to a 10-3 victory in which the Dodgers center fielder, Pete Reiser, suffering episodes of vertigo that he kept to himself, misplayed four balls. Red Smith wrote in the *New York Herald Tribune* that Reiser "had appalling difficulties with the sun. This at least he will be spared when the carnival moves on to Ebbets Field for Game 3. The sun no longer shines in Brooklyn."

The Dodgers won Game 3 and tied the Series in a suspenseful Game 4 in which Yankees starter Bill Bevens walked 10 Dodgers. (No other pitcher has walked that many batters in a World Series game.) With two outs in the bottom of the ninth inning, the Yankees had a 2-1 lead and Bevens had not given up a hit. The Dodgers, however, had two run-

Hank Bauer played in nine World Series for the Yankees — five against the Dodgers. "They had an expression on the Yankees, 'Don't screw with our money' because we were going to the bank every October,'" said Bauer.

Hank BAUER
OUTFIELDER

Bauer was a World War II Marine with a reputation for toughness and, as once described by the great sportswriter Jim Murray, the face of a clenched fist. He played right field on Casey Stengel's teams from 1948 through 1959, usually in a platoon role with Gene Woodling. Bauer, a right-handed batter, hit for a high average, was selective at the plate, had real power, and was a fine fielder with a strong throwing arm. Three things kept Bauer from becoming a big star: World War II, which delayed the start of his career by several years; Yankee Stadium, which cost him several home runs a year; and the abundance of talent on the Yankees, which kept him from being an everyday player.

ners on base, and both scored when pinch-hitter Cookie Lavagetto drove a double to the right field wall, giving the Dodgers a 3-2 victory. Rud Rennie wrote in the *Herald Tribune*: "Bill Bevens, in the most strangely beautiful performance ever seen in a World Series, broke three records only to have Lavagetto break his heart."

Game 5 went to the Yankees, and Game 6 turned in the Dodgers' favor on a catch in a distant reach of the outfield. Brooklyn held an 8-5 lead in the bottom of the sixth inning when DiMaggio came to bat with two runners on base. "I'm playing him to pull, which in the Stadium means in close," said left fielder Al Gionfriddo, who had entered the game that inning for his defensive skills. "He hit the ball to left center, very deep. I mean, Joe really hit it. He took some swing. I put my head down and I ran. The ball is going to the bullpen gate, 415 feet out. I'm left-handed so the glove is on my right hand. I make a jump. I'm turning in midair, turning and reaching, and I catch the ball. I crash the gate. I hit it hard against a hip. I hold the ball." And the Dodgers won, 8-6.

The Gionfriddo catch often is compared to Willie Mays' great catch at the Polo Grounds in the 1954 World Series. "But Mays had plenty of room," DiMaggio said years later. "Running back, all he had to worry about was the ball. On my drive, Gionfriddo had to worry about the ball and those iron bullpen gates. He had to worry about running out of room, about getting hurt. With all that, I say Gionfriddo made the greater catch, the greatest, as far as I know, in the whole history of the Series."

A day later, the Yankees won the World Series for the 11th time, taking the seventh game, 5-2. Sportswriter Al Laney summed it up in the *Herald Tribune*: "This extraordinary Series, which has provided perhaps more thrills and more hysteria than any other, finally came down to a sunny, pleasant afternoon on which people could sit back and enjoy an ordinary ballgame without having their nerves worn raw or their emotions too heavily involved. This was a straightforward game with reason and logic in it and never once did panic sit up and make noise."

By the time the Yankees and the Dodgers met in the 1949 World Series, day-to-day control of the Yankees had passed from MacPhail to George Weiss, and Stengel, who never had brought a major league team home in the first division, was the manager. In his first spring training with the Yankees, Stengel began pairing players in platoons at various positions. DiMaggio later told Yankees shortstop Phil Rizzuto, "With this guy managing, we can't possibly win."

DiMaggio was a better ballplayer than he was a prophet. The Yankees won the pennant by one game after a tense and exciting race against the Boston Red Sox. In Brooklyn, Rickey continued adding African-American players to the roster, with Roy Campanella and Don Newcombe joining the squad. The Dodgers also won the pennant by one game.

The 1949 Series began with two brilliant games. The Yankees' Allie Reynolds and Newcombe matched shut out innings into the bottom of the ninth at the Stadium. Then Tommy Henrich pulled a Newcombe fastball into the right field seats, and the Yankees won this fine game, 1-0. The next day, Preacher Roe of the Dodgers won a 1-0 decision against Vic Raschi. Roe was a thin, angular left-hander whose pitches included a slider, a variety of change-ups, and, as he later revealed to *Sports Illustrated* in an interview for which he was paid $2,000, a spitball.

The Yankees won the next three games and the Series. In Game 3 at Ebbets Field, Branca pitched well until the ninth, when the Yankees scored three runs and took a 4-1 lead. Brooklyn scored twice in the bottom of the ninth, but could get no closer than 4-3. After taking a 6-4 victory in Game 4, the Yankees took command of Game 5 by scoring 10 runs in the first six innings. The Dodgers cut the score to 10-6 in the seventh, but couldn't get any more against Yankees reliever Joe Page. Brown, the Yankees' resident medical student, led all hitters in the Series with a .500 average. (He later became a cardiologist and then president of the American League.)

Gil McDougald hit four of his seven World Series home runs against the Dodgers.

Gil McDOUGALD
INFIELDER

McDougald was the greatest bench player in baseball history and certainly one of the Yankees' most valuable players in the 1950s. He was a rare athlete who performed as well at second base, third base, or shortstop as any other player in the league, yet never groused about not getting an opportunity to remain at one position. McDougald is one of only five players who have logged at least 115 games in one season at each of his three positions. A right-handed hitter with some pop in his bat, McDougald was a career .276 hitter and reached double figures in home runs almost every year. He might have hit 20 to 25 home runs a year if his home park had not been Yankee Stadium.

Tommy Henrich's ninth-inning home run off Brooklyn's Don Newcombe gave the Yankees a 1-0 victory in the first game of the 1949 World Series.

Tommy HENRICH
OUTFIELDER

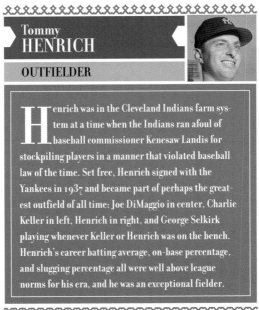

Henrich was in the Cleveland Indians farm system at a time when the Indians ran afoul of baseball commissioner Kenesaw Landis for stockpiling players in a manner that violated baseball law of the time. Set free, Henrich signed with the Yankees in 1937 and became part of perhaps the greatest outfield of all time: Joe DiMaggio in center, Charlie Keller in left, Henrich in right, and George Selkirk playing whenever Keller or Henrich was on the bench. Henrich's career batting average, on-base percentage, and slugging percentage all were well above league norms for his era, and he was an exceptional fielder.

The Yankees-Dodgers' World Series in 1952 was on a par with the teams' great 1947 match. Dodgers manager Charlie Dressen surprised many by starting his ace relief pitcher, Joe Black, in the first game. Reynolds, who started for the Yankees, couldn't throw his curveball for strikes, which enabled the Dodgers to look for fastballs. Jackie Robinson hit one into the left field seats in the second inning. Duke Snider hit a two-run homer — the first of four he would hit in the Series — in the sixth. Black pitched a six-hitter and became the first African-American to win a World Series game, claiming a 4-2 decision.

The following day, the Yankees knocked around Dodgers starter Carl Erskine and tied the Series with a 7-1 victory. In Game 3 at Yankee Stadium, Roe gave up home runs to Yogi Berra and Johnny Mize, but the Dodgers still won, 5-3.

Reynolds pitched a four-hitter and struck out 10 in Game 4, beating Black, 2-0. Robinson, who struck out three times, had a loud statement for sportswriters who entered the Dodgers clubhouse after the game. "You can't hit what you can't see," he shouted.

Sunday, October 5, was memorable: a crowd of 70,536 at Yankee Stadium and, as Red Smith wrote, "Eleven tremendous innings." Erskine took a 4-0 lead into the fifth inning, only to have his control abandon him. The Yankees scored five runs. "And here comes Dressen," Erskine said. "I'm thinking, Oh, no. I got good stuff. I look at Dressen coming closer, and I think the numbers are against me. October fifth. My fifth wedding anniversary. The fifth inning. The fives have done me in. Then Dressen says, 'Are you gonna take Betty out and celebrate tonight?' I can't believe it. But I tell him, 'Yes, we're going to go to some place quiet.' Dressen says, 'Then see if you can get this game over before it gets dark.'" Erskine retired the next 19 Yankees batters, and the Dodgers won, 6-5, in 11 innings.

I thought the rivalries were great back then. Some people thought the players were each other's enemy. Nope, not at all. I used to go barnstorming with a lot of Dodgers guys in the offseason. Pee Wee Reese, Duke Snider, guys like that—we went to Japan. Campanella, of course, was a good friend of mine.

The Giants and the Dodgers weren't rivals, being in the National League. You need to play people a lot to get to be rivals. So even though both teams played near the Yankees, neither was really against us often enough to make it nasty.

Don't get me wrong, when it came time for the World Series, we always seemed to be playing the Dodgers. And when we played them, we wanted to win...a lot. And the Dodgers always wanted to beat the Yankees. But after the games are done and the Series is over, you go home and shake hands — just like the fighters do. You get beat, or you beat them, and you shake their hands. That's that.

We even had fun against Brooklyn in exhibition games. We'd play the Dodgers in Florida seven or eight times for spring training, and both teams enjoyed it, I think.

The one time they won the Series against us was when Sandy Amoros in 1955 robbed my hit at the end. He had taken over for Don Zimmer. Be sure to check with Zim about it—he loves talking about that one.

I get asked if the Dodgers might not have beaten us ever, if not for 1955. You forget, there were a lot of close calls before and after that. Those were some close World Series against Brooklyn.

The best thing about having World Series against Brooklyn so often was not having to travel. Travel then wasn't what it is today. At the end of the season, when you've played every day and not had days off, not having to go farther than across the city was great for both sides. We lived in the Edison Hotel and would take the subway wherever we had to go. We'd ride with everyone else to Ebbets Field, Yankee Stadium, or the Polo Grounds. You could win the World Series and have the entire season over by October 6.

With both the Giants and the Dodgers in the other league, we'd pay some attention to them when the end of the season rolled around. Yankees guys usually pulled for the Giants—not because we liked them any better, but because of the money.

See, Dodger Stadium only held thirty-thousand-something, but the Polo Grounds held more than 50,000. More people in the stands meant higher gate, which meant more for World Series shares for players. Back when our salaries were so small, you needed that Series check. I remember my first one in 1947 was for $5,000.

We always won back then, so if you ask the Yankees about that time, everybody's always going to look back with no negativity.

— *Yogi Berra*

3
NEW YORK CITY
DODGERS · YANKEES · GIANTS

I joined the Brooklyn Dodgers in 1954. We had a good team while I was there. From 1953 to 1957, there was great baseball in Brooklyn. Somehow we always wound up playing the Yankees in the World Series, but in the end we'd come up a little short.

Of course in 1955 we had Johnny Podres and we finally beat 'em in the seventh game. So nowadays if I'm speaking at a banquet or something, I tell everyone—especially if it's a New York City event—how instrumental I was in that Series.

I started at second base in that Game 7. Podres was pitching for us, and Tommy Byrne was going for the Yankees. We got ahead early and were up 1-0. Junior Gilliam was playing left field, me at second. We put a man on third in the sixth with one out. I came up to bat, and Casey Stengel took out Byrne, a lefty, and put in a right-hander to face me. Then our manager, Walter Alston, took me out for a pinch-hitter. Nothing happened, and we didn't score.

But by taking me out, he brought Gilliam in to play second base and used Sandy Amoros in left field. Amoros was a left-handed thrower, so he had his glove on the right hand. That's how he was able to make that remarkable catch down the left field line of Yogi's liner late in the game. Had Amoros been wearing the glove on the other side, like me, a righty, that catch never could've been made.

Amoros got the catch, and we finally beat the Yankees, 2-0, and got our first World Series. So I've been saying ever since how important I was in that game, simply by being taken out of it.

Then here's what happened in 1956: I was on the bench for the World Series, again, the Yankees and Dodgers were in it, because that was the year I had gotten hit in the face with a pitched ball and was out the rest of the year. But Alston got permission from Stengel to have me sit on the bench in uniform—which was significant because it meant I was sitting on the bench when Don Larsen pitched his perfect game.

As a result, they tell me I've been the only person in uniform for all three Yankees perfect games. Once when someone pointed that out, Joe Torre jumped up and said, "No, I was, too. I saw all three games in person." That was correct, however, Joe didn't see all of them in uniform. He came as a fan to the first one.

As far as players being mean or ornery towards each other, that wasn't the Dodgers and the Yankees. It was Yankees and the Red Sox. As players, we couldn't have that kind of bitterness against a team we only faced in spring training or the World Series.

One of things that always stuck with me about playing against the Yankees had to do with two of their pitchers, Allie Reynolds and Vic Raschi, who were hard-throwing tough guys. Our catcher, Roy Campanella, on the other hand, was one of the nicest, sweetest guys you ever could meet. And whenever the Dodgers would play the Yankees—be it in the World Series or spring training—if either Raschi or Reynolds was pitching, they would knock Campy on his rear end. They'd flip him upside-down every time he came to the plate. So Campy would come back to the bench after getting dusted each time, clean himself off, and say over and over again, in that kindly, high-pitched voice of his, "Yeesh...what'd I ever do to those guys? Why are they always laying me out?" But that was more comical than a serious thing. It was just hard-nosed baseball between the Dodgers and the Yanks.

— *Don Zimmer*

Brooklyn got a little help that day from first base umpire Art Passarella, who called out Johnny Sain on a close play in the 10th inning. Red Patterson, the Yankees' adroit publicist, later displayed an enlarged photo of the play at press headquarters. The picture clearly showed Sain's foot creasing the bag while the baseball was still several feet from the glove of Gil Hodges. After the Series, Passarella resigned. "So it turns out," New York sports writer Dick Young told a colleague, "that young Mr. Erskine retired 19 Yankees and one umpire."

The Yankees won Game 6 in Brooklyn. In Game 7, Stengel, now accepted as a virtuoso, used his three best starters — Ed Lopat, Reynolds, and Raschi — in the first seven innings. Down by two runs, the Dodgers loaded the bases with one out in the seventh, and Stengel called for little-known left-hander Bob Kuzava. Snider popped out, and Robinson, on a full count, hit another pop-up, this one toward the right side. First baseman Joe Collins lost the ball in the sun, but second baseman Billy Martin made a splendid, sprinting, knee-level catch, saving the victory for the Yankees.

"Them Brooklyns is tough in this little ballpark," Stengel said after the Yankees had clinched the Series with a 4-2 victory. "And now you're gonna ask me why I left in the left-hander [Kuzava] to face the right-handed feller [Robinson]. Don't I know percentages and etcetera? The reason I left him in is the other man [Robinson] has not seen hard-throwing left-hand pitchers much and could have trouble with the break of a left-hander's hard curve. Which is what happened."

● ● ●

The 1953 Dodgers were the best of all the Brooklyn teams. They won the pennant by 13 games and led the league in batting, fielding, home runs, and stolen bases, and scored 169 more runs than any other National League team. But that October, the Yankees were even better. Martin, hardly the best of Yankees hitters, became the most opportunistic in the Series. He batted .500 with two homers and two triples, and he won the deciding sixth game with a ninth-inning single that gave the Yankees a 4-3 victory. It was the Yankees' fifth consecutive World Championship under Stengel.

● ● ●

Both the Yankees and the Dodgers were starting to show wear by 1955, but each made it to the World Series. Reynolds and Raschi, the Yankees' great power pitchers, had moved on. Rizzuto was nearing the end of his playing days. Mickey Mantle had a damaged leg and was able to play in only three of the seven games. "If Mantle says he hurts," said Sid Gaynor, the Yankees' orthopedist, "believe me, he hurts. His pain threshold is remarkable, 10 times higher than DiMaggio's."

The Series went to the seventh game. The Dodgers were without Robinson, who had a foot injury, and Snider was at less than 100 percent because of a sprained left knee. With Johnny Podres pitching masterfully, the Dodgers had a 2-0 lead going into the bottom of the sixth inning at Yankee Stadium. Dodgers manager Walter Alston had started Jim Gilliam, normally an infielder, in left field. Now, Alston moved Gilliam to second base and put left-handed Sandy Amoros in left field.

The Yankees' first two hitters reached base, then Yogi Berra sent a drive down the left field line. Amoros ran at full speed, and the ball fell into his glove, which was on his right hand. A right-handed outfielder would have had a more difficult time, having to make the catch backhanded. Amoros threw to Reese, who spun and threw a perfect relay to Hodges at first. Berra's smash, which started out looking as if it would be a double, became a double play. Podres made the 2-0 lead stand up, and Brooklyn won its first World Series.

● ● ●

The memorable 1956 Series began as a mirror image of 1955, with the Dodgers winning the first two games. The Yankees won the next two games, setting the stage for Game 5 on October 8. Don Larsen, the starting and losing pitcher in Game 2, was on the mound again. The previous night, Larsen went out with a group that included Yankees reserve outfielder Bob Cerv. "I left him at 4 a.m.," Cerv said. "I called his hotel in the morning to make sure he got out of bed. At the ballpark, he took a whirlpool bath, a cold shower, and had a rub. You know what happened next."

Sal Maglie was marvelous for the Dodgers, limiting the Yankees to five hits. Larsen was better by a wide margin, pitching the only perfect game in Series history. Shirley Povich wrote in the *Washington Post*: "The million-to-one shot came in. Hell froze over. A month of Sundays hit the calendar, Don Larsen today pitched a no-hit, no-run, no-man-reach-first game in a World Series."

Clem Labine beat the Yankees and Bob Turley, 1-0, in 10 innings in Game 6 in Brooklyn. The seventh game matched the Yankees' Johnny Kucks, who had won 18 games that season, against Newcombe, who had led the majors with 27 victories. Kucks pitched a three-hitter, and the Yankees knocked Newcombe out of the game in the third inning on their way to a 9-0 victory and their 17th World Championship.

The Battle of the Boroughs, an American saga, had come to the end. Two years later, the Dodgers were in Los Angeles and the Giants in San Francisco. The Yankees were the unchallenged monarchs of New York baseball. Their fans would say, with some justification, this was nothing new.

Bill SKOWRON

FIRST BASEMAN

Skowron, like Hank Bauer, a teammate on the 1950s Yankees, was handicapped by being a right-handed power hitter in Yankee Stadium. A career .282 hitter, Skowron hit a career-high 28 home runs in 1961, all but seven on the road. He further was limited by Casey Stengel's platoon system, which afforded him more than 480 at-bats in only two of his nine seasons with the Yankees. Most of Skowron's contemporaries knew him as "Moose," a nickname he picked as an infant from a grandfather who thought he resembled the Italian dictator Mussolini.

Written by Pat Jordan

I was born in 1941 in a three-family tenement house in the Italian ghetto of Bridgeport, Connecticut.

When I was five, my family became the first from that ghetto to move to a colonial house in the leafy suburb of Fairfield, Connecticut. To celebrate, my parents invited my aunts and uncles to our new home for a cookout in the backyard. My father grilled hot dogs while my uncles — short, swarthy men in shimmering sharkskin suits — smoked crooked Toscano cigars and sipped Scotch whiskey. The women played poker for a penny a point at a picnic table shaded by a Cinzano umbrella. Some wore wide-brimmed hats because it was a hot, sunny day and they didn't want to get their olive-colored faces any darker than they were.

Propped inside a half-open kitchen window was a radio broadcasting a New York Yankees–Boston Red Sox game. My father and my uncles stood around the barbecue grill and talked, half in Italian, half in English. Every so often they went silent to listen to the radio. None of my uncles or my father had played baseball, nor had they had much interest in that American game until the 1940s. The women, chattering at their table, sipping Scotch, and smoking Chesterfield cigarettes, certainly had not played baseball either — but like my father and my uncles, they now had a passionate interest in it, too.

In the eighth inning of a tie game, Joe DiMaggio came to bat for the Yankees. Suddenly our backyard was silent, and all heads were turned toward the radio. When Joe D. hit a home run, my aunts and uncles and parents let out a cheer.

A few years later, my parents bought our first television — a big, round, black-and-white set in a mahogany cabinet — and placed it in the living room of our home. They again invited my aunts and uncles to our house for a celebration. I helped my mother in the kitchen. I carried a big jug of red wine to the table and then a Cassatta cake. My mother stood at the stove, stirring spaghetti sauce, and they stood around the kitchen talking in Italian and English.

Their conversation was about Italians. Local Italians who had become doctors and lawyers, and famous Italians like DiMaggio, who had become American heroes. Italian-Americans of the 1940s worshipped the Yankees, for many were of Italian descent: DiMaggio, Phil Rizzuto, Frank Crosetti, Tony Lazzeri, Yogi Berra, and Vic Raschi. And we were not alone. Most immigrants in the Northeast in the 1940s, especially the most recent ones, saw in the Yankees proof of "The American Dream." They saw immigrants like themselves who had succeeded at the great American pastime and become heroes to all Americans. It didn't matter how removed those Italian-American Yankees were from the mother country; it mattered only that they seemed like us, with their dark hair and swarthy complexion, and vowels at the end of their name.

The Yankees were seen as hard-working, blue-collar men — except for the great Joe D., who never gave anyone the impression he wore a blue-collared shirt unless it was made of silk. We viewed them in their pinstriped uniforms as silent, stoic, self-deprecating, classy men. And most of all, they were successful, the best sports team in the world. For us, they obliterated the stigma that had cursed Italian-Americans, who were stereotyped as loud, thuggish, too passionate. They dispelled the myth that every Italian was a member of the Mafia or a supporter of the fascist Mussolini, and never would be able to assimilate into the American melting pot. In those days, it was not unusual to see a sign in a storefront window advertising a job that included the admonition, "No Italians Need Apply."

DiMaggio almost single-handedly cleansed the image of Italian-Americans, not only because he had mastered the quintessentially American game of baseball, but also because in doing so he had mastered all things American. He played baseball and glided through life with a style, grace, and silent dignity that made Italian-Americans incredibly proud.

Soon, my father and uncles went to the living room to watch the Yankees game on our new television set. They settled into the easy chairs and lit Chesterfields, hunching forward when Berra came to bat. Berra was squat, taciturn, hardworking. The men loved him because he was an Italian-American and exemplified the American work ethic. The women had little interest in Berra; they worshipped the angular DiMaggio, who was handsome, elegantly dressed, and immaculately barbered.

"That Yogi," said Uncle Ben. "He's a tough one. A clutch batter."

"Not as good as Campanella," said Uncle Ken. The two men argued over the relative merits of Berra and Roy Campanella, the Brooklyn Dodgers catcher. My father intervened.

"What difference does it make?" he said. "They're both Italians."

The men nodded in agreement.

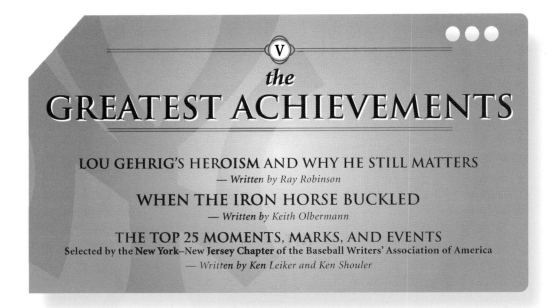

the

GREATEST ACHIEVEMENTS

LOU GEHRIG'S HEROISM AND WHY HE STILL MATTERS
— *Written by Ray Robinson*

WHEN THE IRON HORSE BUCKLED
— *Written by Keith Olbermann*

THE TOP 25 MOMENTS, MARKS, AND EVENTS
Selected by the **New York**–New **Jersey Chapter** of the Baseball Writers' Association of America
— *Written by Ken Leiker and Ken Shouler*

For a team that has won so often for so long, the most memorable events, moments, and performances become decidedly relative. Each new season produces its share of moments, though always against the backdrop of what has come before. The New York–New Jersey Chapter of the Baseball Writers' Association of America voted on 25 of the most compelling Yankee memories. Author and historian Ray Robinson's essay centers on a man that matters as much today as he did more than 60 years ago. For the first time in print, Keith Olbermann recounts a prescient conversation with the man who replaced Gehrig at first base for the Yankees, and how he saw the signs of a debilitating disease in Gehrig years before Gehrig was forced to give up the game. Ken Leiker and Ken Shouler revisit moments, events, and performances that bring to life the history of sport's greatest franchise.

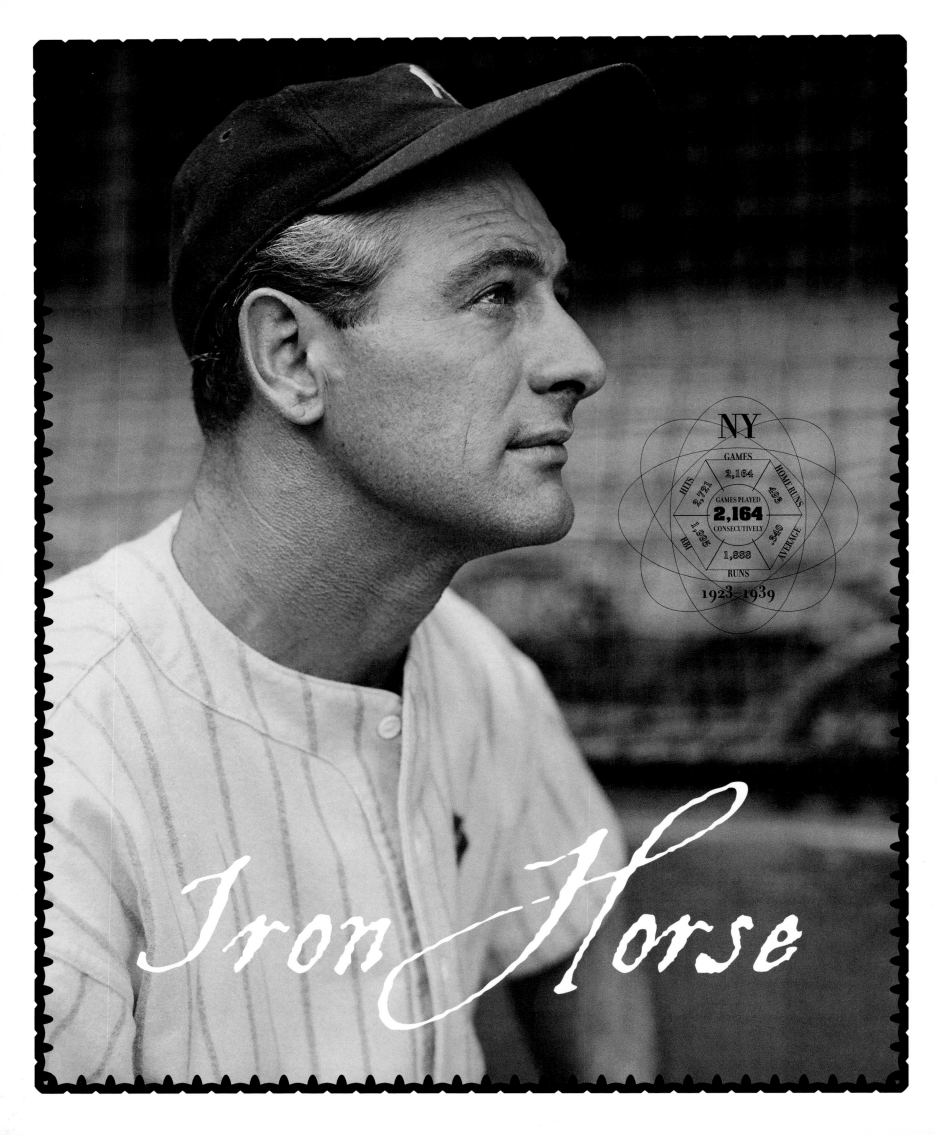

NY

GAMES
2,164

HITS
2,721

HOME RUNS
493

GAMES PLAYED
2,164
CONSECUTIVELY

RBI
1,995

.340
AVERAGE

1,888
RUNS

1923–1939

Iron Horse

LOU GEHRIG

Written by Ray Robinson

The seemingly indestructible Lou Gehrig, the Percheron-esque first baseman of the New York Yankees from 1925 to 1939, spent his Major League Baseball career in the shadow of those other Yankees icons, Babe Ruth and Joe DiMaggio. The Babe, certainly the most implausible sports figure of all time, became the savior of baseball after eight Chicago White Sox players fixed the outcome of the 1919 World Series between the White Sox and the Cincinnati Reds. Ruth's towering and frequent home runs and outsized persona quickly made people forget the game's loss of innocence.

ehrig and Ruth were close friends in their first years together with the Yankees, but it was inevitable that their striking personality differences would polarize them. Gehrig never could fully appreciate the Babe's uninhibited carousing and bombast, even as the public preferred the Rabelaisian Ruth to the introverted Gehrig.

"The Babe took a host of Walter Mittys with him as he rounded the bases," historian Bruce Catton wrote. Gehrig, though one of the most productive ballplayers of all time, did not arouse such fantasies in fans. Even on the day in 1932 when he became the first player of the 20th century to hit four home runs in a game, Gehrig took a backseat. John McGraw picked that same day to resign his 30-year position as manager of the New York Giants. McGraw was in all the headlines of New York City's newspapers, while reports of Gehrig's four home runs in a Philadelphia ballpark received little coverage.

DiMaggio came along in the 1930s. The enigmatic and elegant young center fielder quickly stole the attention away from Gehrig, even though Gehrig was the Yankees' captain. DiMaggio was the type of smooth

performer that attracted everyone's eye. All Gehrig could offer was his daily commitment to show up on time and play as well as he possibly could. Gehrig was the rock in the Yankees lineup, but DiMaggio with his incredible batting eye, flawless fielding ability, and a natural appeal to a growing number of Italian-American fans, quickly won more headlines and more money.

Despite being relegated to the role of second fiddle for most of his career, Gehrig would seem today to possess a legacy every bit as enduring as that of Ruth or DiMaggio. This is sadly due in no small part to the sudden, tragic cut-off to Gehrig's consecutive games streak at 2,130, and the manner in which he confronted certain death at a young age.

It was between games of a doubleheader at Yankee Stadium on July 4,

1939, that the diffident Gehrig, dying of amyotrophic lateral sclerosis, a disease that would later bear his name, delivered a farewell speech that became baseball's most eloquent and remembered address. The speech was rendered with such dignity and honesty (and without notes, although the previous night Gehrig's wife, Eleanor, had helped him construct an outline), that it is included in many compendiums of memorable speeches.

Commenting on the speech and its impact, author Wilfrid Sheed wrote: "All present in Yankee Stadium that day had been given a license to love a fellow human being to the limit, without qualifications, and to root for that person as they had never rooted for themselves. If the Stadium had emptied out suddenly, and he had been left standing there alone, Gehrig would have felt no less lucky, because the appearance merely confirmed what he already knew — that he was having a very good day … a day like that was worth a thousand of the old ones."

I was present on that melancholy occasion in 1939, a 19-year-old Gehrig fan among the 60,000 or so who had turned out at Yankee Stadium. Some years earlier, as a kid in a Manhattan public school, I had written a letter to Gehrig asking if I might interview him for my school newspaper. He replied almost at once, employing a penmanship surprisingly delicate for a person of such strength. "I'll be happy to talk to you," wrote Gehrig. "Just use this letter to come to our clubhouse."

Unfortunately, when I journeyed with a friend to Yankee Stadium the following day, we were denied entrance to the sacred enclave of the Yankees clubhouse. Certainly, if we had not been so young and naive — was Gehrig equally naive in this instance? — we would have anticipated that we'd be turned away, even with the precious letter from Gehrig in hand. We waited outside the Stadium all afternoon, listening eagerly for crowd noises that might have hinted how the Yankees of those glory days were doing. When we heard a swelling roar, we were convinced that Gehrig must have hit a home run. As the sun went down, the game was over, and some time later Gehrig strode out into the street, a man in the prime of his life. He was, as I still remember, deeply tanned, and his thick brown hair was damp from his postgame shower. I waved his letter, and Gehrig stopped. Taking a quick glance at the paper, he realized he had written it.

"Did you enjoy the game?" Gehrig asked.

We responded with some embarrassment that we had not been admitted into the ballpark. Gehrig appeared genuinely sorry, but he added that he was in a hurry. "I'd be happy to give you the interview some other time," he said. He reached into his pocket and pulled out a pair of crumpled tickets. "These will be good for another day," he said, handing them to us. With that, he waved at us and was gone.

Here I am, some 70 years later, and I still recall the incident with clarity. It inspired me to write a biography of Gehrig, and I can only hope that it was a fair-minded assessment of the man.

●　●　●

From among the greatest Yankees, Gehrig was the native New Yorker, until Whitey Ford came along in 1950. Gehrig was born on June 19, 1903, in Manhattan's Yorkville section, the only child of Christina and Heinrich Gehrig to survive infancy. Money was hard to come by in the Gehrig household, but Christina, who took on odd jobs to provide for the family, adamantly rejected the notion that the Gehrigs were poor. Heinrich had mechanical skills and earned decent wages when he worked, but often he was more devoted to the pursuit of beer, causing him to miss many workdays. One can't escape the irony here, for Gehrig ultimately won a large measure of his fame as baseball's most durable man, a fellow who never failed to show up for work. Gehrig was devoted to his mother and relied greatly on her well into his 20s, until he met Eleanor Twitchell of Chicago and married her in 1933.

Gehrig excelled at football and baseball as a youth, displaying enough

promise in both sports to arouse the interest of Columbia University. Gehrig's parents were beside themselves with joy. They long had dreamed of their son becoming "a college man," envisioning that he would study to be an engineer or an architect, but Columbia wanted him only for its football team.

Indeed, when Gehrig enrolled at Columbia, he played football, both on the line and in the backfield. But it was on the baseball diamond that Gehrig truly distinguished himself. After two years he decided to leave school and join the upstart ballclub in town, the Yankees, who were challenging John McGraw's Giants for New York sports supremacy.

The Yankees, in 1921, paid a bit more than $2,000 to Gehrig's parents for the privilege of having their son join Babe Ruth and other Boston Red Sox luminaries who had been lured to the Yankees. Thus, Gehrig took his place as one of Columbia's three most celebrated dropouts, the other two being American Revolutionary hero Alexander Hamilton and tough-guy actor James Cagney.

Gehrig's consecutive games streak began on June 1, 1925, and didn't end until May 2, 1939. He played through many painful injuries. It is said that at one time or another each of his fingers was broken. He once suffered a concussion from a beanball in an exhibition game but made the Yankees lineup the following day.

Gehrig hit 493 home runs and compiled a batting average of .340. He was one of the most prolific run-producers in history, with seasons of 175, 174, and 184 RBIs. Yet all the while, the out-sized Ruth out-roared, out-ate, out-publicized, and out-drank entire platoons of ballplayers, including the reserved Gehrig.

Gehrig didn't share publicly his feelings about Ruth. Gehrig was not one to engage in shouting matches, and his ego always took second place to his profound sense of himself as a responsible public figure. This self-imposed role may have at times cost him dearly in his relationships with teammates, opponents, and the ubiquitous media. Certainly his relationship with the Babe, whom Gehrig worshiped for a time, was severely damaged by Ruth's outspoken disparagement of the consecutive games streak. "The streak is a lot of baloney," Ruth had publicly announced, a cut that no doubt hurt Gehrig deeply.

The consecutive games streak ended rather abruptly. Gehrig had a subpar season in 1938, batting less than .300 for the first time since 1925. He went to 1939 spring training determined to regain his form, but his body seemed to be in revolt. His wife referred to it as "a creeping mystery."

"I'm just not feeling right," Gehrig would say. One afternoon in spring training, he climbed atop a bench to gaze out of a clubhouse window, lost his balance, and fell awkwardly backward, landing painfully on his back. Pitcher Wes Ferrell asked Gehrig if he was hurt, and Gehrig tried to brush off the incident as an accident. Ferrell, however, sensed an uncertainty in Gehrig's tone. The following day the two men played golf together, and Ferrell noticed that Gehrig was wearing tennis sneakers instead of golf cleats. "Lou was shuffling his feet as he played," Ferrell said. "It was not pleasant to watch."

A week into the 1939 season, Gehrig was not only failing as a ballplayer, but was also having trouble performing tasks such as tying his shoes and

"The Babe is one fellow, and I'm another and I could never be exactly like him. I don't try. I just go on as I am in my own right."
— **LOU GEHRIG**

shuffling a deck of playing cards. In Detroit, for a series with the Tigers, Gehrig approached Yankees manager Joe McCarthy, who respected Gehrig more than any other player who ever worked under him, and told him what McCarthy fully anticipated Gehrig was about to say.

"I'm going to bench myself," Gehrig said hoarsely.

After a moment's silence, McCarthy asked, "Why, Lou?"

"For the good of the team, Joe. Nobody has to tell me how bad I've been and how much of a drawback I've been to the club. I've been thinking ever since the season opened, when I couldn't start the way I hoped I would, that maybe the time has come for me to quit."

McCarthy understood, yet it was difficult for him, too, to let go. "Take some time off, maybe you'll feel better in a week or so," he said. "Any time you want to get back in there, it's still your job."

The following day, May 2, Ellsworth "Babe" Dahlgren, a slick-fielding first baseman, was assigned the unenviable task of succeeding Gehrig, baseball's Rock of Gibraltar. Gehrig never would play again.

At this critical moment in his life, Gehrig wrote Eleanor a letter, revealing the depth of his feeling for his wife and his own sensitivity to the cloud over his future. This is part of what Gehrig wrote to Eleanor:

"My sweetheart — and please grant that we may ever be such, for what the hell else matters — that thing yesterday I believe and hope was the turning point of my life for the future as far as taking life too seriously is concerned. It was inevitable, although I dreaded the day, and my thoughts were with you constantly — and how the thing would affect you and I — that was the big question and the most important thought underlying every thing. I broke before the game because I thought so much of you. Not because I didn't know you are the bravest kind of partner but because my inferiority grabbed me and made me wonder and ponder if I could possibly prove myself worthy of you. As for me, the road may come to a dead end here, but why should it? Seems like our back is to the wall now, but there usually comes a way out. Where and what, I know not, but who can tell that it might not lead to better things. Time will tell."

LG

WRITTEN BY **KEITH OLBERMANN**

On a wet afternoon at Fenway Park in 1935, Lou Gehrig rapped a single to right field and rounded the first base bag. His spikes slid across the slick base and jammed into the muddy infield. Gehrig fell, and he did not rise immediately.

The rookie first baseman of the Red Sox was startled that Gehrig did not seem able to get up. The Yankees captain lay in the mud, one foot stretched back to the base. *That's funny,* the rookie thought to himself. *He's the Iron Horse, he never misses a game, he doesn't look hurt. Something's wrong with him.*

Finally, the rookie spoke up: "Lou? Can I help you?"

The response was muffled. "Just let me take care of it," Gehrig said. He flattened his palms and pushed himself up with his fingers and knees. Once on his feet again, Gehrig wiped his hands on his pants legs and breathed deeply. He smiled wanly at the rookie. "Thanks, kid. What's your name again?"

The rookie swallowed hard. "Lou, I'm Dahlgren," he said. "Babe Dahlgren."

Less than four years later, on May 2, 1939, Dahlgren would succeed Gehrig as first baseman for the Yankees, after Gehrig decided he no longer could help the team and ended his playing streak at 2,130 games. A few weeks later Gehrig was diagnosed with amyotrophic lateral sclerosis, an incurable disease that breaks down the nerves and tissues of the body.

Half a century later, on May 2, 1989, Dahlgren related the Fenway Park incident to me in an interview on a Los Angeles television station. His memory of Gehrig's struggle to rise from the mud brought up the question: When did the disease that killed Gehrig first begin to eat away at his body?

"I've always thought in my heart that maybe this thing was acting on him as early as '35," Dahlgren told me.

"He was probably sick in 1935. I think I knew something was really wrong when the Yankees bought me (in 1937). Me? What did they need me for? I was really upset when they got me. I thought I'd never play. Then in my mind I saw Lou in the mud like that, not able to get up. And I knew something was terribly wrong. And I think we all knew."

If Gehrig truly was in the early stages of his disease in 1935, what he did the rest of his career was nothing short of incredible. He continued to play every day, in 626 consecutive games. He hit 145 home runs, drove in 545 runs, batted .330. He was the Most Valuable Player in 1936. All perhaps while he was dying.

On the day he replaced Gehrig, Dahlgren dropped down next to the Iron Horse in the dugout in the seventh inning of what would be a 22-2 Yankees victory. Dahlgren urged Gehrig to reconsider and keep the streak alive. "I told him he wouldn't be hurting the team, that this'd at least give him another day to get better. He just smiled and told me the team was doing fine, and shook my hand."

Dahlgren repeated his request to Gehrig in the eighth inning, and again his idol turned him down. Before heading out to the field for the bottom of the ninth, Dahlgren made one final plea. "I asked him to do it for me, that I didn't want to be the one to break his streak. I put it on those terms."

Gehrig's opaque eyes gazed past Dahlgren. "I appreciate it, Babe," he said. "But I'm done."

Gehrig went to the Mayo Clinic in Minnesota to find out what was wrong with him. The diagnosis, couched in the sterile, bloodless language of medical speak, was dreadful. He was suffering from amyotrophic lateral sclerosis, an incurable and relatively unknown disease. It was never clear if Gehrig knew he had been handed a death sentence. Eleanor knew; the Mayo doctors had told her. It is possible that she chose to withhold the news from her husband. Yet, it is not unreasonable to assume that as Gehrig's body continued to fail, even though his brain remained sharp and alert, he was aware of the hopelessness of his condition.

"I had him for over eight years and he never gave me a moment's trouble. I guess you might say he was kind of my favorite."
— **JOE McCARTHY, Yankee manager (right)**

he offered him a post on the New York City parole commission. The mayor reasoned that the famous Gehrig might be an inspiration to the city's wayward youngsters in need of rehabilitation.

After some reluctance because he didn't feel he was qualified for the position, Gehrig accepted and delved into books on criminology, psychology, and sociology with the same dedication and enthusiasm that he had played baseball. The pay for his new job was $5,700 a year; not a meager stipend at the time, but only a few dollars more than Gehrig's share of the 1939 World Series proceeds.

Gehrig remained with the Yankees for the rest of the 1939 season, traveling with the team and holding his title of team captain, even though his playing days were over. While the Yankees were beating the Cincinnati Reds in the World Series, Gehrig was becoming acquainted with New York mayor Fiorello LaGuardia, who was so impressed with Gehrig's intelligence and tenacity that

Gehrig earned the reputation of a thoughtful man in his new role. He seemed inclined to give many a second chance and was never excessively punitive. "We must play fair with these fellows," he said. "But we must also consider the rights of the taxpayers and our duties toward them. We don't want anyone in jail who can make good."

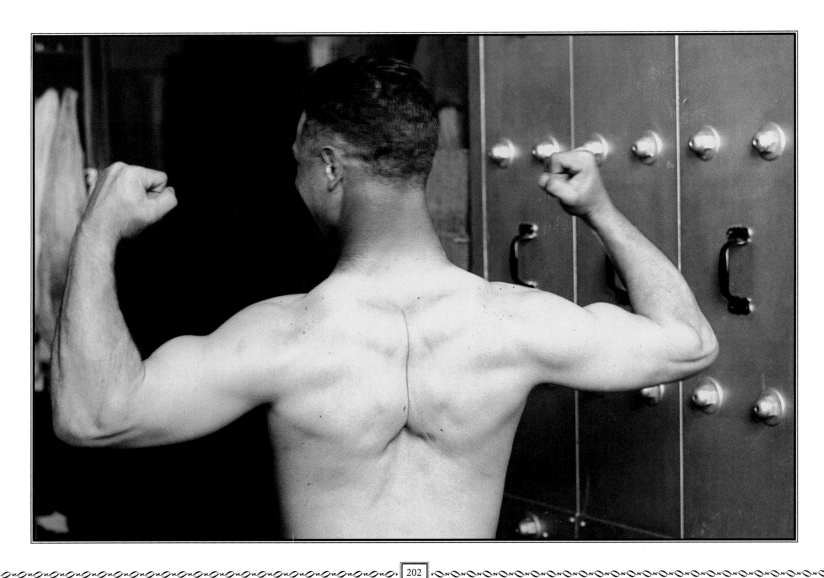

One person who failed to gain Gehrig's compassion was 19-year-old Rocco Barbella; a swaggering hoodlum who had been incarcerated on a statutory rape charge. Gehrig studied Barbella's case conscientiously, and it was clear to him that Barbella had caused his mother considerable grief. This weighed heavily on Gehrig, whose loyalty and lifetime devotion to his mother was legendary. Gehrig's decision was swift: Barbella was to be returned to reform school. As he was taken away, the enraged Barbella shouted at Gehrig that he was a "bastard." Years later, Barbella became Rocky Graziano, a hugely successful and popular middleweight boxing champion, and he credited Gehrig for helping "to straighten me out."

By the spring of 1941 Gehrig's relentless disease had destroyed his body to the point where he could no longer perform his parole board assignment satisfactorily. Eleanor had been his chauffeur, driving him every morning to his office in lower Manhattan. His legs, once sturdy and fleet enough that he stole home 15 times in the major leagues, could no longer bear his weight, and his trembling fingers could not properly sign documents. Yet his mind remained active and attentive. Neurologists who have treated this incurable disease say that for the victim it is like attending his own funeral.

On June 2, 1941, 17 days before his 38th birthday, Gehrig died in his sleep at home. It had been a little more than two years since his condition had been diagnosed at the Mayo Clinic. President Franklin D. Roosevelt, himself a survivor of polio and a man with a fondness for baseball, sent flowers. LaGuardia ordered that all New York City flags be flown at half-mast. At Gehrig's funeral, his longtime on-the-road roommate with the Yankees, catcher Bill Dickey, succinctly summed up the feelings of those who had known Gehrig. "Lou didn't need tributes from anyone," Dickey said. "His life and the way he lived were tribute enough; he just went out and did his job every day."

"Lou was the kind of boy that if you had a son, he's the kind of person you would like your son to be."
— **SAM JONES**, teammate

"I'm not a headline guy. I know that as long as I was following Ruth to the plate I could have stood on my head and no one would have known the difference."
LOU GEHRIG

TRIPLE CROWN · AMERICAN LEAGUE ·
HR 49
RBI 165
AVG. .363
1936

• • •

What were the sources of Gehrig's strength of character? As author Donald Honig wrote, "He was as unvarying and ongoing as a railroad track." Perhaps that did not make Gehrig an appealing figure to many. Yet it was his unwavering commitment as a husband, patriot, team player, and son that steeled him as a person of rare integrity. Always respectful and never particularly assertive, Gehrig nevertheless quietly defied the prejudice of his era by taking a stand for the right of African-Americans to play Major League Baseball. Gehrig once thanked Detroit Tigers catcher Birdie Tebbetts for having gotten in a few well-aimed punches at Ben Chapman. Gehrig and Chapman had been teammates for seven years, and Gehrig regarded Chapman as a bigot.

"Would you fight him again?" Gehrig asked Tebbetts.

"Yes, sir," Tebbetts responded. "I would."

"Well, if you ever do, and you land a couple of good punches, I'll buy you the best suit you'll ever own," Gehrig said.

This exchange, recounted by the late Tebbetts in his autobiography, casts Gehrig in a different mold than we had come to expect. But it shows that he was not impassive or incapable of honest emotion. Gehrig simply did not often reveal this side of his personality.

There is no doubt that Gehrig derived much of his temperament from his dominating mother; a wife who appreciated and respected his qualities of mind and heart; and from two strong-willed, manipulative managers, Miller Huggins and Joe McCarthy, both of whom relied heavily on Gehrig's stolid persona.

Gehrig's legacy must be judged by the totality of his 38 years, not just by his accumulation of batting and fielding statistics, as remarkable as they may be. He was constantly nagged by feelings of insecurity — a New York writer once said that Gehrig had confided that each time he made a hit or a home run he was convinced it would be his last — yet his talent and strong fiber saw him through remarkably well. He believed in always striving to do his best, which made him a commanding presence on and off the baseball field. And when it came time to die, harsh as the circumstances were, he departed life with exemplary grace. Should anyone have expected less?

To call Gehrig a ballplayer would be to sell him considerably short. Columbia University well understands that he transcended the field of play. Gehrig is the only athlete included in Columbia's pantheon of "Living Legacies," an elite group selected as part of the school's celebration of its 250th anniversary, in 2004. There he is, the solid man himself, the immortal Iron Horse, among the scientists, the philosophers, the poets, the Nobel Prize winners, the authors, the teachers, the songwriters, the warriors, the educators. And Gehrig is probably the one being asked for his autograph.

Lou Gehrig with his mother, Christina.

Save perhaps for Willie Keeler and late-1800s pitcher Mickey Welch, Lou Gehrig was the first New Yorker to star for a New York baseball team since the game went professional after the Civil War.

Babe Ruth was from Baltimore. Christy Mathewson, the idol of the Giants, was from Pennsylvania, as was John Ward, the Giants' 1880s superstar. Keeler, born and raised in Brooklyn, gained most of his fame playing for the Baltimore Orioles, although he also had good seasons with the Dodgers and the Yankees. Welch, from Brooklyn, won 238 games for the Giants. John McGraw of upstate Truxton, the Giants' manager for 30 years, was all but done as a player when he left the Orioles.

As a New York homegrown hero, Gehrig has never been truly replaced. Phil Rizzuto and Whitey Ford are New Yorkers, and both are in the Hall of Fame, but neither would claim to be in a league with Gehrig.

Gehrig was the Yankees' captain for many years, and for many New Yorkers that title went into the grave with the Iron Horse in 1941. It wasn't until the 1970s that the Yankees again named a captain, a catcher from Ohio named Thurman Munson.

★

"No other club could afford to give the amount the Yankees have paid for him,

AND I DO NOT MIND SAYING I THINK THEY ARE TAKING A GAMBLE.

The Boston club can now go into the market and buy other players and have a stronger
and better team than if Ruth had remained with us."

— HARRY FRAZEE, Red Sox owner, when Ruth's sale to the Yankees was announced on January 3, 1920

Major League Baseball's integrity was seriously compromised in 1919, when some members of the Chicago White Sox conspired with gamblers and threw the World Series. The plot was unraveled in a courtroom drama the following year, and disbelieving fans expressed betrayal and outrage. Some swore off the game forever; others demanded to know why they should ever again take baseball seriously. As the game's leadership speculated on how badly baseball had been damaged and whether it could thrive again, little did they know that the seeds of recovery were being sown.

JANUARY 3, 1920

BABE RUTH
Leaves the Red Sox for the Yankees

NEW YORK, NY
NEW YORK YANKEES
AMERICAN LEAGUE

On the day after Christmas, in 1919, Harry Frazee unwittingly saved baseball. Frazee's intentions were not so pure when he arranged a clandestine meeting that day with the principals of the New York Yankees, whose office was within shouting distance of his own in New York's theater district. Frazee, owner of the Boston Red Sox — baseball's most successful team over the first two decades of the 20th century; winners of five of the first 15 World Series — had two problems: mounting debt and a charismatic, pigeon-toed slugger who was demanding that his salary be doubled.

Within hours Frazee had signed over Babe Ruth's contract to the Yankees in exchange for $125,000 in cash and a $300,000 loan with Fenway Park as collateral. (The deal wasn't announced until January 3, 1920.) The cash was twice what any player had fetched previously in a sale, but it would prove to be baseball's greatest bargain. Ruth was the best left-handed pitcher of the era and so accomplished a hitter that the Red Sox had taken to using him in the outfield when he wasn't pitching. Upon arriving in New York, he succeeded in getting his salary doubled to $20,000, then took on a larger-than-life status, booming home runs at a stunning clip and living equally large off the field. Fans forgave baseball its transgressions and returned to ball-

parks in droves to see the Babe, who became one of the defining symbols of the Roaring '20s. In 1920 the Yankees became the first team to surpass 1 million in home attendance, and within a few years the Yankees were the most powerful and famous team in baseball, representing the most powerful and influential city in the world.

Ruth's role in luring fans back to baseball cannot be overestimated. Performing at a level above his peers, which has never been matched by any athlete in any sport — and likely never will be — he was an irresistible attraction. Consider the following: Ruth hit 54 home runs in his first season with the Yankees, more than the total of any team except his own and the Philadelphia Phillies; when he hit his 700th homer, no one else had hit even 300; and when he died in 1948, he held 56 Major League Baseball records.

As for Frazee, he remains a reviled figure in New England lore for his role in shifting baseball's balance of baseball power from Boston to New York. The Red Sox trail the Yankees 26-0 in World Series titles since Ruth moved south. The Babe's legend was growing to mythic proportions in New York, when one day Frazee hailed a Boston taxi for a ride to Fenway Park. Upon learning the identity of his passenger, the cabbie took a swing for all of New England. He dropped Frazee with one punch.

America never has been riveted to baseball quite like it was for two months in the summer of 1941. It was an unsettling time in the world, the uneasy calm before the storm. Hitler and the Nazis ruled Germany and were plotting to take the rest of Europe. The Japanese were the silent enemy across the Pacific. President Roosevelt challenged Congress to prepare for national defense. The American public needed respite from the grim news of the real world and found it in a sporting drama that became more gripping with each passing day. "Did he get a hit?" became the most popular refrain in the country.

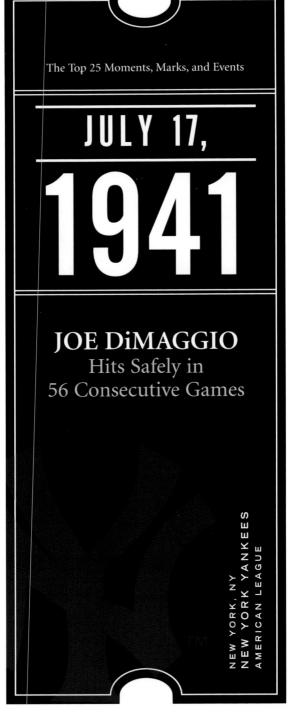

The Top 25 Moments, Marks, and Events

JULY 17, 1941

JOE DiMAGGIO
Hits Safely in 56 Consecutive Games

NEW YORK, NY
NEW YORK YANKEES
AMERICAN LEAGUE

Joe DiMaggio, the gifted and graceful center fielder of the mighty New York Yankees, was getting a hit every day. Starting on May 15, 1941, and winding through June and into July, DiMaggio hit safely in 56 consecutive games, a streak that many regard as the most remarkable achievement in sports history. More than 60 years have passed since DiMaggio's feat, and no one has come closer than 44 games. That's still 20 percent short, two weeks' worth of games.

DiMaggio's streak was the signature achievement of his sterling career, yet it served to measure him more as an American icon than a ballplayer, broadening an audience that was mesmerized by his excellence, elegance, and charisma. Except for Babe Ruth, no ballplayer has ever captivated and fascinated the American public like DiMaggio did. He was poised, confident, proud, humble, detached, seemingly above human frailties. He rarely showed emotion on the field, reacting to success and failure in the same stoic manner. Baseball contemporaries spoke of him in reverent tones. DiMaggio never disappointed his adoring public, yet he was a private man who left much unsaid,

which only added to the mystique about him.

DiMaggio was performing like a common ballplayer before he launched his 1941 hitting streak on May 15, batting only .306 after batting-championship seasons of .381 in 1939 and .352 in 1940. He had few close calls in the streak, needing a hit in his final at-bat only a few times. When pitchers became loath to throw DiMaggio strikes, Yankees manager Joe McCarthy allowed him to swing away on 3-and-0 counts. DiMaggio had a .408 batting average (91 for 223), 15 homers, and 55 RBIs during the streak, and after it ended he had a hit in each of the next 16 games, which meant that he had hit safely in 72 of 73 games.

The 56-game streak ended on July 17 in Cleveland, in front of a crowd of more than 67,000. Indians third baseman Ken Keltner twice robbed DiMaggio of hits. In his final at-bat, DiMaggio sent a hard grounder to the left side that kicked up late, but shortstop Lou Boudreau was able to snatch the ball near his shoulder and flip to second baseman Ray Mack in time to start a double play. Befitting his image, DiMaggio showed no emotion, taking the disappointment "like a man," as the saying went.

LONGEST
HITTING STREAKS

PLAYER	YEAR	TEAM	STREAK
Joe DiMaggio	1941	New York (AL)	56
Willie Keeler	1897	Baltimore (NL)	44
Pete Rose	1978	Cincinnati	44
Bill Dahlen	1894	Chicago (NL)	42
George Sisler	1922	St. Louis (AL)	41
Ty Cobb	1911	Detroit	40
Paul Molitor	1987	Milwaukee (AL)	39
Tommy Holmes	1945	Boston (NL)	37
Billy Hamilton	1894	Philadelphia (NL)	36
Fred Clarke	1895	Louisville (NL)	35
Ty Cobb	1917	Detroit	35
Luis Castillo	2002	Florida	35
George Sisler	1925	St. Louis (AL)	34
George McQuinn	1938	St. Louis (AL)	34
Dom DiMaggio	1949	Boston (AL)	34
Benito Santiago	1987	San Diego	34
George Davis	1893	New York (NL)	33
Hal Chase	1907	New York (AL)	33
Rogers Hornsby	1922	St. Louis (NL)	33
Heinie Manush	1933	Washington	33
Ed Delahanty	1899	Philadelphia (NL)	31
Nap Lajoie	1906	Cleveland	31
Sam Rice	1924	Washington	31
Willie Davis	1969	Los Angeles	31
Rico Carty	1970	Atlanta	31
Ken Landreaux	1980	Minnesota	31
Vladimir Guerrero	1999	Montreal	31
Cal McVey	1876	Chicago (NL)	30
Elmer Smith	1898	Cincinnati	30
Tris Speaker	1912	Boston (AL)	30
Goose Goslin	1934	Detroit	30
Stan Musial	1950	St. Louis (NL)	30
Ron LeFlore	1976	Detroit	30
George Brett	1980	Kansas City	30
Jerome Walton	1989	Chicago (NL)	30
Nomar Garciaparra	1997	Boston (AL)	30
Sandy Alomar Jr.	1997	Cleveland	30
Eric Davis	1998	Baltimore	30
Luis Gonzalez	1999	Arizona	30

When it came to hitting a baseball in the 1920s, every batter but one felt the fierce tug of gravity. Babe Ruth was on a different level, above the exosphere, his head poking through the ether, competing at a level of his own making. A new headline language of wallops and swats, clouts and blasts, booms and bams was invented to describe his feats.

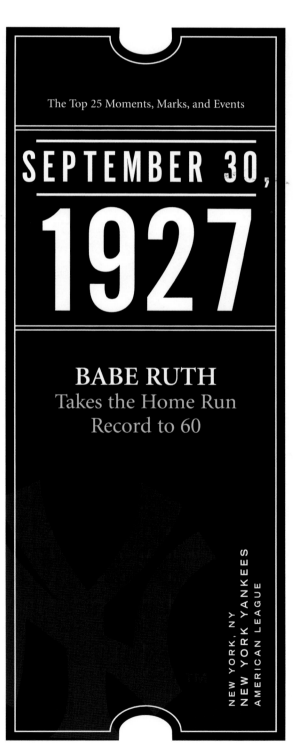

The Top 25 Moments, Marks, and Events

SEPTEMBER 30,
1927

BABE RUTH
Takes the Home Run Record to 60

NEW YORK, NY
NEW YORK YANKEES
AMERICAN LEAGUE

Ruth changed the game by taking quantum leap upon quantum leap over his peers. His 29 home runs in 1919 set an all-time record. His 54 the following year shattered the previous record that had defined baseball; the next man in line hit 19. Just one of 15 teams beside his Yankees hit as many as Ruth hit alone. The runner-up hit 24 in 1921 and couldn't see Ruth in the distance; he hit 59.

Few measured Ruth against others. Ruth was the Sultan of Swat and would forever be judged, trapped even, by the lofty standards he set in his mid-20s. Whatever the reasons — peerless fame, wealth (his income from baseball, motion pictures, vaudeville, barnstorming, syndicated ghost-written columns and endorsements was more than $250,000 in 1926) or insatiable indulgence — Ruth didn't approach his record of 59 for five years. How likely was it that Ruth, his girth swelling, would set a new standard in 1927?

Ruth was motivated by a painful loss to the St. Louis Cardinals in the 1926 Series. He tried to steal second base and was thrown out — the final

out of the Yankees' one-run loss in Game 7. "The only dumb play I ever saw you make," Yankees general manager Ed Barrow told Ruth.

Ruth had 43 homers when the 1927 calendar flipped to September, and he hit nine in the following two weeks. The Yankees clinched the pennant on September 13 and would win 110 games. One drama remained: Could Ruth hit eight home runs in the remaining 14 games? He tied his record of 59 by hitting two on the third-to-last day of the season.

The following game, on September 30, Ruth connected with a low, inside fastball from Tom Zachary of the Washington Senators and drove it just inside the right-field foul pole and halfway up the bleachers in Yankee Stadium. Hats and confetti rained onto the field. As Ruth went to right field for the next inning, he received a handkerchief salute from the bleacher denizens. Ruth playfully returned a series of military salutes.

In the clubhouse after the game, Ruth bellowed, "60 homers! — let's see some sonofabitch match that." Nobody did for 34 years.

There were 152,666 Major League Baseball games played in the 20th century, which means that 305,332 pitchers had an opportunity to achieve a perfect game — retiring all batters without any of them reaching base. Only 14 did.

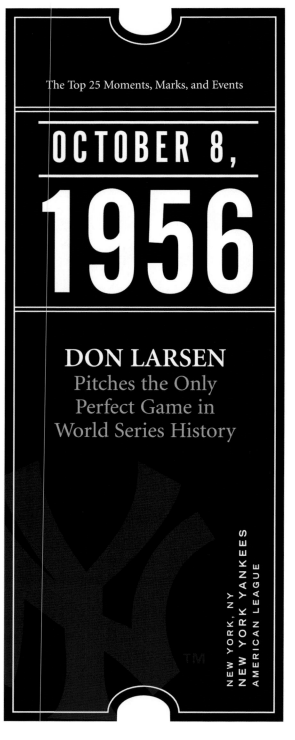

The Top 25 Moments, Marks, and Events

OCTOBER 8, 1956

DON LARSEN
Pitches the Only Perfect Game in World Series History

NEW YORK, NY
NEW YORK YANKEES
AMERICAN LEAGUE

On average, it happened once every seven years, once every 10,900 games. The list of 14 includes five Hall of Fame pitchers — but it does not include the likes of Christy Mathewson, Lefty Grove, Grover Cleveland Alexander, Warren Spahn, Walter Johnson, Roger Clemens, Steve Carlton, Whitey Ford, Nolan Ryan, Bob Gibson, or Tom Seaver. Those immortals on their greatest day were not as good as Don Larsen was on his greatest day. Even among the perfect-game pitchers, Larsen stands alone, for he was the only one to achieve the feat on baseball's biggest stage, the World Series. No one else, in fact, has ever pitched a no-hitter in the World Series or in the postseason series that now precede it.

Larsen pitched for 14 seasons in the major leagues and ended his career with a modest 81-91 record. One year he went 3-21. For every nine innings he pitched, he gave up an average of eight hits and four walks. Larsen clearly had talent, but he also had a reputation for losing focus and purpose on the mound. Teammates called him "Gooneybird." He was a voracious reader of comic books and had an affinity for the nightlife. After Larsen wrecked his car during the wee hours of the morning one spring, Yankees manager Casey Stengel deadpanned, "He must've been going to the post office to mail a letter."

If a New York Yankees pitcher was destined to achieve perfection in 1956, it surely would have been 19-game winner Whitey Ford, 18-game winner Johnny Kucks, or 16-game winner Tom Sturdivant. Larsen went 11-5 — it would prove to be the best season of his career — but he didn't make it through the second inning against the Brooklyn Dodgers in the second game of the World Series. Stengel sent out Larsen again for the fifth game on the afternoon of October 8.

No one, least of all Larsen, knows what came over him that day. He worked from a stretch position because he had lost confidence in his ability to pitch from a traditional windup. Inning by inning, batter by batter, he pitched with the skill, guile, and poise he had never known. Larsen sat down a lineup that included Jackie Robinson, Pee Wee Reese, Duke Snider, and Roy Campanella, all Hall of Fame–bound players. He went to a ball-three count only once, and the Yankees made only three plays behind him that were considered above the norm.

For two hours and six minutes, the 27-year-old Larsen practiced the craft of pitching better than almost anyone ever had. When it was over, the Yankees had a 2-0 victory and the tall, broad-shouldered Larsen had Yogi Berra in his arms, a celebratory embrace that is one of the most lasting sports images of the era. The next year, the perfect pitcher became Don Larsen again, a condition he could live with because he had proved there is a cure: Anything was possible.

Here is the Brooklyn Dodgers lineup that Don Larsen faced on October 8, 1956, and their statistics for the regular season. Reese, Snider, Robinson, and Campanella are in the Hall of Fame.

PLAYER	POS	G	HR	RBI	SB	BA	PLAYER	POS	G	HR	RBI	SB	BA
Junior Gilliam	2B	153	6	43	21	.300	Sandy Amoros	LF	114	16	58	3	.260
Pee Wee Reese	SS	147	9	46	13	.257	Carl Furillo	RF	149	21	83	1	.289
Duke Snider	CF	151	43	101	3	.292	Roy Campanella	C	124	20	73	1	.219
Jackie Robinson	3B	117	10	43	12	.275	Sal Maglie	P	28	0	2	0	.129
Gil Hodges	1B	153	32	87	3	.265	Dale Mitchell	PH	57	0	7	0	.204

Roger Maris arrived in Keokuk, Iowa, during the summer of 1954, climbing the minor-league ladder. Keokuk manager Jo-Jo White watched the strapping, young left-handed batter hitting the ball to all fields and quickly interrupted. "Look, boy," White bellowed, "you're not a singles hitter. You're big and you've got power. Pull that ball to right field and see what happens."

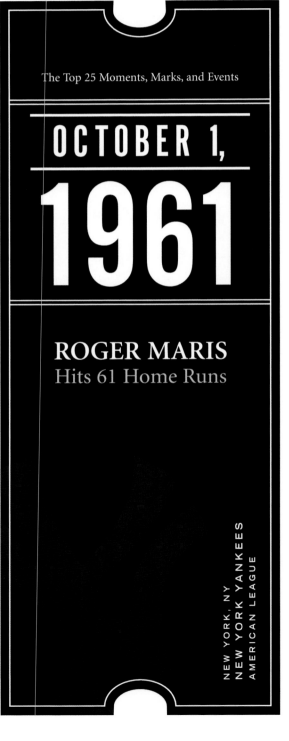

The Top 25 Moments, Marks, and Events

OCTOBER 1,
1961

ROGER MARIS
Hits 61 Home Runs

NEW YORK, NY
NEW YORK YANKEES
AMERICAN LEAGUE

W hite's sage advice would carry Maris to unprecedented heights in the game — and also bring him unwarranted pain and revilement.

No other ballplayer has ever pulled the ball quite as effectively and efficiently as Maris did during the 1961 season. He had joined the New York Yankees the previous season and proved to be a fine player. Maris played with a burning intensity, was a superb right fielder with an exceptionally strong arm, and rarely made a mistake while running the bases. But his greatest attribute was a quick pull swing with a slight uppercut that was ideal for Yankee Stadium, where the right field bleachers sat little more than 300 feet from home plate. Few of Maris' home runs traveled as far as 400 feet; most dropped into the early rows of seats in the lower deck of the Stadium.

The 1961 season promised to be an offensive awakening, especially in the American League, which had new teams in Los Angeles and Washington, D.C., and with them at least 20 pitchers who otherwise wouldn't be considered major league quality. In addition, the schedule had been extended from 154 to 162 games. No one, though, expected an assault on the most hallowed record in sport: Babe Ruth's 60 home runs in a season. Maris and his more celebrated teammate, Mickey Mantle, took up the chase, and both were still on pace for the record in late August.

Mantle dropped out in September because of a hip injury, leaving Maris to go it alone. The public and press had been chilly to Maris' mounting home run total, all along favoring Mantle, a larger-than-life and charismatic player in the great tradition of Yankees legends. Once Maris became the only threat to Ruth, the environment about him was charged with hostility and even hatred. The relentless pressure caused his hair to fall out in clumps and turned his personality sour. The career .260 hitter found solace only in the batter's box, where he could slip into the one-on-one battle with a pitcher and erase everything else from his consciousness.

The homers kept coming. On October 1, the final day of the season, the battle-weary Maris connected with a 2-and-0 fastball from Tracy Stallard of the Boston Red Sox and dropped it some 340 feet into the right field seats at Yankee Stadium for his 61st homer. The crowd that day was a mere 23,154, a third of the Stadium's capacity. Baseball almost seemed ashamed of Maris' feat. Commissioner Ford Frick had decreed that Maris would have to set the record in 154 games for it to be official, and Yankees management declined to promote Maris' chase — all in deference to the godlike Ruth, who had held the season home run record for 42 years.

Maris was the first to reach 60 homers in 34 years. And it would be 37 years before both Mark McGwire and Sammy Sosa surpassed Maris' record in 1998.

BEST TO NEXT

Roger Maris' second-best home run total was 39. The following list shows players who had the greatest difference between their best and second-best home run seasons.

PLAYER	BEST	SECOND BEST	DIFF.
Brady Anderson	50 (1996)	24 (1999)	26
Luis Gonzalez	57 (2001)	31 (2000)	26
Richard Hidalgo	44 (2000)	19 (2001)	25
Davey Johnson	43 (1973)	18 (1971)	25
Barry Bonds	73 (2001)	49 (2000)	24
Roger Maris	61 (1961)	39 (1960)	22
Alfonso Soriano	39 (2002)	18 (2001)	21
Joe Charboneau	23 (1980)	4 (1981)	19
Ken Hunt	25 (1961)	6 (1963)	19
Terry Steinbach	35 (1996)	16 (1987)	19
Willard Marshall	36 (1947)	17 (1953)	19
Buzz Arlett	18 (1931)	————	18
Bob Cerv	38 (1958)	20 (1959)	18
Jim Baxes	17 (1959)	————	17
Jay Bell	38 (1999)	21 (1997)	17
Andre Dawson	49 (1987)	32 (1983)	17
Hack Wilson	56 (1930)	39 (1929)	17

GEHRIG'S FAREWELL SPEECH

" FOR THE PAST TWO WEEKS YOU HAVE BEEN READING ABOUT A BAD BREAK.
BUT TODAY I CONSIDER MYSELF THE LUCKIEST MAN ON THE FACE OF THE EARTH.

I have been in ballparks for 17 years and have never received anything but kindness and
encouragement from you fans.

Look at these grand men. Which of you wouldn't consider it the highlight of his career just to associate with them for even one day?
Sure I'm lucky. Who wouldn't consider it an honor to have known Jacob Ruppert? Also, the builder of baseball's greatest empire,
Ed Barrow? To have spent six years with that wonderful little fellow, Miller Huggins? Then to have spent the next nine years with
the best manager in baseball today, Joe McCarthy?

Sure I'm lucky. When the New York Giants, a team you would give your right arm to beat, and vice versa,
sends you a gift — that's something. When everybody down to the groundskeepers and those boys in
white coats remember you with trophies — that's something.

When you have a wonderful mother-in-law who takes sides with you in squabbles with her own daughter — that's something.
When you have a father and a mother who work all their lives so you can have an education and build your body — it's a blessing.
When you have a wife who has been a tower of strength and shown more courage than you dreamed existed — that's the finest I know.

I MIGHT HAVE BEEN GIVEN A BAD BREAK,
BUT I'VE GOT AN AWFUL LOT TO LIVE FOR. THANK YOU. "

Few have personified the American Dream like Lou Gehrig did. The son of poor German immigrants, he grew up to be the star first baseman of his hometown New York Yankees, perhaps the best first baseman in history. No matter how rich and famous he became, Gehrig never failed to give his best every day.

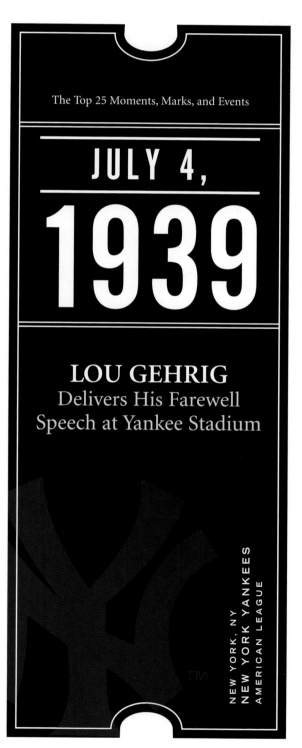

The Top 25 Moments, Marks, and Events

JULY 4, 1939

LOU GEHRIG
Delivers His Farewell Speech at Yankee Stadium

NEW YORK, NY
NEW YORK YANKEES
AMERICAN LEAGUE

For 14 years he was as regular as the postman, except the postman got Sunday off and Gehrig didn't. Through it all, he maintained a quiet dignity, never boasting or showing a crass side, never envious of the spotlight dominated by Babe Ruth, his more celebrated teammate. Ruth might be the best ballplayer in history, but he was not the captain of the Yankees. Gehrig was; he engendered that level of respect.

Gehrig's legend began when the Yankees used him as a pinch-hitter on June 1, 1925, and a day later he was playing at first base. The next time he missed a game was May 2, 1939. For 2,130 consecutive games, Gehrig's name appeared in the Yankees boxscore. He played through broken bones, back spasms, concussions, and illness. His hands were X-rayed late in his career, and doctors found 17 different fractures that had healed while Gehrig continued to play. In the history of professional sports, only Cal Ripken Jr. has played in more consecutive games than Gehrig had.

Gehrig was a big man for his era, about 6 feet tall, 200 pounds. Naturally strong, he had broad shoulders, a powerful back and massive thighs. Gehrig looked every bit the he-man in the double-breasted suit of the era and even better in the pinstriped uniform of the Yankees. His body, however,

began to betray him in spring training 1939. Balls that Gehrig hit right on the screws looped over the infield rather than soar out of the ballpark. His motor skills slipped; he had trouble tying his shoelaces and routine plays at first base required extraordinary effort from him. It got worse after the regular season started, and after eight games Gehrig took himself out of the lineup. He never would play again.

The big man went to the Mayo Clinic in June 1939 and came away with a grim diagnosis: amyotrophic lateral sclerosis, an incurable form of paralysis that destroys the central nervous system and has come to be known as "Lou Gehrig's Disease." He was 36, and he had two years to live.

The story could end right here, and Gehrig would be remembered as one of baseball's greatest treasures. Instead, the chapter that virtually every American has come to know was written on July 4, 1939, Lou Gehrig Appreciation Day at Yankee Stadium. The quiet man stood at home plate and in measured, heartfelt words delivered a message from his soul, the most famous address in baseball history. With dignity and grace, he told more than 60,000 spectators in the stadium and many thousands more listening on the radio: "Today I consider myself the luckiest man on the face of the earth."

"I must admit: when Reggie hit his third home run and I was sure nobody was looking,
I APPLAUDED IN MY GLOVE."

—STEVE GARVEY, after Game 6 of the 1977 World Series

The New York Yankees were staging a renaissance of their glorious past in the mid-1970s. Aided by the advent of the free-agent players' market and owner George Steinbrenner's largesse, the Yankees had a good enough team in place to win the American League pennant in 1976, for the first time in 12 years. But losing the World Series to the Cincinnati Reds in four games pushed the determined Steinbrenner to dig even deeper. He was the winning bidder for the services of Reggie Jackson, the ranking power hitter of the day, and the game's most flamboyant personality.

The Top 25 Moments, Marks, and Events

OCTOBER 18, 1977

REGGIE JACKSON
Slams 3 Home Runs
in Game 6 of the
'77 World Series

NEW YORK, NY
NEW YORK YANKEES
AMERICAN LEAGUE

Amid great fanfare and expectation, Jackson strode into a posh New York hotel on November 29, 1976, took a seat in a gilded chair, and signed what then was the most lucrative contract in baseball history: $2.9 million for five years. Never short on self-promotion, he remarked that he probably would have a candy bar named after him.

Jackson's adjustment to a Yankees team rife with seasoned veterans resentful of his celebrity and managed by the fiery Billy Martin proved to be a summer-long ordeal. Jackson certainly didn't endear himself to his new clubhouse when, prior to the season, he told a magazine writer, "I'm the straw that stirs the drink," adding that respected team captain Thurman Munson "thinks he can be the straw that stirs the drink, but he can only stir it bad."

Yet when they took the field, the Yankees managed to put aside their differences and perform as one. Jackson, most of all, relished the refuge he found four or five times a night when he strode to home plate and cocked his menacing bat. He achieved one of his best seasons — 32 home runs, 110 RBIs, 20 game-winning hits — and the Yankees again advanced to the World Series, this time against the Los Angeles Dodgers.

After five games, the Yankees held a 3-2 lead and Jackson had two home runs. As the teams prepared for Game 6 at Yankee Stadium on October 18, Jackson was a man possessed during batting practice, blasting pitch after pitch into the seats. "Save some of those for the game," said Willie Randolph. Jackson shot a glare at his teammate and said defiantly, "There are more where those came from." Were there ever. During the next three hours, Jackson put on the greatest show ever by a batter in the World Series. After walking in his first at-bat, he drilled home runs on the first pitch in each of his next three trips to the plate. The third home run was a majestic blast that soared like a rocket toward center field, cleared the fence, and bounced crazily among the black unoccupied seats — more than 450 feet from home plate. As Jackson circled the bases in his signature swaggering trot, the crowd of 56,407 was deafening in its "Reggie! Reggie! Reggie!" salute. Twenty minutes later, the Yankees clinched their first World Championship since 1962.

Jackson's five home runs — and fourth in four official at-bats going back to the eighth inning of Game 5 — is a record for a World Series. As great a player as he was, he rose to a higher level when performing in October on baseball's grandest stage. Jackson's batting average for his six World Series is 95 points better than his season average (.357 to .262) and his slugging average of .755 is a Series record.

The playoff game mirrored the 1978 season. The Boston Red Sox jumped ahead, seemed to be in control, fell behind, rallied, and fell short. New Yorkers witnessed the Yankees in a wholly unfamiliar role: the underdog. As much as the Yankees had achieved in 75 seasons — including winning 21 World Series — they had never made up so much ground chasing someone else.

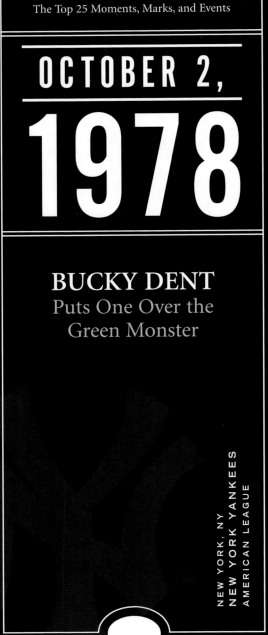

The Top 25 Moments, Marks, and Events

OCTOBER 2, 1978

BUCKY DENT
Puts One Over the Green Monster

NEW YORK, NY
NEW YORK YANKEES
AMERICAN LEAGUE

The American League pennant race appeared settled three weeks earlier, during a weekend gruesomely stamped the "Boston Massacre." No need for the exaggerating effects of time to make that story larger. The weekend assumed mythic dimensions the moment it happened. The Yankees entered Fenway Park, a den of fear and loathing for opposing pitchers, and cold-cocked the Red Sox four straight by a score of 42-9. After losing two in Yankee Stadium the following weekend, Boston was 2 1/2 games behind with nine to go.

This reversal was incredible. Boston had been 51-19 and held a 14-game lead on July 19. Following the All-Star break, the Sox lost 11 of 14, and half of their lead disappeared. Meanwhile, the Yankees, under the calming influence of manager Bob Lemon, who had replaced the volatile Billy Martin in late July, won 52 of their last 73 games. The Red Sox regrouped in time, won their final eight games, and pulled even.

In the winner-goes-on, loser-goes-home game on October 2, 1978, the Red Sox sent to the mound Mike Torrez, who had won two World Series games for the Yankees the previous year. Torrez took charge, holding a 2-0 lead into the seventh. It would have been 4-0 except that in the sixth inning, Yankees right fielder Lou Piniella, cheating toward the foul line on a hunch that pitcher Ron Guidry was tiring, snatched Fred Lynn's sizzling line drive before it could reach the right field corner.

Two Yankees reached base in the seventh, and then up came Bucky Dent, the ninth batter in the lineup. Torrez's fastball was much too true. Dent connected and the ball took flight toward the Green Monster in left field. "I didn't know it cleared the wall till I got past first," Dent said of his three-run homer that put the Yankees in charge 3-2.

With a runner on third base, Goose Gossage got the final out for the Yankees in the bottom of the ninth, paralyzing Carl Yastrzemski with a hard-boring fastball that Yaz meekly popped into the air. The final score was 5-4 — ending another chapter in the curse of the Red Sox, who had sold the mighty Babe Ruth to the Yankees in 1920 and were still being punished for such foolhardiness 58 years later.

"You know you dream about things like that when you're a kid.

WELL, MY DREAM CAME TRUE."

— BUCKY DENT

Lou Gehrig went about baseball with such unflagging persistence that he undersold his own magnificence. He was the immutable background rhythm that accentuated Babe Ruth's blare of trumpets.

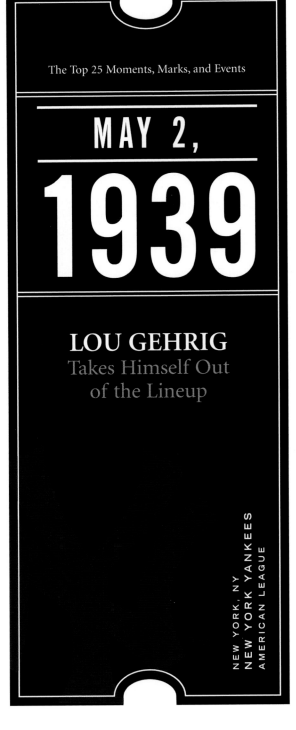

The Top 25 Moments, Marks, and Events

MAY 2, 1939

LOU GEHRIG
Takes Himself Out
of the Lineup

NEW YORK, NY
NEW YORK YANKEES
AMERICAN LEAGUE

Gehrig got his Iron Horse nickname from a superior locomotive of his time. That a 35-year-old man suddenly would lose the singular strength that was the foundation for his streak of consecutive games played was as unlikely as Sir Isaac Newton awakening to find that a propensity for math had deserted him between discovery of the second and third laws of motion. Yet it happened.

Forever second in notoriety, Gehrig joined a team that had won a World Series and whose celebrity was due to Ruth. Ruth and Gehrig would become the most formidable pair on the same team in baseball history, but there never was any doubt about who held the leading role and who was the supporting actor.

In a fabled 1927 season, the two staged a neck and neck race for the home run title. Ruth pulled away in September and prevailed, 60 to 47. In the forlorn words of one writer, "Gehrig was the one who hit all those homers the year Ruth broke the record." In the 1928 World Series, Gehrig swatted a then-record four homers; more often what is recalled is that Ruth hit three in the final game to seal the sweep of the St. Louis Cardinals.

While closing in on Everett Scott's record of 1,307 consecutive games in 1932, Gehrig became the first player in the 20th century to hit four home runs in a game. John McGraw resigned as the New York Giants manager that same day, so while McGraw made page one, Gehrig made the sports page. Ruth's two homers in the third game of the Series that year, including the famed called shot, rendered Gehrig's pair in the same game all but forgotten.

For one foreboding month in 1939, Gehrig got all the attention. He had played in every Yankees game from June 1, 1925, to April 30, 1939 — 2,130 consecutive games. But Gehrig was slumping, and when a teammate praised him for a routine play, Gehrig knew the end had come. On May 2, in the Book-Cadillac Hotel in Detroit, he told manager Joe McCarthy of his decision. "I'm going to bench myself," he said. McCarthy asked why. "For the good of the team, Joe," Gehrig said.

Wally Pipp, the player Gehrig replaced 14 years earlier and now a businessman, coincidentally was in the hotel that day. When the announcement that Gehrig wasn't playing in the lineup came over the public address in Detroit's Briggs Stadium, a crowd of 11,000 honored him with a two-minute ovation.

Gehrig's replacement was someone named Babe. Ellsworth "Babe" Dahlgren homered in New York's 22-2 rout of Detroit in that first game without Gehrig, who cried while sitting in the dugout that day. Gehrig never played again. He retired from baseball in June, following the disclosure that he had an illness that would kill him. The Iron Horse had come to a halt, but the Yankees rolled on uninterrupted, winning their fourth consecutive World Series in 1939.

On May 2, in the Book-Cadillac Hotel in Detroit, he told manager Joe McCarthy of his decision.
"I'M GOING TO BENCH MYSELF."

— LOU GEHRIG

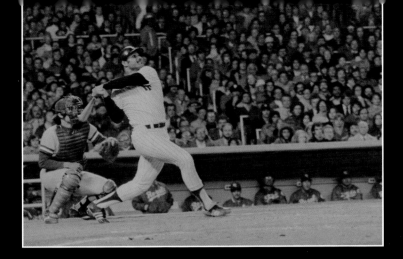

Chambliss dug in, connected on the first pitch from Mark Littell,
AND LIFTED A TANTALIZING FLY TO RIGHT FIELD.

A home run by Chris Chambliss, the Yankees' 1970s quiet man, didn't just win a game — it ended 12 years without a pennant. As the 1976 season approached, the Yankees were enduring their longest span without a pennant since the Highlanders-turned-Yankees went 18 years before finishing first for the first time in 1921.

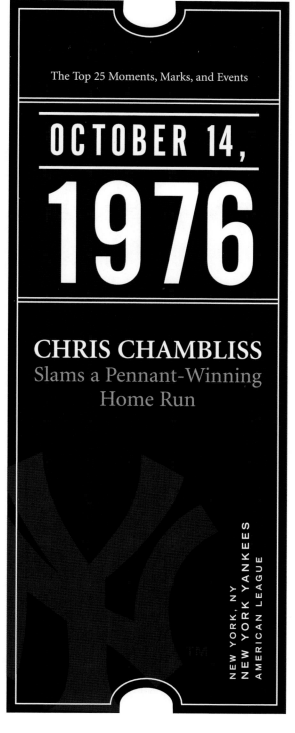

The Top 25 Moments, Marks, and Events

OCTOBER 14, 1976

CHRIS CHAMBLISS
Slams a Pennant-Winning Home Run

NEW YORK, NY
NEW YORK YANKEES
AMERICAN LEAGUE

Over the next 44 years they won 29 pennants and 20 World Series. If you rooted for the Yankees from 1921 through 1964, your team had a two-in-three chance of winning a pennant and a 45 percent chance of winning the World Series.

Then came the collapse. Sixth place in 1965, then 10th (the Yankees' first last-place finish since 1912), then ninth. The team's slump, captured by frames of tens of thousands of empty seats in their three-tiered stadium, mirrored Mickey Mantle's decline. The collapse lasted long past his retirement in 1969. By 1976 the team inhabited a refurbished Yankee Stadium, spiritually if not physically removed from the intimidating ghosts of the Ruth-Gehrig-Huggins monuments and cavernous, unforgiving expanses in center field and left-center.

The new park promised a new start. Only Roy White and Thurman Munson remained from 1970. General manager Gabe Paul had retooled the lineup, acquiring players from the Cleveland Indians (Chambliss, Graig Nettles, Oscar Gamble), California Angels (Mickey Rivers, Ed Figueroa, Rudy May), and Pittsburgh Pirates (Willie Randolph, Dock Ellis). Catfish Hunter had signed a landmark free agent contract in 1974. The new cast won 97 games and the American League East division in 1976.

Next up was a five-game series with the AL West champion Kansas City Royals for the pennant. The Yankees appeared to have control of the fifth game, but George Brett struck a three-run home run in the eighth inning and tied the score, 6-6. The suspense mounted as the Yankees came to bat in the bottom of the ninth, and the noisy crowd was pleading for a hero. Chambliss dug in, connected on the first pitch from Mark Littell, and lifted a tantalizing fly to right field. Al Cowens sped to the fence, leaped, and stabbed for the ball with his glove. The ball eluded him by several feet, dropping beyond the 385-foot marker in right-center field.

Fans swarmed the field, intercepting Chambliss as he circled the bases. He touched second with his hand, just before a fan took the base. Third base was gone, too. Engulfed in a sea of humanity, Chambliss lowered his shoulders and broke for safety. Two hours later, under police escort, he touched the spot where home plate had been. A long, lonely period in Yankees history had come to an end.

When you think of the greatness of a group without recalling a single individual, that is the essence of team play. The 1998 Yankees won 114 games, an American League record, breaking the previous mark of 111 set by Cleveland in 1954 (in 154 games). The Yankees competed less against 29 other teams and more against a lofty standard of their own making. People who have watched baseball for decades could not recall a team that played 162 games like it expected to win them all, at least not until they saw the 1998 Yankees.

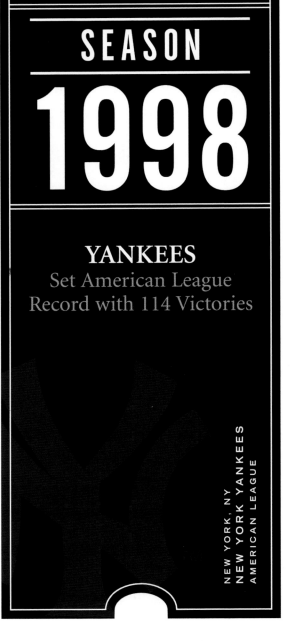

The Top 25 Moments, Marks, and Events

SEASON

1998

YANKEES
Set American League
Record with 114 Victories

NEW YORK, NY
NEW YORK YANKEES
AMERICAN LEAGUE

No one hit 30 home runs. Only one pitcher won 20 games. No one on the roster finished in the top five in doubles, triples, homers, RBIs, walks, or slugging percentage. In a season of team excellence, the only league leader was Bernie Williams, who won the batting title. This wasn't the 1927 Yankees, 1961 Yankees, or 1975 Reds pounding teams into submission with 38-ounce Louisville Sluggers. The 1998 Yankees played offense patiently, waiting for a favorable count to hit, waiting for walks, waiting for a mistake, waiting to make comebacks.

The strategy worked: They scored two runs more a game than they allowed. They were 20 games ahead in the standings by mid-August and won their 100th game on September 4, quicker than any other team in history.

Now immortalized, the club was constructed in a mixed way. David Wells, David Cone, Scott Brosius, Chuck Knoblauch, Tino Martinez, Jeff Nelson, Paul O'Neill, Tim Raines, Chad Curtis, Hideki Irabu, and Luis Sojo arrived in trades. Mike

Stanton and Chili Davis were signed as free agents. Williams, Ramiro Mendoza, Mariano Rivera, Derek Jeter, Shane Spencer, Jorge Posada, and Andy Pettitte were products of the Yankees player-development system. Orlando "El Duque" Hernandez arrived from Cuba on a rickety 19-foot boat.

Twice the Yankees were tested. After they started with a 1-4 record, nervousness seeped into the clubhouse. Who might be traded or lose his job if this Rolls Royce continued to sputter? The question had hardly been uttered when they won eight in a row, then six consecutive, then eight again. By the All-Star break, the Yankees were 61-20.

The next test came in the Championship Series. Down two games to one against the Cleveland Indians, they faced the sobering thought that 114 victories might lead to nothing. Hernandez took the ball at Jacobs Field and overwhelmed the Indians. The Yankees never lost again, finishing off Cleveland and sweeping the San Diego Padres in the World Series. "We weren't Ruth, Gehrig, and DiMaggio — but this is the ultimate team," Cone said.

"We weren't Ruth, Gehrig, and DiMaggio — BUT THIS IS THE ULTIMATE TEAM."

— DAVID CONE

Derek Jeter, Tino Martinez, Mariano Rivera,
and the rest of the 1998 Yankees kept their
game-faces intense.

Major League Triple Crown Winners

PLAYER	YEAR	AVG.	HR	RBI
Mickey Mantle New York Yankees	1956	.353	52	130
Ted Williams Boston Red Sox	1942	.356	36	137
Lou Gehrig New York Yankees	1934	.363	49	165
Rogers Hornsby St. Louis Cardinals	1925	.403	39	143
Ty Cobb Detroit Tigers	1909	.377	39	107

Mickey Mantle's baseball career reached full bloom in 1956. He was just 24, a boy growing into a man. He ran for short bursts like an Olympic sprinter, and he had the strength of Hercules, driving baseballs to distances that amazed both his peers and his fans.

The Top 25 Moments, Marks, and Events

SEPTEMBER
1956

MICKEY MANTLE
Soars to His Greatest Heights, Leading the Major League in Batting Average, Home Runs, and RBIs

NEW YORK, NY
NEW YORK YANKEES
AMERICAN LEAGUE

A s the 1956 season coursed onward, it became apparent that the star center fielder of the New York Yankees was playing at a level above the crowd. When it was over, Mantle not only led the American League in batting average, home runs, and RBIs, but he surpassed everyone in the National League as well. Mantle batted .353 with 52 home runs and 130 RBIs. The only other players who have led the major leagues in all three categories are Ty Cobb in 1909, Rogers Hornsby in 1922, Lou Gehrig in 1934, and Ted Williams in 1942.

Williams challenged Mantle in the batting race, but was undone by Yankees pitchers, who limited him to 11 hits in 56 at-bats. Al Kaline fell two short of Mantle in the RBIs race. Duke Snider, the closest challenger in home runs, was nine behind Mantle, who became just the seventh player in history to reach the 50-homer level.

Mantle's legend took on greater proportions on a regular basis in 1956. His greatest day of the season — perhaps the greatest day of his career — came in a May doubleheader against the

Washington Senators. In the first game, he drove a ball to right field that crashed off the facade atop the third deck, failing by less than three feet to become the only ball ever hit fair out of Yankee Stadium — "The best ball I ever hit left-handed," a self-satisfied Mantle said later. Engineers estimated the ball would have traveled 550 to 600 feet had its flight not been interrupted. In the second game, he sent a drive to the base of the scoreboard in the right-center field bleachers, about 465 feet from home plate. In addition to the majestic blasts, the fleet and nimble Mantle dropped down a drag bunt that day and easily was safe at first — one of 12 drag bunts he executed that season.

His signature season continued into October. In Game 5 of the World Series, Mantle hit a home run and also got on his horse and pulled down a long drive by Gil Hodges in left-center field. All in a day's work for Mantle, but his labor on that day helped Yankees pitcher Don Larsen achieve the only perfect game in World Series history. Mantle hit three home runs in the Series, which the Yankees won in seven games against the Brooklyn Dodgers.

A crowd of more than 74,217 — another 15,000 were turned away by the fire department — began flowing into Yankee Stadium on April 18, 1923, three hours before the 3:30 start. It was the largest gathering ever to watch a major league game. Some arrived by car; most spent a nickel for subway fare.

The Top 25 Moments, Marks, and Events

APRIL 18, 1923

YANKEE STADIUM
Opens to Rave Reviews

NEW YORK, NY
NEW YORK YANKEES
AMERICAN LEAGUE

They braved a raw, breezy day to behold the grand new home of New York's American League baseball team, a triple-tiered arena shaped like a horseshoe. The upper deck was trimmed with a 16-foot copper frieze, a distinctive look that would become the Stadium's signature.

There was no arena in the world to compare to the brand new Yankee Stadium. The image of such a grand edifice, towering just off the Harlem River and visible for miles, signaled that baseball was in the chips and the Yankees were at the forefront. Babe Ruth surveyed his new digs that day and remarked, "Some ballyard, huh?"

Ruth's three-run home run christened the park, propelled the Yankees to a 4-1 victory and launched the team's golden age. The Yankees won half of the next 40 World Series, maintaining excellence over three distinct eras.

Yankee Stadium was built on 11 acres of farmland purchased for $600,000 by Colonel Jacob Ruppert, an owner of the team. The Yankees needed a place of their own because they no longer were welcome tenants at the Polo Grounds, home of the National League's New York Giants. Since the arrival of Ruth in 1920, the Yankees had steadily become the more popular team and drew bigger crowds than the Giants in the Giants' own park. Caving to the demands of his manager, John McGraw, Giants owner Charles Stoneham evicted the Yankees. "The Yankees will have to build a park in Queens or some other out-of-the-way place," McGraw said. "Let them go away and wither on the vine."

They didn't go far. Yankee Stadium was built in the Bronx, just across the Harlem River from the Polo Grounds in northern Manhattan. The *New York Times* described the new stadium as "a skyscraper among ballparks." Fred Leib, a sportswriter of the day, was the first to call the place, "The House That Ruth Built."

As Ruth changed the look of the game by hitting the ball higher and farther than anyone else, the turnstiles spun faster at Yankee Stadium than in any other ballpark. The Yankees soon were attracting a million paying customers annually. Most teams didn't draw half of that.

Colonel Ruppert threw a party at the downtown Hotel Commodore to celebrate the opening of Yankee Stadium and crowed, "This is a wonderful occasion. I now have baseball's greatest park, baseball's greatest players and baseball's greatest team." He was right on all counts.

The most impressive thing about Babe Ruth's called shot in the 1932 World Series was that he was on the downslope of his career when he pulled it off. The Wrigley Field atmosphere that day was charged with hostility. Moments before Ruth connected, a storm of vitriol flowed from both dugouts. The torrent of emotion that fueled both the Chicago Cubs and the Yankees was about to boil over.

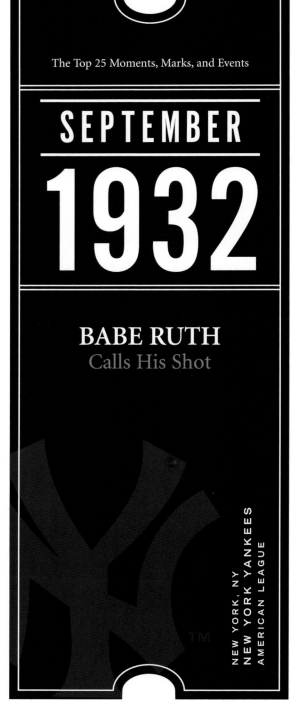

The Top 25 Moments, Marks, and Events

SEPTEMBER

1932

BABE RUTH
Calls His Shot

NEW YORK, NY
NEW YORK YANKEES
AMERICAN LEAGUE

The pot started simmering during the first two games of the Series in New York. The Cubs had acquired shortstop Mark Koenig, formerly a Yankee, from the Pacific Coast League in August. Koenig played brilliantly down the stretch, yet the Cubs players voted to award him only a half-share of their World Series loot. The Yankees were livid. As the Cubs filed through the Yankees dugout to their side prior to the first game, Ruth lit into them. "Hey, you lousy bunch of cheapskates," Babe boomed. "Why do you associate with a bunch of bums like that, Mark?" After Ruth knocked nine balls into the Wrigley bleachers prior to Game 3, he sneered, "I'd play for half my salary if I could hit in this dump all my life."

The Cubs, in turn, harassed Ruth mercilessly, calling the 37-year-old "Grandpops" and making jokes about his ballooning girth. Ruth always had let the ribbing of opponents slide off his back. Even remarks from players like Ty Cobb didn't get to him. He laughed at everyone, but mostly at himself.

But this was different. This was not the Ruth of five years previous who after launching his 60th home run crowed, "Let's see some sonofabitch match that." By anyone else's standards, Ruth was still a force. But a leg injury and appendicitis had

laid him up for 21 games during the season, and for the first time in seven seasons he was not the American League home run king, his 41 far behind leader Jimmie Foxx's 58. The Chicago newspapers hit below the belt, one carrying this commentary on the Cubs' opponent in the Series: "One of their outfielders is a fat, elderly party who must wear corsets to avoid immodest jiggling, and cannot waddle for fly balls, nor stoop for grounders."

The taunts continued. "By the middle of the third game, it had got just plain brutal," said Yankees third baseman, Joe Sewell. "I'd never known there were so many cuss words or so many ways of stringing them together." Standing at home plate and in the eye of the storm, Ruth audaciously held up two fingers to indicate the number of strikes, knowing that pitcher Charlie Root would have to be man enough to throw near the plate to get a third one. "I'm going to hit the next pitch down your goddamned throat," Ruth roared.

Root accepted the challenge, and Ruth drove a bent offering into the center field bleachers, the ball traveling 436 feet before landing. The game's most outsized player and beloved personality, the mythmaker without peer, had outdone his own standards for drama.

After Ruth knocked nine balls into the Wrigley bleachers prior to Game 3, he sneered,
"I'D PLAY FOR HALF MY SALARY IF I COULD HIT IN THIS DUMP ALL MY LIFE."

Jack Chesbro, whose fame followed the unpredictable path of his spitball, won 41 games in 1904 for the New York Highlanders, who would come to be known as the Yankees. No one had a clue that the 30-year-old right-hander had set a record that would hold up for the rest of the 20th century and beyond.

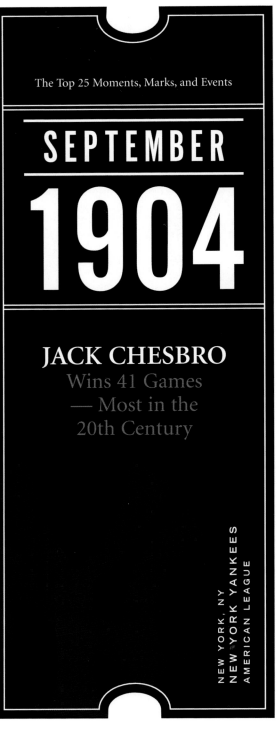

The Top 25 Moments, Marks, and Events

SEPTEMBER
1904

JACK CHESBRO
Wins 41 Games
— Most in the
20th Century

NEW YORK, NY
NEW YORK YANKEES
AMERICAN LEAGUE

Chesbro completed 48 of his 51 starts in 1904, both records that still stand. He struck out 239, a franchise record until Ron Guidry broke it in 1978.

Chesbro was known as "Happy Jack," a nickname he picked up in his 20s while working as an attendant at a Middletown, New York mental hospital and pitching for the hospital baseball team. The 5-foot-9-inch, 195-pound pitcher with an omnipresent smile arrived in New York in 1903, at the same time as the Highlanders, who had moved from Baltimore. Chesbro had gone 28-6 for the Pittsburgh Pirates in 1902 and was lured by the promise of more pay to jump to the fledgling American League.

He also was among the hardest workers in an era when pitchers routinely worked upward of 300 innings a season. He reached that level four times, peaking at an astronomical 454 in 1904.

Wee Willie Keeler's hitting and Chesbro's pitching in 1904 thrust the Highlanders into the franchise's first pennant race. Until Chesbro was knocked out of a game in August, he had pitched 30 consecutive complete games. On the final day of the season, the Highlanders trailed the Boston Pilgrims by 1 1/2 games, and, as fate would have it, the teams were playing a doubleheader at Hilltop Park, the New York team's first home.

The score was tied 2-2 in the first game and Boston had a runner at third base with two outs in the ninth inning. Chesbro got two strikes on the batter, then unleashed a spitball that sailed over the catcher's head. The man on third raced home with the winning run, and Boston had the pennant. The Highlanders would not be a serious pennant contender again until acquiring Babe Ruth from that same Boston team in 1920.

Chesbro had several good years for the Highlanders after 1904, but they paled in comparison to his 41-12 season. He pitched until 1909 and was constantly reminded of the wild pitch he threw that eliminated the Highlanders from their first pennant race.

Chesbro died in 1931 at age 57. His widow lobbied for years to have the wild pitch officially changed to a passed ball, but her efforts were unsuccessful.

PLAYER, TEAM	YEAR	RECORD	PLAYER, TEAM	YEAR	RECORD
Jack Chesbro, New York Highlanders	1904	41-12	Joe Wood, Boston Red Sox	1912	34-5
Ed Walsh, Chicago White Sox	1908	40-15	Cy Young, Boston Red Sox	1901	33-10
Christy Mathewson, New York Giants	1908	37-11	Christy Mathewson, New York Giants	1904	33-12
Walter Johnson, Washington Senators	1913	36-7	Walter Johnson, Washington Senators	1912	33-12
Joe McGinnity, New York Giants	1904	35-8	Pete Alexander, Philadelphia Phillies	1916	33-12

The weather was cool and misty. Babe Ruth, dressed in his old Yankees uniform with the familiar No. 3 on the back, sat in a chair in the tunnel behind the visitors' dugout at Yankee Stadium, a camelhair overcoat draped on his shoulders. When the rain subsided, he rose wearily and began his final walk onto the famous field.

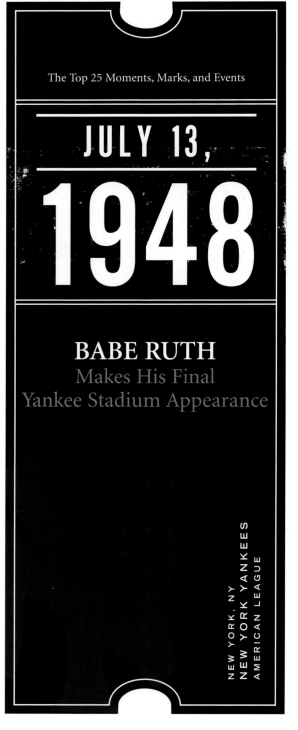

The Top 25 Moments, Marks, and Events

JULY 13,

1948

BABE RUTH
Makes His Final Yankee Stadium Appearance

NEW YORK, NY
NEW YORK YANKEES
AMERICAN LEAGUE

The Yankees had marked Sunday, June 13, 1948, to celebrate the 25th year of Yankee Stadium. The crowning moment of the festivities would be the announcement that Ruth's uniform number was to be retired, never again to be worn by a player in Yankees pinstripes. Great Yankees past and present were there, and the grand ballpark had almost 50,000 seats filled. The mood, however, was somber, for everyone knew that the Babe was seriously ill. Ruth's once broad shoulders were sloped and narrow, and his cheeks that had once swelled to the size of a pumpkin with a boyish grin were now gaunt.

As the P.A. announcer introduced Ruth to a growing ovation, Bob Feller pushed a bat into Ruth's hands as the Babe struggled up the dugout steps. Feller, who was pitching for the Cleveland Indians that day against the Yankees, thought Ruth might use the bat for support. Ruth doffed his cap as he took the field. "He walked out into that cauldron of sound he must have known better than any other man," said sportswriter W.C. Heinz.

Ruth stopped along the third base line. Photographer Nat Fein of the *New York Herald Tribune*, unable to get in front of Ruth, instead snapped a photo from behind at an angle that caught the Babe in a dignified pose below the majestic sweep of the distinctive Stadium facade. It remains one of the most famous pictures in sports history.

The large crowd roared its gratitude, over and over. Will Harridge, president of the American League, conducted the No. 3 retirement ceremony. A Hall of Fame representative accepted treasure from Ruth's bounty: a uniform, glove, spikes, and the bat the Babe used when he hit his 60th home run in 1927.

Finally, the Babe took the microphone. In a voice hoarse from the ravages of throat cancer, he thanked everyone for the memories and mentioned his pride in being the first to have hit a home run in the Stadium 25 years earlier. He then began a long, labored walk off the field in what to this day is known as "The House That Ruth Built," never to return. One month later, the Babe was dead.

"He walked out into that cauldron of sound
HE MUST HAVE KNOWN BETTER THAN ANY OTHER MAN."

— W.C. HEINZ, *sportswriter*

The Yankees of the late 1970s were consummate professionals. They routinely overcame distractions and won significant games. From 1976 to 1978 they won the American League pennant every season and twice prevailed in the World Series. Those teams had a core of talented and experienced players who truly understood how to put differences aside and play as one when they were between the white lines.

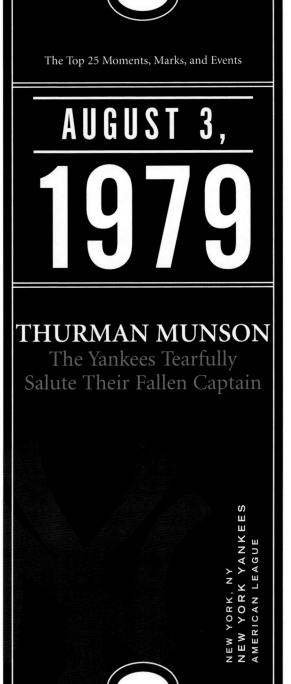

The Top 25 Moments, Marks, and Events

AUGUST 3, 1979

THURMAN MUNSON
The Yankees Tearfully Salute Their Fallen Captain

NEW YORK, NY
NEW YORK YANKEES
AMERICAN LEAGUE

Graig Nettles, Ron Guidry, Willie Randolph, Reggie Jackson, Chris Chambliss, Bucky Dent, Brian Doyle, Jim Beattie — superstars and obscure players alike, all had something to contribute.

The toughest of them all was Thurman Munson, the man behind the plate who ran the show. He was a block of intensity and resolve, constantly prodding for excellence. "He told me where I should play this hitter, told the center fielder where he should play, and communicated with the pitcher besides," Chambliss said. "A lot of guys looked up to Thurman's hard-nosed kind of play. With him, you just thought you were going to win."

Munson's standing among those who wore the world's most famous pinstripes became evident in 1976; the walrus-mustachioed catcher was appointed captain of the Yankees, the first to hold that position since Lou Gehrig. Munson was the American League MVP that year, as the Yankees won their first pennant in 12 years, and he hit .529 in the World Series.

A year later, Munson batted .308 and drove in 100 runs — the first AL player to achieve .300 and 100 RBIs for three consecutive seasons since Ted Williams in the late 1940s. Munson was behind the plate when the Yankees won the World Series in 1977 and 1978. For his career, he batted .357 in 30

postseason games. He won three Gold Gloves for his generalship behind the plate.

Then one summer day in 1979, the Yankees captain was gone forever, dead at age 32, his major league career frozen in its 11th season. Munson was killed in Canton, Ohio, on August 2, 1979, when he crashed his private aircraft while practicing takeoffs and landings. He had purchased the plane for the convenience of commuting from New York to Canton to be with his wife and three children on days when the Yankees didn't play.

The following evening more than 51,000 turned out at Yankee Stadium and saluted the fallen captain with an eight-minute ovation. The Yankees stood on the field, heads bowed and caps in their hands. Jackson, who had his differences with Munson but greatly admired the catcher's mettle, wept openly. The Yankees announced that Munson's uniform No. 15 and his clubhouse locker never again would be used by the team.

The Yankees finished fourth in the AL East in 1979, lost to Kansas City in the 1980 AL Championship Series, and lost to the Dodgers in the 1981 World Series. What if Munson had been in the lineup for those seasons? "Had he lived," Jackson said, "I believe we would have won two more World Series, both in 1980 and 1981. Very few people have been the leader he was."

YANKEES CAPTAINS™

Hal Chase
★ 1912 ★

Roger Peckinpaugh
★ 1914 to 1921 ★

Babe Ruth
★ May 20, 1922 to May 25, 1922 ★

Everett Scott
★ 1922 to 1925 ★

*Lou Gehrig
★ April 21, 1935 to June 2, 1941 ★

Thurman Munson
★ April 1, 1976 to August 2, 1979 ★

Graig Nettles
★ January 29, 1982 to March 30, 1984 ★

**Willie Randolph
★ March 4, 1986 to October 2, 1989 ★

**Ron Guidry
★ March 4, 1986 to July 12, 1989 ★

Don Mattingly
★ February 28, 1991 to 1995 ★

* **Lou Gehrig died on June 2,1941**
** Named co-captains on same day

The 2001 World Series offered something new for the Yankees, difficult as that is to imagine, considering that they were playing on baseball's biggest stage for the 38th time, more than any other two teams combined. Down two games to one to the Arizona Diamondbacks, the Yankees tied Game 4 with a home run in the bottom of the ninth inning and won with a home run in the 10th.

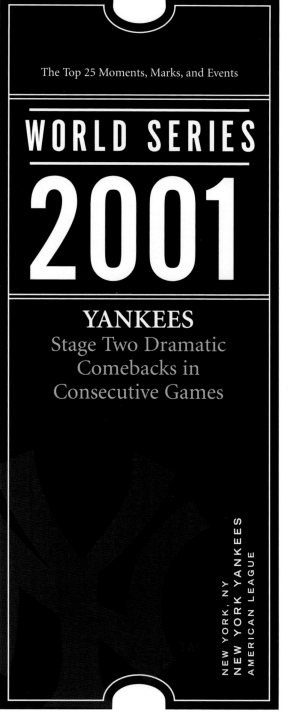

The Top 25 Moments, Marks, and Events

WORLD SERIES
2001
YANKEES
Stage Two Dramatic
Comebacks in
Consecutive Games

NEW YORK, NY
NEW YORK YANKEES
AMERICAN LEAGUE

It was the first time in 97 World Series that scenario had played out. A day later, the Yankees continued their unbelievable performance. Again they tied the score with a home run with two outs in the bottom of the ninth then won in extra innings.

From the time President Bush threw out the ceremonial first pitch for Game 3 at Yankee Stadium until Chuck Knoblauch scored the decisive run on Alfonso Soriano's hit in the 12th inning of Game 5, baseball offered grief-stricken New Yorkers a chance to celebrate the city's undaunted spirit and valor. In the seven weeks since the attack on the World Trade Center, the Yankees and the Mets had provided welcome relief for New Yorkers in need of a diversion from real-world issues.

The upstart Diamondbacks had a 3-1 lead with two outs in the bottom of the ninth inning of Game 4. It had been a miserable Series for Yankees hitters, who had managed but a .143 average against Arizona pitchers. The Yankees had a runner on base, and Tino Martinez was the batter. Byung-Hyun Kim, a 22-year-old sidewinder from Korea, tried to sneak a belt-high fastball past Martinez, but Martinez sent the ball into the night and over the center field fence, tying the score. Fifteen minutes later, Kim failed again, delivering a 10th-inning gopher ball to Derek Jeter that left the Yankees improbable 4-3 winners.

As if they were Broadway thespians, the Yankees staged a repeat performance less than 24 hours later. Kim again was on the hook for the Diamondbacks with two outs in the ninth inning, charged with holding a 2-0 lead. Again he caved, his offering dropped over the left field fence by Scott Brosius. An hour later, Soriano drove home the decisive run with a single. On consecutive nights, the Yankees had overcome two-run deficits in the ninth inning and won — an achievement equaled only four previous times in the World Series.

The Series ran its course in the Arizona desert, and the Yankees had no magic remaining for the final two games. The Diamondbacks won the war — but the two battles won by the Yankees in stunning fashion were symbolic of a great city that refused to be conquered.

Hank Bauer, Yogi Berra, Billy Martin, and Joe Collins (left to right) celebrate after the Yankees win the first game of the 1953 Series.

The 1953 World Series was a chance for the Yankees to scale still another level of greatness. They had been the dominant team in Major League Baseball since the 1920s. From 1936 through 1939 they won every World Series; no other team had ever won more than two straight.

From Ruth to Gehrig to DiMaggio, the Yankees wove a tapestry of excellence. DiMaggio retired after the 1951 season; after the team won the World Series for the third consecutive year. There would be no break in the chain. Mickey Mantle stepped in as the next larger-than-life presence on America's greatest team. The Yankees beat the Brooklyn Dodgers in the 1952 Series, and the same teams were the last ones standing again in 1953. Someone calculated the odds of one team winning every World Series from 1949 to 1953 — an unprecedented five straight — at 1,048,576 to 1.

Long odds never applied to the Yankees, though the same can't be said for the hero of the 1953 Series. Mantle, Yogi Berra, and Phil Rizzuto were bound for the Hall of Fame, yet none ever had a Series to match Billy Martin's performance in 1953. Martin was a career .257 hitter who drifted through seven teams in his 11 years in the major leagues.

He was best known for his combative and cantankerous personality, and his escapades with best-friend Mantle. Martin rose far above his journeyman station in the 1953 Series, batting .500 and delivering 12 hits, a record for a six-game Series. His final blow was a ringing single up the middle of the diamond in the bottom of the ninth inning of the sixth game. It brought home the decisive run, ended the Series, and gave Martin 23 total bases for the Series. "When I crossed first base and realized that we had won it, a thousand sensations seemed to

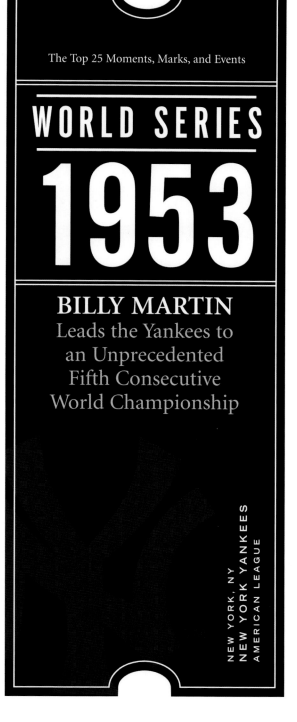

The Top 25 Moments, Marks, and Events

WORLD SERIES

1953

BILLY MARTIN
Leads the Yankees to an Unprecedented Fifth Consecutive World Championship

NEW YORK, NY
NEW YORK YANKEES
AMERICAN LEAGUE

pass through my body all at once," Martin said. "You did it kid! — that's what I kept telling myself over and over again. But I just couldn't believe it."

Twelve players shared in the five consecutive World Championships: Berra, Rizzuto, Hank Bauer, Jerry Coleman, Joe Collins, Ralph Houk, Eddie Lopat, Johnny Mize, Vic Raschi, Allie Reynolds, Charlie Silvera, and Gene Woodling. Players come and players go, and in the Yankees' case, those coming always were equal to those they were replacing. DiMaggio, Tommy Henrich, and Joe Page departed; Mantle, Gil McDougald, and Whitey Ford arrived.

The Yankees had grown so mighty that it had become fashionable to root against them. Emanuel Celler, a U.S. congressman from Brooklyn, claimed the Yankees were a monopoly and protested in a verse published in the *New York Times*, a day after the 1953 Series ended. The musical *Damn Yankees* hit Broadway in May 1955 and ran for 1,019 performances — on stage, at least, the Yankees could be beaten.

Few doubted the Yankees could win again in 1954. "The Yankees, as they are now constituted, have a good chance to win the pennant in 1954 — unless the other clubs get stronger," said Casey Stengel, their astute manager.

Indeed, the Yankees won big in 1954, claiming 103 victories, their best total since 1942. But it was good for only second place; Cleveland won 111, the American League record at the time. A year later, the baseball world was back to normal: The Yankees won the pennant, the first of four in a row.

It was Yogi Berra Day at Yankee Stadium. The pregame ceremonies honoring the greatest catcher in Yankees history ended with Berra behind the plate, receiving the ceremonial first pitch from Don Larsen, a reprise of sorts of that October 1956 afternoon when Larsen pitched the only perfect game in World Series history.

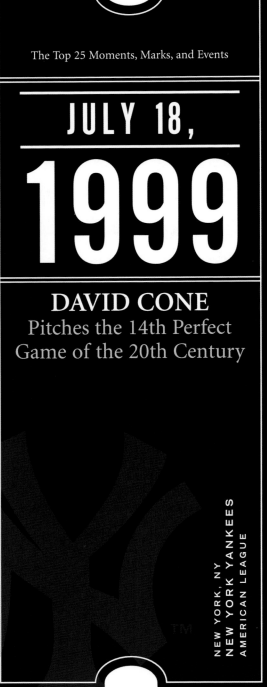

The Top 25 Moments, Marks, and Events

JULY 18,
1999

DAVID CONE
Pitches the 14th Perfect Game of the 20th Century

NEW YORK, NY
NEW YORK YANKEES
AMERICAN LEAGUE

Then the old teammates and almost 42,000 fans settled in for a ballgame between the Yankees and the Montreal Expos. As the innings passed by on Sunday afternoon, July 18, 1999, Berra and Larsen must have glanced at each other on occasion in wide-eyed amazement. For out on the mound, David Cone was retiring the Expos 1-2-3, without incident, inning by inning.

It was Cone's 14th season, and he had not won a game in nearly three weeks. Cone had ridden great talent to great heights. He had won 177 games, struck out 19 in a game, nearly pitched a no-hitter in his first start after recovering from surgery to repair an aneurysm in his right arm. He had pitched in four World Series, won eight postseason games. Now Cone was 36, and his fastball had lost its hop. He had to rely more on guile and gumption, and a variety of pitches thrown at varying speeds and from different arm angles. Once asked about his chances of making the Hall of Fame without having 200 wins, Cone, who would finish his career with a 193-123 record, replied confidently, "It's the quality of the stats, not the quantity, that counts."

On this Sunday afternoon, Cone was crafting a performance of quality that would have been rare for a pitcher in his prime, much less a 36-year-old of faded glory. Though Montreal held an unimpressive place in the standings, the result might have been the same had Cone been facing the best team of Berra's era. Cone kept the Expos' hitters on the defensive, getting ahead in the count with breaking pitches that bent impossibly and following with fastballs that painted the corners. This approach was so effective that by the sixth inning Orlando Cabrera, the ninth batter in the Expos' order, had reached a dreaded conclusion. "I'm going to be the last out," Cabrera told a teammate.

Cone had his closest call in the eighth inning. Jose Vidro lashed a grounder that appeared headed for center field, but second baseman Chuck Knoblauch fielded the ball on his backhand and made the throw to first base in time. Finally it was Cabrera's turn in the ninth. The 27th batter lifted a popup that nestled into the glove of third baseman Scott Brosius for the 27th out.

David Cone had pitched the 14th perfect game of the 20th century. And there to witness it were the pitcher and catcher of the greatest perfect game in history. Only the Yankees could pull off such high drama.

Three days short of his 35th birthday, in "The House That Ruth Built,"
Wells had accomplished a feat that had eluded all but 12 others,

INCLUDING HIS IDOL.

David Wells once said he could never pitch a no-hitter because he threw the ball over the plate too frequently. Wells was wrong. On the afternoon of May 17, 1998, he not only pitched a no-hitter, but it was the 13th perfect game of the 20th century. Wells befuddled the Minnesota Twins with fastballs and sharp-breaking curves thrown with precise control. His idol would have been proud of him.

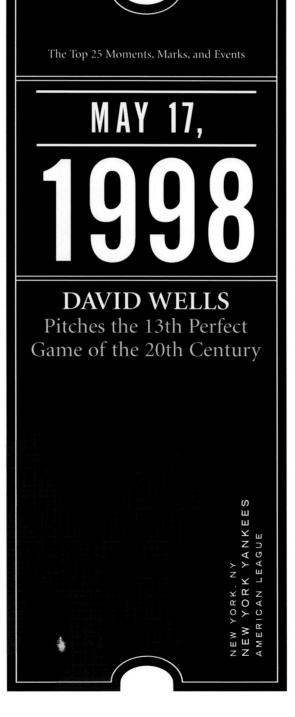

The Top 25 Moments, Marks, and Events

MAY 17,
1998

DAVID WELLS
Pitches the 13th Perfect
Game of the 20th Century

NEW YORK, NY
NEW YORK YANKEES
AMERICAN LEAGUE

Wells was a great admirer of Babe Ruth. Though separated in age by more than 60 years, the two had much in common. Both were accomplished left-handed pitchers, had round faces, portly physiques, mischievous grins, and were noted free spirits. Wells once took the mound for the Yankees wearing a flat cap that Ruth had worn in the 1920s, and he asked if he could wear uniform No. 3 in honor of the Babe. The request was denied, so Wells settled for No. 33.

When he took the mound against the Twins that May day, Wells was a pitcher merely trying to find his way. His work had been inconsistent. Two starts previous, he had surrendered most of a 9-0 lead and didn't finish the game. The Yankees manager, the ever-optimistic Joe Torre, tried to buoy Wells' confidence and spirit, mentioning that the lefty had ability enough to pitch a no-hitter.

Sure enough, Wells found his pitching rhythm against the Twins and began a high-level game of pitch-and-catch with Jorge Posada. Wells went to a three-ball count with only four batters. He struck out 11, and his fielders made no exceptionally tough plays.

As is the custom when a pitcher has gone deep into a game without giving up a hit, the Yankees did not mess with Wells in the dugout. Nobody wanted to jinx him — ridiculous, maybe, but a time-honored tradition. Torre did joke to pitching coach Mel Stottlemyre after the seventh inning that Stottlemyre ought to inform Wells he was through for the day and the bullpen would finish up. The always chatty David Cone was the only player who spoke to Wells, suggesting, with as straight a face as he could muster, that Wells try out the knuckleball he had been working on.

Wells spent the bottom of the eighth inning sitting alone in the dugout, stretching his neck and arms. The Yankee Stadium crowd of 49,820 afforded him a standing ovation as he left the dugout to pitch the ninth inning.

Wells got two outs in routine fashion. The last batter was Pat Meares, who swung late and hit a lazy fly to Paul O'Neill in right field. The crowd grew quiet for a moment and then roared as O'Neill made the catch. Wells pumped his arm madly as the Yankees swarmed him in celebration near the pitcher's mound. Three days short of his 35th birthday, in "The House That Ruth Built," Wells had accomplished a feat that had eluded all but 12 others, including his idol.

Two strikes on Bobby Grich. Ron Guidry backed off the pitcher's mound at Yankee Stadium and onto the grass, making him look 5-feet-8-inches tall instead of the official 5-feet-11-inches. At either height, he was a reed with pipe-cleaner legs. He stretched his arms mightily and swung them in a starfish motion.

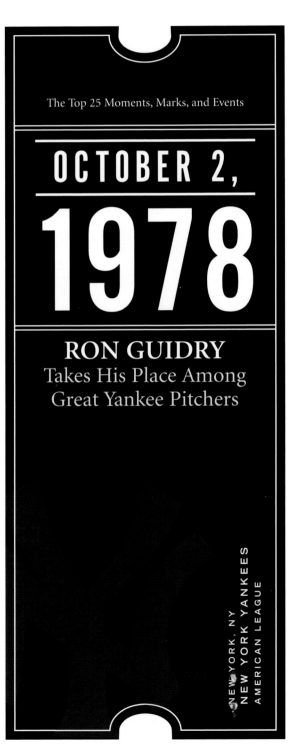

The Top 25 Moments, Marks, and Events

OCTOBER 2, 1978

RON GUIDRY
Takes His Place Among Great Yankee Pitchers

NEW YORK, NY
NEW YORK YANKEES
AMERICAN LEAGUE

Ready to pitch again, Guidry climbed back atop the mound to growing, rhythmic clapping from fans anticipating what was about to happen. Guidry rocked into his motion and let go a slider that approached home plate at belt-level, then dove suddenly. Too late for Grich to react; his swing was a foot above the ball. It was June 17, 1978, and Guidry was crafting one of the finest pitching performances in Yankees history. He set a club record that night by striking out 18 batters.

Every aspect of pitching came easily for Guidry in 1978. He had nine shutouts, a Yankees record and the most in the major leagues by a left-hander since Babe Ruth pitched nine in 1916. Guidry won his first 13 decisions, and by the time the season had run its course he had a 25-3 record, a winning percentage of .893, the best of all time among 20-game winners.

Guidry edged aside several Yankees greats in 1978. His 248 strikeouts was a team record, breaking the 74-year-old mark of Jack Chesbro, who had 239 strikeouts and a 1.82 ERA in 1904.

The previous best winning percentage for a Yankees' 20-game winner was held by Whitey Ford, who went 25-4 (.862) in 1961.

Guidry's 1.74 ERA was the lowest for a major league left-hander since Sandy Koufax's 1.74 in 1964 and 1.73 in 1966. Unlike Guidry, Hubbell didn't face a lineup that included a designated hitter. The DH has increased American League run production by about half a run a game. Adjusting ERAs accordingly, no one since Bob Gibson in 1968, who had a 1.12 ERA, has been as stingy as Guidry.

Guidry's victories in 1978 had pennant-race implications, too. The Yankees once trailed the Boston Red Sox by 10½ games but made up the gap, and the teams met in the famous playoff game decided by Bucky Dent's home run.

Guidry pitched three shutouts in September, two against the Red Sox in a week. He kept the Yankees alive with a 3-1 win over the Toronto Blue Jays on September 28, and after three days' rest he was on the mound in Fenway Park for the game to decide an American League East champion. With a little help from Dent, he won his 25th game that afternoon.

BEST WINNING PERCENTAGE FOR 20-WIN SEASONS

PLAYER, TEAM	YEAR	W-L	PCT.
Ron Guidry, New York Yankees	1978	25-3	.893
Lefty Grove, Philadelphia Athletics	1931	31-4	.886
Preacher Roe, Brooklyn Dodgers	1951	22-3	.880
Fred Goldsmith, Chicago Cubs	1880	21-3	.875
Smokey Joe Wood, Boston Red Sox	1912	34-5	.872

Under Steinbrenner's rule,
THE FAMED PINSTRIPED UNIFORM AGAIN WOULD
COME TO REPRESENT SUSTAINED EXCELLENCE.

On January 3, 1973, a limited partnership headed by George M. Steinbrenner III as the managing general partner purchased the Yankees from the CBS television network. The most famous franchise in professional sports had fallen on hard times, but the change of ownership set the Yankees on the road back to glory.

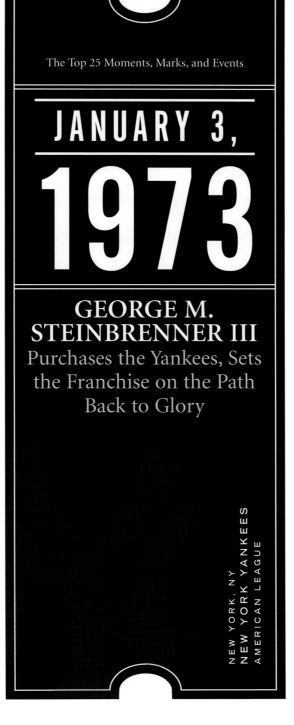

The Top 25 Moments, Marks, and Events

JANUARY 3, 1973

GEORGE M. STEINBRENNER III

Purchases the Yankees, Sets the Franchise on the Path Back to Glory

NEW YORK, NY
NEW YORK YANKEES
AMERICAN LEAGUE

Within four years, prudent trades and player acquisitions from the free-agent market had rejuvenated the team. The Yankees returned to freshly renovated Yankee Stadium in 1976, and a year later won the World Series for the first time in 15 years.

Steinbrenner's group paid $10 million for the Yankees, $3.2 million less than CBS paid for the franchise in 1964. The performance of the Yankees from 1965 through 1972 — they finished no higher than third in those years — was the chief reason for the reduced price. "I think CBS suffered some small embarrassment in buying a club at its peak and then having it fall from first place in the league, to sixth place (1965), and then to 10th (1966). The bottom fell out," said Michael Burke, Yankees president from 1966 to 1973.

The 1972 Yankees had made a spirited run, only to falter and finish fourth in the American League East. Their low place in the standings was not the only troubling reality. Yankees attendance in 1972 fell to 966,000, the first time since 1945 that the team had fewer than 1 million spectators. Steinbrenner, though, hardly was deterred. Rather, he saw buying into a franchise that had won 29 pennants and 20 World Series in the 45 years from 1920 to 1964 as an opportunity of gigantic proportions.

"It's the best buy in sports today. I think it's a bargain," he said at the time.

Steinbrenner grew up in Cleveland, an Indians fan, but he appreciated the buzz that accompanied the Yankees wherever they went. "When the Yankees came to town, it was like Barnum and Bailey coming to town," he said. "It was the excitement. Being in Cleveland, you couldn't root for them, but you would boo them in awe."

The Steinbrenner era began with finishes of fourth, second, and third in the standings. Then came a pennant in 1976, achieved in dramatic fashion when Chris Chambliss cracked a home run in the bottom of the ninth inning of the final game of the Championship Series.

Under Steinbrenner's rule, the famed pinstriped uniform again would come to represent sustained excellence. Dynasties in Major League Baseball were expected to go the way of the dinosaur when the rule that enabled teams to control player movement was struck down in court. Yet through 2002, 30 years under Steinbrenner's stewardship, the Yankees had won nine pennants and six World Series. The next most successful Series teams during that span were Oakland and Cincinnati, each with three World Championships.

The ball shot off Mickey Mantle's bat on a screaming line. It soared beyond the left-center field fence at Griffith Stadium in Washington, D.C., high above the 391-foot marker. The ball ticked a football scoreboard mounted atop a 50-foot-high wall that stood 69 feet behind the outfield fence and soared onward.

The Top 25 Moments, Marks, and Events

APRIL 17,
1953

MICKEY MANTLE'S
Griffith Stadium Blast

NEW YORK, NY
NEW YORK YANKEES
AMERICAN LEAGUE

TM

When the ball struck pavement, it bounced over a two-story building and finally came to rest behind a house at 434 Oakdale Street, a block from the stadium. Donald Dunaway, a 10-year-old boy who had seen the ball clear the stadium, ran to pick it up.

Yankees public relations director Red Patterson left the stadium to find where the ball landed. As the story goes, he then calculated the distance as best he could, by taking into account the acknowledged measurements inside the stadium and pacing off the rest of the distance. His estimate was 565 feet though no one knows for sure where fact left off and fiction took over.

A man with a name eminently suited for comic-book fame, Mickey Mantle was 21 when he crunched that ball beyond the sight lines of everyone inside Griffith Stadium on April 17, 1953. Over the next 15 years, from both sides of the plate, he would strike blows just as famous and perhaps just as far. But this one helped launch the Mantle legend.

Mantle was bigger than that game, and he would transcend games to come. The towering blast in the nation's capital afforded baseball fans a glimpse of what this muscular kid from Oklahoma could do. Of all Mantle's talents that contribute to his mythic stature as an American hero, none was greater than his awe-inspiring ability to make a ball disappear into the far reaches of the sky.

A report in the *New York Times* the following day said Mantle's home run was the longest in major league history, except for one hit by Babe Ruth in Detroit's Navin Field, in 1926, that traveled 600 feet. The distance of Ruth's clout was not measured, though several witnesses swore to it in an affidavit. The newspaper also mentioned a 587-foot shot by Ruth during a 1919 exhibition game in Tampa.

The boy who found Mantle's 565-foot home run ball gave it to Patterson in return for money, and Patterson gave it to Mantle. The curator of the Hall of Fame asked Mantle for the ball to display it in Cooperstown, and Mantle agreed. Mantle hit his most famous homer with a bat borrowed from teammate Loren Babe, and that, too, was sent to the Hall of Fame.

The Yankees had won 19 World Championships and were on the verge of another. All they had to do was protect a one-run lead in the bottom of the ninth inning in the seventh game of the 1962 World Series at San Francisco's Candlestick Park.

The Top 25 Moments, Marks, and Events

OCTOBER 16,
1962

BOBBY RICHARDSON
Grabs Willie McCovey's Screaming Liner for the Final Out of the 1962 World Series

NEW YORK, NY
NEW YORK YANKEES
AMERICAN LEAGUE

The Giants had challenged the Yankees relentlessly throughout the Series, and well they should have. Willie Mays was in his prime, and he'd been joined in the San Francisco lineup by young sluggers Orlando Cepeda and Willie McCovey. All three ended up in the Hall of Fame.

The Series lasted 13 days, which included a four-day rain delay between games five and six. Four games were played in Candlestick Park, a wind tunnel that whipped fly balls into spinning dervishes chased with great uncertainty by harried outfielders. Pitcher Stu Miller once was blown off the Candlestick mound by a sudden gust in the dead of summer.

Candlestick's unpredictability and Ralph Terry on the mound were the cause of great uneasiness for Yankees fans as the Giants came to bat in the ninth inning, trailing 1-0. Terry was a 23-game winner that season, yet just two Octobers previous he had yielded Bill Mazeroski's seventh-game, ninth-inning homer in Pittsburgh that had won the Series for the Pirates.

Matty Alou led off with a bunt single. Terry got two outs, then Willie Mays sent a line drive toward the right field corner. Roger Maris cut off the ball before it reached the fence and threw a quick relay to Bobby Richardson. Alou made third, but he certainly would have scored if not for Maris' nifty work in right field. Mays was at second.

Next up was the menacing McCovey, a powerful left-handed hitter who would clout 521 home runs in his career. First base was open, but in a lively conversation on the mound, Terry convinced Yankees manager Ralph Houk that he could retire McCovey with "good stuff just outside the strike zone." Richardson, the second baseman, moved a yard toward first base from where he normally played and ignored Houk's gesture to assume his usual position. McCovey's bat met Terry's third pitch flush, as a gun discharging a bullet. The ball shot on a screaming line toward right field, only to slam into Richardson's glove at chest level. "A yard to one side or the other and I wouldn't have had a chance at that ball," Richardson said.

Candlestick fell silent, except for the celebratory exchanges among the Yankees on hostile ground. Terry tossed his glove and cap into the air, and his teammates lifted him atop their shoulders and carried him off the field. The Yankees had repelled another challenge to their supremacy and gained a hard-earned World Championship—the 20th for the storied franchise.